THE LEGAL AID MARKET

Challenges for Publicly Funded Immigration and Asylum Legal Representation

Jo Wilding

P

First published in Great Britain in 2023 by

Bristol University Press
University of Bristol
1-9 Old Park Hill
Bristol
BS2 8BB
UK
t: +44 (0)117 374 6645
e: bup-info@bristol.ac.uk

Details of international sales and distribution partners are available at bristoluniversitypress.co.uk

© Bristol University Press 2023

British Library Cataloguing in Publication Data
A catalogue record for this book is available from the British Library

ISBN 978-1-5292-5849-7 hardcover
ISBN 978-1-4473-5850-3 paperback
ISBN 978-1-5292-5851-0 ePub
ISBN 978-1-5292-5852-7 ePdf

Cover design: Robin Hawes
Front cover image: borchee /iStock

Contents

List of figures and tables

Figures

Tables

List of terms and abbreviations

ASA   Advance Skeleton Argument. A document required
                        to be submitted before an appeal is listed for hearing,
                        under new Tribunal appeal procedures introduced
                        in 2020.

Advice deserts/   Areas in which there is a lack or a shortage of advice
droughts   and representation. An advice desert is generally
                        considered to be a geographical area with one or
                        no providers in a category of law, while an advice
                        drought is a term coined in this research for a
                        geographical area which appears to have provision
                        in a category of law, but where advice is unavailable
                        in practice.

BAJ   The Business of Asylum Justice study.

BSB   Bar Standards Board.

BVT   Best-Value Tendering. A proposed system of
                        bidding for contracts under which organisations
                        would compete to offer the lowest price or the best
                        value for money according to criteria set by the
                        government or agency.

Carter Review   A government-commissioned review by Lord Carter
                        of Coles, published in 2006, which recommended
                        market-based procurement of legal aid work,
                        moving towards a system of Best-Value Tendering
                        for contracts.

CCMS   Client and Cost Management System.

Domestic   A provision in paragraph 289A of the Immigration
Violence rule   Rules whereby a person granted limited leave
                        to remain in the UK as a spouse, civil partner or
                        unmarried partner, whose relationship breaks down
                        as a result of domestic abuse, can apply for indefinite
                        leave to remain in the UK. There is also a concession
                        whereby a person who would otherwise be destitute
                        as a result of leaving the relationship, can access
                        public funds while they apply under this rule. The
                        purpose of these provisions is to protect any person
                        from having to remain in an abusive relationship.

ECF   Exceptional Case Funding. A category of legal aid
                        funding for cases which are outside the scope of
                        mainstream legal aid, but where there would be a

breach (or risk thereof) of a person's human rights or European Union rights if legal aid were not made available.

Green Form scheme   A scheme providing for legal advice and assistance by solicitors, who could undertake a capped amount of work on any category of law which was not expressly excluded from scope, for any eligible person, with minimal oversight. In operation from 1973 until it was replaced by Legal Help in 1999.

IAS   Immigration Advisory Service.

ILPA   Immigration Law Practitioners' Association.

Inter partes   Costs awarded between the parties according to the general principle that the losing party pays the winner's legal costs.

Immigration Bar   Those barristers in England and Wales who include immigration and asylum work as a specialism.

JR   Judicial review.

LAA   Legal Aid Agency.

LASPO Act   Legal Aid, Sentencing and Punishment of Offenders Act (2012).

Legal Help   A stage or type of civil legal aid which allows for advice and negotiation but does not include representation at court. In immigration and asylum work, this would normally apply to the application stage of a case. Once a decision is made, the case would move onto the Controlled Legal Representation stage for representation on appeal to the Tribunal.

LSC   Legal Services Commission (replaced by Legal Aid Agency in 2013)

Matter starts   Cases which a provider is permitted to open in a contract year.

NAO   National Audit Office. An independent Parliamentary body which scrutinises public spending and audits government departments and agencies, including the Home Office and Legal Aid Agency.

NASS   National Asylum Support Scheme. Accommodation and subsistence financial support available to people who are in the process of claiming asylum in the UK, under sections 95 and 98 of the Immigration and Asylum Act 1999, as they are excluded from all mainstream welfare benefits. Accommodation is on

	a no-choice basis anywhere in the country. Support is also available in very limited circumstances for those whose asylum appeal rights are exhausted, under section 4 of the same Act. Also referred to as 'asylum support'.
OISC	Office of the Immigration Services Commissioner.
QALSS	The Quality of Asylum Legal Services provided by Solicitors research.
RLC	Refugee Legal Centre (name changed to Refugee and Migrant Justice in 2009).
RMJ	Refugee and Migrant Justice (formerly the Refugee Legal Centre).
SQM	Specialist Quality Mark.
SRA	Solicitors Regulation Authority.
UKIAS	United Kingdom Immigration Advisory Service.

Acknowledgements

Although this book draws heavily on my PhD, almost all of the writing was done during the 2020–21 lockdowns. I initially thought that the cancellation of everything else would make it easier to sit at home and write. I was, of course, wrong and I would like to thank my postdoc mentor Mary Darking for encouragement and support, socially distanced sessions in my garden while the university was closed, and even bringing around a printed copy of the whole draft when I couldn't look at a screen anymore. Heartfelt thanks also to the multi-talented Rosaria Gracia, for reading and commenting far beyond the call of duty, at a time when I was almost hyperventilating with lockdown writing stress. Thank you as well to Howie Rush for gentle but constructive critique and Dan Newman for your generosity during the final revisions process.

I would like to thank Professor Marie-Bénédicte Dembour, for inspiration, for believing in me and giving me the opportunity to become a researcher, for bringing in the funding that became my PhD studentship and being my lead supervisor. Thank you to Phil Haynes and Alex Newbury, my other two PhD supervisors: I can honestly say I enjoyed every single supervision session and your input was invaluable. Thanks also to Kepa Artaraz for multiple readings of my thesis and insightful comments, and to Hilary Sommerlad, who examined my PhD and is an inspiration.

I am enormously grateful to all the legal aid lawyers who took the time to discuss their work and their businesses with me despite the immense pressures on them. They are not named, for reasons of confidentiality, but each one of them is extraordinary. I also want to thank Rosie Brennan for the opportunity and support to research the legal aid desert in Devon, the Joseph Rowntree Charitable Trust, who funded the *Droughts and Deserts* report and seminar, and everyone who took part in that event or took the time to offer feedback on the report. Each of those conversations has helped to make this a better book.

The support of the Economic and Social Research Council (ESRC) is gratefully acknowledged. My postdoctoral fellowship, through the South Coast Doctoral Training Partnership, gave me the opportunity to write this book. Thank you to Helen Davis at Bristol University Press for support and guidance as I developed the proposal and wrote the book (and for the deadline extension).

Finally, thank you to my Postdoc Sisters, Josie Maitland and Claire Warrington, for coffee, plants and moral support, and my Nemesisters,

Naomi Blackwell and Kate Jessop, without whom I would have neither started nor finished the book (not to mention the soundtrack), and to Lars, Spike, Billie, Lily and my mum for being there through my writing fog and making me step away from the computer occasionally. My dad died while I was writing the book, depriving the world of an endless source of unrepeatable short poems, but I think it was from him that I inherited the stubborn obsessiveness needed to get this done.

1

Introduction

This book is a close investigation of the immigration and asylum legal aid market in England and Wales, based on six years of empirical research (set out in more detail later in this chapter). It explores the interactions of demand, supply, quality of services, financial viability for legal aid practitioners and organisations, and clients' access to advice and representation. Above all, it argues for a whole-system perspective on legal aid, but one which is informed by evidence and a detailed understanding of the participants in the market.

The focus on one sector, across the branches of the legal profession, helps to understand legal aid as one part of a whole system. It enables assumptions about markets and legal aid to be examined in context. The frameworks for understanding demand and supply in immigration and asylum law should be equally applicable to any category of law and, to some extent, other public services. They should also be relevant over time, although policy changes rapidly. The core concepts of demand, supply, client access and quality will remain central to any systems for governing migration, justice, social welfare and legal aid, and this book aims to offer a toolkit for interpreting the human and economic costs and benefits of reforms.

The Lord Chancellor has a legal duty to secure the availability of legal aid services in certain categories of law. They also have a duty to appoint a senior civil servant as Chief Executive of the Legal Aid Agency (LAA), the executive agency of the Ministry of Justice (MoJ), which is responsible for administering legal aid. The LAA employs around 1,450 people across England and Wales, according to its website. It carries out procurement for legal aid services by geographical area every three to five years. This 'market-based procurement' of legal aid services was adopted at the time of the Carter Review in 2006, and was intended to keep quality up and costs down, via providers competing for contracts and clients.

Despite legal duties, high-level management and a sizeable workforce, the market-based system for procuring legal aid services in England and Wales is failing to secure either adequate access to legal aid or adequate quality in immigration and asylum work. This argument contradicts the government's response to the MoJ's 2019 *Post-Implementation Review of*

Part 1 of LASPO, that the legal aid market (as a whole) is sustainable at present (paragraph 52). But it is justified by a close analysis of demand and supply, quality, financial viability and client access in the immigration and asylum sector.

To what extent is the market, in its current form, capable of ensuring that supply meets demand and the quality of work done on legal aid is adequate? Market theories predict that supply will increase to equal demand where price is adequate, via existing suppliers expanding or new ones entering the market. Instead, there are large parts of England and Wales where no advice is available at all, and others where advice appears to be available, but is inaccessible to would-be clients in practice.

The fee regime creates a conflict between quality and financial viability, which can only be reconciled at the expense of client access. It results in fewer and fewer organisations doing legal aid work, leaving shortages. For example, at the time of writing, Plymouth, in the south west of England, has only one legal aid immigration and asylum lawyer: one organisation, with one caseworker. There used to be two people, until the supervising caseworker resigned. They shared a single-room office, so they had to take turns working from home, enabling the other to meet clients in that one room. When they tried to recruit a replacement supervisor, they received no applications. There are no providers in Cornwall, to the south, nor in Somerset and Dorset, to the north, all the way up to Bristol. Apart from Bristol, the only other provider in the South West region is in Swindon, in the county of Wiltshire, to the north east of Devon. That provider, however, has been unable to do any immigration cases in the two years since getting the legal aid contract, because it cannot recruit a solicitor to do the work. This recruitment crisis is a recurring theme throughout the country.

In 2004, the Citizens Advice Bureau published its *Geography of Advice* report (Citizens Advice, 2004), drawing attention to 'advice deserts' around the UK and concluding that bureaucracy discouraged providers from the legal aid market. This prompted an inquiry by the House of Commons Constitutional Affairs Committee into shortcomings in the organisation of the system, confirming that there were advice deserts, even before the reforms which explicitly marketised legal aid procurement, and several rounds of legal aid fee cuts.

At the time of that inquiry, civil legal aid costs were roughly constant year on year. Personal injury had been removed from its scope, but immigration and asylum appeals had come in. Immigration legal aid costs rose from £81.3 million in 2000–01 to £174.2 million in

2002–03 (LCD, 2003). The reasons for these rising costs are discussed in subsequent chapters, particularly Chapter 5, which explores demand, and Chapter 2, on the proliferation of immigration law since the early 1990s. The Constitutional Affairs Committee noted that:

> At present there appears to be no coherent or transparent way in which the Government factors in the cost to the civil legal aid budget of new initiatives and rights for citizens. If this is not done, many of these rights will in practice be unenforceable. (House of Commons Constitutional Affairs Committee, 2004: paragraph 15)

This goes beyond immigration and asylum work: in the LAA's 2018 contract tender, 39 procurement areas, covering 61 local authorities in England and Wales, received insufficient bids for housing and debt advice (LAG, 2018a), and the education and discrimination tender was abandoned (LAG, 2018b). The market has particularly lost not-for-profit providers (Refugee Action, 2018), with more than half of the 97 legal advice centres operating in 2013 having closed by early 2020.

As for quality, the House of Commons Public Accounts Committee published severe criticism of the MoJ and LAA over legal advice across the board:

> The Agency's own quality assurance processes indicate that the quality of face-to-face legal advice is unacceptably low, with almost one in four providers failing to meet the quality threshold. This has serious implications in terms of both value for money for the taxpayer and access to justice for legal aid claimants. The Agency could not explain why these results were so bad, or whether they are related to the reduction in fees paid for civil legal aid. It seems to have done nothing to understand why some providers are falling short of the quality standards expected. (2015:p6)

Although this is a critique of an often-dysfunctional system, the focus is not on apportioning blame for the flaws that exist, but on understanding the market and how to operationalise it more effectively. Too often, reforms have shunted costs around the system, reduced costs at the expense of effectiveness, or failed to produce the change they were intended to produce, because each part of the system was treated in isolation or because reforms were motivated and shaped by politics of blame rather than by evidence.

There remains an urgent need for a more detailed, more accurate and more nuanced understanding of the market, on which to base policy. What drives demand? How does that demand manifest itself? How can demand be mapped or monitored? How well does supply match demand? How do lawyers decide which services to supply and to whom? How do demand and supply interact with quality and financial viability? To what extent is the market, in its current form, capable of ensuring that the quality of work done on legal aid is adequate? This book seeks to give a detailed, evidence-based picture of what is happening in the market of practitioners and organisations doing immigration legal aid work, to identify the gaps in data, and to draw out the implications for policy.

At the core of this critique is the concept of **monopsony**, first described by the economist Joan Robinson (1933) as the situation where there are multiple sellers or suppliers and only one buyer. It is the converse of a monopoly, where there is only one seller or supplier for multiple buyers, like the formerly state-owned utilities (water, gas, and so on). Either of these creates an imperfectly competitive market and potential market failure because the single buyer or seller has excessive power. Monopsony enables the buyer to obtain goods or services at prices below the marginal cost of supplying them, and to impose other terms on suppliers, who must comply or leave the market.

In legal aid work, the transition to a monopsony market was facilitated first by franchising and then contracting, and by the extent of specialism imposed on suppliers by requirements like the Specialist Quality Mark (SQM) and accreditation. That meant that the overall industry of legal aid work was increasingly fragmented into separate markets: housing, welfare, immigration, police actions, and so on. The concept of monopsony is key to understanding the market in immigration and asylum legal aid and will arise throughout the book.

Some earlier work looked at either incentives or system factors, and occasionally both. Given a monopsony, however, all providers are subject to similar financial incentives, audit incentives and system factors at any given time. These, combined with substantive and procedural legal rules, make up the boundaries of the system, or the parameters within which providers operate. But it is clear that providers do not all respond in the same way to either the incentives or the system factors and boundaries.

This book introduces the sector with a brief introduction to the history, politics and context of the immigration legal aid market (Chapter 2). It follows this with a micro-level introduction to the market, through the organisations which participated in the Business of Asylum Justice (BAJ) research which informs this book (Chapter 3).

Chapter 4 discusses in detail the threats to financial viability and some of the incentives and obstacles those threats create. A detailed framework for understanding demand follows in Chapter 5, which proposes that some practitioners or organisations respond more closely to demand, whereas others respond more closely to incentives. The survival strategies adopted by providers are addressed in Chapter 6, showing how those affect clients' access to good-quality legal advice. This develops the explanation of advice droughts and how these arise, showing why clients are unable to access advice even when they are eligible. In Chapter 7, the focus shifts to how the market, as structured, has lost any power it might have had to maintain quality. Finally, Chapter 8 pulls together all of these issues, demonstrating why a whole-system perspective is essential.

The book aims to be accessible to a wide range of readers and also to draw on themes from different disciplines including economics, socio-legal studies and public policy in order to better analyse the market. There is a risk, in crossing disciplines, of disappointing everybody as depth gives way to breadth. That means some of the conceptual questions in each discipline give way to a more pragmatic approach, and undoubtedly some writers are excluded whose ideas are relevant, but it allows us to pull on a greater variety of disciplinary threads. The aim is to break out of silos of discipline, practice and policy and reach a multifaceted understanding – and perhaps encourage others to pick up on some of the conceptual questions the book raises.

To this end, the book adopts Cornford's (2016) useful working description of access to justice: the extent to which individuals are able to obtain the legal services they need to protect and uphold their legal rights. Access to justice extends beyond access to legal advice, but the focus here is on the latter, and two key dimensions in particular: the availability of legal assistance and the quality of that assistance (OECD, 2019). As for defining or measuring quality, the peer-review criteria adopted by the LAA have been validated in other research as useful proxies for substantive quality. They are applied by both practitioners and funders for substantive quality assessments, so are treated as a reasonable framework for discussing quality in the book.

This story from Emma, a migrant support worker seeking advice for a client, illustrates the challenges surrounding access to immigration legal aid:

> 'I've got a client who has leave to remain but she has No Recourse to Public Funds. So she's here lawfully, but she can't claim any benefits, housing assistance, nothing, and

she needs to apply for leave to remain under the Domestic Violence rule. Her husband is very controlling and won't pay for her prescriptions, which she needs because of chronic pain, or for sanitary towels, or anything. We were paying for her prescriptions and giving her toiletries out of our crisis fund.

We found a solicitor who could make an application for her No Recourse condition to be lifted, but his fee to do that was £170. The local authority is reluctant to help. They've said unless the husband hits the child, it's not enough to override the money it would cost them to support her and the child.

I've been told it probably would be possible to challenge the local authority, to judicially review it, but there's no one in [the next two counties] who can do judicial review work. There's a solicitor in [city] who does it, but I work 30 hours a week. I haven't got time to make applications to people outside the area to take on a case. I feel like I'm letting the clients down, but I don't have time and I can't just give the clients the phone number and expect them to do it themselves.

Sometimes there's only a very specific time and date I can speak to a client, because of when the husband is around, and top of that there's the language barrier and finding a female interpreter and then arranging a meeting. All of that is just to get legal aid, not their actual leave to remain.

There is a firm up the road but they don't do legal aid. I phoned everywhere and no one was taking on new cases. For the last three months I've been unable to refer clients to any legal advisers in the [region]. It's really hard and there are less and less people I can go to for advice.'

On the face of it, Emma's client was eligible for legal aid for advice and assistance with the domestic violence issue. On the face of it, she was eligible for legal aid to challenge the local authority's decision not to help her and her child escape the violence. On the face of it, the lawyer who offered to assist with the removal of her No Recourse condition should have applied for Exceptional Case Funding instead of charging for the work, but the requirement to apply for that funding created yet another barrier. The reality was that there was simply no one available to provide advice, meaning Emma's client and her young child could not flee the abusive relationship – even though both the immigration laws and the legal aid rules intend that they should.

Research basis

The book is based primarily on research for the Business of Asylum Justice (BAJ) study; a three-year project on the immigration and asylum legal aid market in England and Wales, across the branches of the legal profession. The fieldwork, conducted between June 2016 and January 2018, consisted of 74 interviews organised around four main case studies (one not-for-profit, one private firm, the publicly funded Immigration Bar, and the now-closed Refugee Legal Centre) and four subsidiary case studies (two not-for-profits and two private firms). These included a mixture of London and non-London practices. The Bar case study consisted of 20 barristers and four staff in six sets of chambers, both in and outside London.

One of the private firms was selected because it was withdrawing from legal aid and offered the opportunity to understand some of the reasons why firms leave the market. All of the other case-study participants were invited on the basis of quality criteria. For the Bar and private firms, they were ranked (either individually or as an organisation) in the *Chambers and Partners Directory* of leading practitioners; for not-for-profits they had a level-one or level-two peer review, or were cited by at least two interviewees in earlier research (detailed later) as high-quality providers. These selections were also approved as high-quality providers by the advisory group members for the study, based on their knowledge of the market.

The analysis is also informed by discussions with policy officials from a range of organisations at a seminar and a series of meetings as part of the *Droughts and Deserts* project, funded by the Joseph Rowntree Charitable Trust, where the key findings of the BAJ study were discussed, following the publication of the report (Wilding, 2019). This was followed by a project in Plymouth, in the south west of England, involving discussions with stakeholders to form a clear understanding of the obstacles to increasing legal aid capacity in Devon, followed by solution-focused meetings to try to overcome those obstacles. It also draws on extensive data from the Quality of Asylum Legal Services provided by Solicitors (QALSS) study, commissioned by the Solicitors Regulation Authority (SRA) and the Legal Ombudsman. The research team (of which the author was a member) interviewed 123 asylum seekers and 42 'key informants' in practice, policy, non-governmental

(NGO) and regulatory positions, and carried out 45 case-file reviews (35 of which related to asylum seekers interviewed for the research) from August to December 2014 (Migration Work et al, 2016).

The system

Certain features of the English and Welsh legal system may be unfamiliar to non-lawyers and overseas readers, but are crucial to understanding the parameters of 'the system' and will be relevant throughout the book.

First, it is an **adversarial** system. Much of the world employs some kind of **inquisitorial** system, whereby some or all of the work of gathering evidence is done by court employees, and the judge oversees the whole process. In an adversarial system, that work is done by the parties' lawyers: gathering evidence, carrying out legal and factual background research, preparing statements and written arguments, compiling bundles of case law, and so on. Very little of the preparation work for the hearing is done by the court or judge, and judges are not expected (or allowed, in most cases) to carry out or initiate their own investigations. Each model has advantages and disadvantages, but this largely determines where in the system the costs fall: international comparative data suggest that higher legal aid costs in adversarial systems are offset to a great extent by lower spending on courts and other parts of the justice system (Bowles & Perry, 2009).

Second, as a common law system, precedent cases play a much more important role in legal cases in England and Wales than they do in civil law systems. When Parliament makes a law, the courts have to interpret it and apply it to the facts of whatever case comes to them. A decision made by a superior court – the High Court, Court of Appeal or Supreme Court – is a **legal precedent** and is binding on a lower court. So a decision made by the High Court binds the Immigration and Asylum Tribunal, and it has to act consistently with the higher court's decision. That can be overturned by the Court of Appeal or Supreme Court, but all lower courts have to apply the law as set out by the higher one. In practice, that means a lawyer needs to consider not only what statutes apply to their client's case, but also how previous cases have interpreted those statutes, cite the relevant cases in written and oral argument, and provide copies to the opponent and the judge. It will be immediately apparent that this increases the amount of work the parties' lawyers have to do.

Third, the legal profession is split. Although many countries have a single legal qualification, the UK has a distinction between solicitors, who litigate or run the case on behalf of the client, and barristers ('advocates' in Scotland), who advise and carry out advocacy, but do not 'have conduct of' the case. That has implications for lawyers' business models, as well as the structure of the legal system.

Fourth, unlike most countries, the UK does not have a written or codified constitution. It has constitutional law, which is often described as resting on three pillars: the rule of law; legislative supremacy of Parliament; and the (incomplete) separation of powers. At the time of writing, all legislation was required to comply with the European Convention on Human Rights and the domestic Human Rights Act, though the courts can only declare the law incompatible with such compliance – they cannot strike it down, as many other countries' constitutional courts can. The protected rights include the right to a fair trial, although this does not apply to immigration cases. But we cannot talk about a *constitutional right* to legal aid in the way that, for example, Belgium and the Netherlands do (Hubeau & Terlouw, 2014).

Fifth, the structure of the UK is unusual. Most countries are either unitary states – one central government with power over the entire territory – or federal states in which some power is held by the federal or central government, but the states or provinces hold other powers independently, so that different laws apply in different parts of the country. The UK is a unitary state, but has devolved legislatures for Wales, Scotland and Northern Ireland, each of which has different powers depending on what has been delegated to them by the UK government. England has no devolved government or powers. There are separate justice and legal aid systems for England and Wales, Scotland, and Northern Ireland, although the UK Supreme Court is the highest court of appeal for all parts of the country. Wales is likely to develop a devolved justice system and break away from England. Immigration and asylum law, though, remains the same for the whole UK, with the Immigration and Asylum Chamber of the Tribunal having jurisdiction over appeals for all four nations.

On top of these peculiarities of the UK's legal system, it sits partly within and partly outside the Common European Asylum System, which has developed since 1999 (IARLJ, 2016). The system was created to standardise EU states' substantive and procedural approaches to asylum in an era of borderless transit across Europe. The UK opted into the first phase of Directives, setting out minimum standards, but not into the recast Directives, which attempted to harmonise the way people seeking asylum were treated. It is unclear, at the time of writing, what aspects of this common system the UK will retain now it has left the EU.

Finally, a word on terminology. Asylum law, and all of social welfare law, deals with fundamental human rights on a daily basis. Legal aid is about access to *justice*, not about access to *services*, and lawyers seek to uphold human and constitutional rights rather than selling services to consumers in a market. The right to life, to freedom from torture or inhuman treatment, to freedom from slavery, to liberty, to private and family life, to freedom of religion, expression, association, the right to marry a person of one's own choosing (or *not* to marry a person of someone else's choosing) are the day-to-day work of asylum lawyers and the life experiences of their clients. These are often life-and-death cases for extremely vulnerable people who are sometimes compelled to choose between domestic violence and destitution.

The adoption of economic or market-focused analytical terms is not intended to displace the focus on access to justice or fundamental rights, but rather to clarify what is happening and to speak to those tasked with trying to design policies which work, within the budgets they are given, as well as to practitioners trying to make their businesses work, and to academics seeking to understand marketised public services, without meaning any disrespect to the human beings who are caught up in the system.

2

Evolution of immigration law, legal aid and lawyers

This book argues throughout for a whole-system approach to legal aid, in any category of law. That approach means there is a need to develop frameworks for understanding demand and supply, the conflict between quality, financial viability and client access, and the system factors which drive those. Within such frameworks, rising demand (if unaffordable) can be addressed not by reducing the scope of legal aid (or any other service), but by changing the system to create less need. Building those frameworks requires an understanding of the context and history of the bodies and actors involved. The 'memory' of that history is stored throughout an organisation or system (Cilliers, 2000), so that everyone in a system can act 'dutifully and rationally', yet still experience a bad result (Meadows & Wright, 2008: p5). When history is ignored, there is a risk of developing and attempting to impose solutions and reforms that cannot succeed.

This chapter offers that framework of context, history and politics, beginning with the development of immigration law and the legal profession, then introducing the key stages of legal aid development. The next chapter fills out the framework with the micro-level introduction to individual provider organisations and practitioners.

Emergence of the immigration legal profession

In the late 1800s, as poor Jewish refugees fled persecution in the pogroms of Eastern Europe, the UK Parliament passed the Aliens Act 1905, aiming to stop them entering Britain. That began the development of both the modern system of immigration control in the UK and the right of appeal against immigration decisions. The Act created the Aliens Inspectorate, which was given the power to inspect ships carrying immigrants and refuse entry to those deemed undesirable, generally by reason of poverty, disability or sickness (Clayton, 2016). It gave overall responsibility for the scheme to the Home Secretary. It was augmented with new war-related restrictions in 1914 and 1919, but it was not until after World War II, as the British Empire shrank and migration from the colonies and the new Commonwealth grew, that immigration law began to proliferate and drive the development of an immigration legal profession.

The Joint Council for the Welfare of Immigrants (JCWI) formed in 1967, to campaign for the rights of migrants and provide practical support. JCWI's first employee was stationed at London Heathrow Airport in 1968, to help new arrivals with immigration issues that arose, such as children arriving to join their parents in the UK having their relationship disputed (JCWI, 2017). The Commonwealth Immigrants Acts 1962 and 1968 were criticised for aiming to restrict 'non-White' migration from the former colonies. The Immigration Act which followed in 1971 divided Commonwealth citizens into 'patrial' and 'non-patrial', depending on whether they had an ancestor born in the UK – a distinction which was 'designed to exclude as many black people as possible' (Robertson, 2019). The Society of Labour Lawyers and the Campaign Against Racial Discrimination legal group were among those fighting the new legislation.

The 1967 Wilson Report recommended changes to the system of appeals against immigration officers' decisions that was created by the 1905 Act. It proposed that both Home Office and migrant should be represented, since the process was (and remains) adversarial (Thomas, 2016). The UK Immigration Advisory Service (UKIAS) was founded in 1969 to meet this need for advice and representation, which was not then covered by mainstream legal aid, except in cases involving deportation or liberty (Care, 2016). In 1970, North Kensington Law Centre opened in London, followed by 13 other law centres in 1973–74. These were a product of both the anti-racist movement (John, 2019) and the access to justice movement, which recognised that mainstream legal aid was not yet meeting social welfare needs (Zander, 1978).

The Green Form scheme started in 1973, allowing lawyers to give time-limited advice on any area of law. This opened up the availability of free specialist advice in social welfare areas of law. Both private firms and law centres could advise through the scheme. It did not cover representation in immigration appeals, which were still only funded through UKIAS, but Green Form funding was often used creatively for preparation of cases, alongside pro bono representation at appeal. At this time there were no appeals against asylum decisions, only judicial reviews of decisions to deport a person whose asylum claim was refused.

UKIAS, JCWI and the law centres, then, formed the bedrock of the immigration and asylum legal sector in England, grounded in anti-racism and overtly political in outlook. Many advisers were specialist caseworkers, not legally qualified solicitors or barristers. The barrister

Ian Macdonald wrote the first manual of immigration law, *Macdonald's Immigration Law and Practice*, in 1983. This manual has been described as, '... the foundation of our credibility before those judges uncomfortable with – or downright hostile to – our basic claim to be at court: that immigration should be closely governed by law, and not just left to politicians' (Garden Court Chambers, 2019). In other words, this new sector of the legal profession had to fight even to be recognised as such.

The Immigration Law Practitioners' Association (ILPA) was formed in 1984, although participation in the sector was still limited. Just four firms of solicitors took on 43.6 per cent of all the immigration cases in 1987 (Sterett, 1998). Despite this, by the mid-1980s, 30 per cent of all judicial review cases in the High Court involved immigration (Sterett, 1990; Sunkin, Bridges & Meszaros, 1993), as practitioners sought to defend migrants' legal rights before there was a right to appeal asylum refusals. In this period, refugees arriving in the UK, particularly Tamils from Sri Lanka and Kurds from the Middle East, could be given a cursory interview and put on a return flight within twelve hours of arrival, despite being at high risk of persecution and serious harm. Sterett (1998) describes lawyers applying, in the middle of the night if necessary, for injunctions to prevent removal on the basis that these procedures were unfair (and therefore unlawful); such claims then entered a nine-month queue for a full hearing. More colourfully, Webber describes how she, as a young barrister, literally ran from her office to the High Court to apply for injunctions to prevent the removal of a group of Tamil men, who undoubtedly faced persecution if returned to Sri Lanka, who were at that moment stripping to their underwear on the airport runway to slow the process of putting them on the plane (Webber, 2012). This eventually forced the Home Office to implement more thorough, formalised systems for interviewing and giving reasons for decisions, and to bring asylum cases into the scope of the immigration appeals system, through the Asylum and Immigration Appeals Act 1993.

Asylum attracted frequent legislative attention from the early 1990s. By 1992, there were fewer claimants from former Communist countries and 56 per cent of applicants were African or Asian (Gibney, 2004). Conflicts in Afghanistan, Iraq, Somalia and the Balkans drove up overall numbers (Spencer, 2011). By this time, the government and much of the media had begun publicly accusing asylum seekers of dishonesty (Webber, 2012). Carrier sanctions were introduced in 1987, forcing transport companies into a border control role, on pain of fines. The UK's first asylum-specific legislation, the Asylum and Immigration Appeals Act (1993), was followed by the Asylum and Immigration Act

(1996) and two further Acts in 1999 and 2002. The Human Rights Act entered into force in 2000. These statutes transformed the asylum process, limiting claimants' access to welfare and housing, increasing powers to detain on immigration grounds, providing for vastly greater detention capacity, amending appeal rights and introducing a 'white list' of countries presumed safe, whose nationals would be excluded from the normal asylum process.

Although dedicated immigration detention facilities had existed since 1970, capacity was doubled year-on-year from around 500 in 1999 to over 1,000 by the end of 2000 and over 2,200 by the end of 2001 (see Welch & Schuster, 2005). In 2000, the 400-bed detention centre at Oakington, near Cambridge, was opened specifically to process fast-track asylum claims. Under the Immigration and Asylum Act 1999, people who applied for asylum were no longer eligible for mainstream housing assistance, but were instead accommodated through the National Asylum Support Scheme (NASS) on a no-choice basis, in 'dispersal areas' within local authorities which had agreed to accept asylum seekers (Robinson et al, 2003; Griffiths, Sigona & Zetter, 2005).

These policy changes created pools of demand throughout the UK in places where they had not previously existed, in and around detention centres and in dispersal areas, while the overall number of applicants and the proliferation of laws on detention, safe third countries, asylum support, and so on, created ever more complex and varied legal need. (For a detailed account of these provisions and the cases challenging them, see Webber, 2012.)

In such a committed profession, rising need created a dilemma. Demand for free legal advice exceeded supply. UKIAS split, in 1992, into the asylum specialist Refugee Legal Centre (RLC) and the immigration-focused Immigration Advisory Service (IAS). Those who worked at RLC during this period recall asking asylum seekers to opt for private advice if they could afford it, simply to manage demand. But the very small number of specialist private firms also had more demand than capacity. There was a clear need for more practitioners to get involved. Yet there were also arguments for 'concentrating practice within an organised group of lawyers' (Sterett, 1998:p309), because a poorly chosen or argued case could hold up a large number of similar cases, or even set an unfavourable precedent that might disadvantage numerous others. The level of unmet demand for free advice meant that: 'migrants were frequently gulled into paying thousands of pounds to unqualified high street advisers, who became notorious for exploiting and cheating migrants' (Webber, 2012:p67).

ILPA therefore took on an important role in offering training and a discussion forum which would allow the immigration sector to expand without diluting the level of organisation, knowledge and commitment that was considered necessary. From 1998, legal aid for asylum and immigration appeals increased the availability of free advice. A regulatory scheme operated by the newly created Office of the Immigration Services Commissioner (OISC) enabled non-lawyers to register as providers, and criminalised the provision of immigration advice by anyone who was not qualified and regulated. This, Singh and Webber say, 'cleaned up the field' of the worst quality advisers (2010:p2).

Alongside the development of the legal profession, it is important to briefly mention the professionalisation of the immigration judiciary. Jurisdiction over immigration tribunals passed from the Home Office to the Lord Chancellor's Department in the 1990s. Judicial training became more structured, to meet the challenges of new legislation. The country guidance case system was established to try to ensure consistency in handling cases on similar issues. The Upper Tribunal was designated a Superior Court of Record by the Tribunals, Courts and Enforcement Act 2007, which then opened up a route for Upper Tribunal Judges to be appointed Deputy High Court Judges (Free Movement, 2020). UK judges were at the forefront of founding the International Association of Refugee Law Judges in 1997 (later the International Association of Refugee and Migration Judges), which now has chapters for Europe, the Americas, Africa and Asia Pacific. The development of the Common European Asylum System created some common legal instruments for judges across Europe, and the European Chapter played a key role in judicial training and discussion of emerging issues (Free Movement, 2020).

So far, then, we have seen how the increasing complexity of immigration law and controls drove the growth of the immigration legal profession and professionalisation of the immigration judiciary. Individuals affected by these laws, even if not detained, even leaving aside language barriers, are unlikely to be able to manage applications and appeals alone because of that complexity. This somewhat reflects modern law more generally; though immigration and employment law stand out as particularly dense, one could carry out a similar exercise to those outlined here for welfare benefits, housing, discrimination, or community care law as a foundation for understanding the wider context in which legal aid sits. The focus now moves, however, to legal aid itself and the forces which have shaped it in the years since its foundation.

Development of legal aid: from autonomy to audit

Until 1949, access to free legal advice was mostly a matter of charity. A year after the foundation of the Welfare State (education, housing, National Health Service and welfare benefits), the Legal Aid Act (1949) came into force. It aimed to provide legal advice in courts and tribunals where lawyers would normally appear for paying clients, for those of 'small or moderate means', not only the very poor. It was intended that lawyers should be paid for their services, so that advice was available by right, rather than by donation. What follows is a brief exploration of how legal aid fits into, and has been shaped by, the wider public-service context, to ground an understanding of where we are now, and why. For a comprehensive history of legal aid, see Sir Henry Brooke's detailed Appendix to the Bach Commission report (Brooke, 2017).

Wider public sector reforms, shaped by political ideologies and budgetary considerations, have driven serial reviews and reforms, creating identifiable phases in the public sector generally and in legal aid specifically. These phases are characterised by who can provide services on legal aid, who administers it, its scope, and what services are in fact provided, and help to put legal aid into the wider social policy context. The phases outlined here are not dissimilar in timing from those set out by Brooke (2017) or Hynes (2012), but they differ in emphasis. Broadly, legal aid has transformed from a free market with minimal surveillance into a highly controlled and regulated market, moving with other public services (like health, education and social security which had been directly state-run bureaucracies) through managerialism into marketisation.

Early phase (1949–70)

Legal aid was initially administered by the Law Society, the professional body of solicitors: 'the only private body to dispense public money to its own members' (Hansen, 1992). It was a 'judicare' system, in which any solicitors' firm could do legal aid work and bill the state for it. This was fundamentally different from most public services at the time. It was provider-led in the sense that solicitors chose which areas of law to cover and where. Consequently, it covered mainly criminal and family law, reflecting what solicitors already knew, with very little social welfare provision. Lawyers were self-regulated, with a very high level of autonomy. Near the end of this phase, in 1969, the government-funded UKIAS became one of the very limited exceptions to the general rule that legal aid services were provided by the private sector.

Expansion phase (1970–88)

Legal aid expanded in the 1970s, following the trend in other public services from the 1960s onwards (Burnham & Horton, 2012). As per the previous section, the first law centres took a proactive approach to access to justice and social welfare law (Hynes, 2012), whereas the Green Form scheme, from 1973, allowed solicitors and not-for-profits to give time-limited advice in any area of law, with minimal bureaucracy and surveillance. These expansions in scope and supply radically widened the areas of law in which people could access advice. Lawyers still had near-complete autonomy (Spencer, 2002). Towards the end of this phase, the Police and Criminal Evidence Act 1984 expanded eligibility for criminal legal aid significantly, driving up costs to the legal aid fund.

Early control phase (1988–99)

Private-sector management techniques were introduced to the public sector from the early 1980s in what became known as 'new public management' (Hood, 1991), whereby managers took over certain functions from professionals, with a focus on customer service, spending controls and ideas around efficiency and value for money, leading to the requirement for competition through quasi-markets in public services. Even though legal aid already operated as a quasi-market, it did not escape these changes.

The Legal Aid Act 1988 gave control to the Legal Aid Board, a quasi-autonomous government body under the auspices of the Lord Chancellor's Department. Half of its board of governors were business people (Hynes & Robins, 2009), in line with the new focus on markets, business planning and serving individual customers rather than society as a whole (Jackson & Price, 1994). It set payment rates, ending the discounted private rate which had applied since the start of legal aid. All solicitors' firms were still able to provide via the Green Form scheme, but a voluntary franchising scheme began in 1994. This was the first attempt to ensure a minimum quality standard, initially as a prelude to opening up the legal services market to non-solicitors and not-for-profits (Sherr et al, 1994; Sherr & Paterson, 2008), described as 'third way regulation' (Moorhead, 2001), as distinct from either self-regulation or government regulation. This was part of the move to create consumer choice within public services, allowing different kinds of provider into the legal sector. Although other areas of law were now being subjected to financial cuts, immigration appeals were brought within the scope of the mainstream 'judicare' legal aid scheme for the first time in 1998, as previously explained, to meet the rising demand.

Local planning phase (2000–06)

From 2000, only franchise holders could do legal aid work, marking the beginning of monopsony power in legal aid. The franchise was later replaced by the Specialist Quality Mark (SQM) and Lexcel accreditation (an alternative quality assurance scheme to the SQM). All legal aid providers must hold one or other. They have no relationship to substantive quality of advice (Trude, 2009), but consist of 'proxies' relating to practice management, such as file reviews and risk management.[1] The Legal Services Commission (LSC, a non-departmental public body of the Lord Chancellor's Department) took over administrative control, with specific responsibilities to inform itself about the need for services and plan services to meet that need (Access to Justice Act, 1999, s4). That meant it needed to take action to expand provision; this was the first time that provision had been driven by anything other than practitioners' availability (Hynes, 2012).

The overall number of legal aid providers was reduced, as franchising and contracting compelled providers to specialise (Smith & Cape, 2017), removing the 'dabblers' who did very little legal aid work and often lacked specialist expertise (Hynes & Robins, 2009). There was a 40 per cent drop in the number of legal aid immigration providers, from 380 in 2004 to 234 in July 2006 (Langdon-Down, 2006). The not-for-profit sector was expanded, however, from 42 franchise holders in 1997 (across all categories of law) to more than 400 in 2003. In immigration, the enforced specialisation, combined with the implementation of legal aid for immigration and asylum appeals in 1998, and the new scheme for regulation by the OISC, as mentioned earlier, somewhat 'cleaned

---

[1] Legal Aid Agency (n.d.) 'What is the Specialist Quality Mark?' Available from: http://www.recognisingexcellence.co.uk/sqm/what-is-the-specialist-quality-mark/ [Accessed 4 October 2018].

up the field' of corrupt or incompetent unregulated advisers (Singh & Webber, 2010:p2).

Practitioners interviewed in the BAJ study recall the Commission "throwing money at" immigration advice: providers were encouraged to expand into immigration and asylum law, and one barrister interviewee recalled benefiting from a training and incentive scheme designed by the LSC and Bar Council to attract more barristers into immigration law. Former RLC managers explained that the LSC asked and supported them to move into new regions to meet the demands generated by detention and dispersal.

However, this proactive approach was short-lived and rapidly dismantled. In 2000, for the first time, providers were allocated a limited number of 'matter starts', or cases, which they were permitted to open in a year. New costs limits in 2004 allowed for only three hours' work on immigration cases and five for asylum. At that time, it was especially difficult for a person who was dispersed to find a new representative if the money on the file had been used up (Singh & Webber, 2010), though it later became possible for a new provider in the dispersal area to open a new file. At the same time, lawyers stopped being funded to accompany clients to their asylum interviews, even though these formed the main information-gathering process for the asylum decision. Increasingly, providers were compelled to work at risk, as changes in 2005 meant they were not paid for onward appeals to the Upper Tribunal unless they succeeded in getting permission to appeal. All of this meant that the provider had to either limit the work they did or work unpaid.

In these ways, the task of denying access to people who were nominally entitled to legal aid was delegated to legal practitioners, via serious financial risk which created conflict between organisational survival and caseworkers' professional values (James & Killick, 2010, 2012; Mayo, 2013). Services could (and still can) only be provided to clients who meet the 'merits test'. The precise test varies according to the stage of the case, but essentially an initial asylum claim would usually meet the merits test, whereas appeals require at least a 50 per cent chance of success. Interviewees explained that prospects of success are difficult to pre-judge, not least because so much depends on which judge hears the case (Genn & Genn, 1989; Gill et al, 2015). Key performance indicators (KPIs) apply to all categories of law but, unlike all other areas of law, immigration and asylum providers had a KPI requiring them to succeed in at least 40 per cent of appeals (Ling & Pugh, 2017). That drew criticism as a perverse incentive for providers to cherry-pick simple cases and refuse to represent clients with more complex or labour-intensive cases. It is easy to imagine how a similar provision for criminal trials would result in defendants with more complex cases going unrepresented.

Carter phase (2006–10)

Lord Carter of Coles was commissioned to review the procurement of legal aid services, publishing proposals in 2006, 'directed towards achieving a market-based outcome' (Carter, 2006: Executive Summary). Carter's review was fairly typical of its time: appointment of a reviewer from whom, 'ministers and civil servants would have known exactly what they were likely to get by way of an outcome' (Dingwall, 2010:p79), followed by a rapid move into a market-based procurement system. Competition based on reputation and client choice was intended to ensure quality and, together with peer review, to force poor-quality suppliers out of the market, ensure value for money and make the justice system more efficient as it moved, over a four-year transition period, towards Best-Value Tendering (BVT) – also known as price-competitive tendering, meaning solicitors' firms and other 'providers' of legal aid services would compete for contracts awarded (primarily) on the basis of the lowest price, subject to minimum quality criteria. Carter's proposals began being implemented almost immediately, although BVT was opposed intensely by providers and civil society organisations as likely to lead to a race to the bottom, and remains unimplemented across most of legal aid.

Funding changes, intended as part of the transition to BVT, included fixed fees, payments in arrears when cases closed, and a unified civil contract, placing both firms and not-for-profits on the same terms. Smith and Cape (2017) describe that contract as a means of controlling providers, manifested by preconditions to obtaining contracts, an auditing regime, limits on client eligibility and fees, and restrictions on the number of legal aid cases a contract-holder could open. It was expected to lead to fewer providers, each doing larger amounts of work, reducing the transaction costs for the legal aid funder in contracting with them. Carter was a transformational change in the sector as a whole, and many providers either closed or withdrew from legal aid work.

Meanwhile, independent regulation replaced self-regulation, as it did in many professions in this period (Dingwall, 2010). Following the Clementi report (2004), the Bar Council and the Law Society, as the professions' representative bodies, saw their regulatory roles handed over to the new Bar Standards Board and Solicitors Regulation Authority, in

2006 and 2007 respectively. These regulators and six others are overseen by the Legal Services Board (a non-departmental public body of the MoJ). The Board is advised by the Legal Services Consumer Panel, a statutory body established in 2009 by the Legal Services Act, as was the Legal Ombudsman service, which deals with complaints from the public about legal services. Non-lawyer practitioners and entities are regulated by the OISC, an executive non-departmental public body sponsored by the Home Office. Unlike other professional regulators, OISC is not regulated by the Legal Services Board or any other body.

All of these layers of regulatory activity are paid for by levies on legal professionals. This complex regulatory system is not untypical of public services, leading Burnham and Horton to write that: 'By 2010 ... a huge public sector regulatory industry had emerged and a parallel set of bureaucracies coexisted alongside the public organisations they were designed to control' (2012:p231). Hood et al (1998) described it as the 'regulatory state'.

Towards the end of this period, in October 2009, the National Audit Office (NAO) published a report criticising the LSC for not doing enough to understand the criminal legal aid market, the impact of reforms or the savings, if any, those reforms generated. The report noted that this was partly because of the intention to start procuring legal aid services through BVT, which led it to conclude that it did not need detailed information about providers' costs, profits and geographical variations, because competition would soon begin determining the price (and, presumably, smooth out the geographical variations). The NAO disagreed, and also reported 'tensions in the relationship' between solicitors and the LSC (NAO, 2009:p6), and between the LSC and the MoJ. These difficult relationships between the LSC and its parent department prompted the Magee Review, published in March 2010, which paved the way for the LSC's abolition (Brooke, 2017).

Austerity phase (from 2010)

The announcement of public sector austerity brought rate cuts and scope exclusions across the public sector. A 10 per cent fee cut in 2011 was followed by the LASPO Act 2012, which cut fees further and dramatically reduced the scope of civil legal aid. Providers could only do work which was expressly *included* in scope, inverting the previous position, where they could do anything which was not expressly *excluded*. Almost all non-asylum immigration work was removed from scope, except (to varying extents) cases relating to liberty, domestic violence and trafficking, creating particular difficulties in mixed asylum and immigration cases, where some work would be paid and some not. This proved catastrophic for some providers, since non-asylum cases tended to conclude much more quickly than asylum ones, maintaining cash flow and often cross-subsidising the losses from fixed-fee asylum work. Not-for-profits were badly affected, with 47 out of 94 not-for-profit legal advice centres closing between April 2013 and July 2019 (Bowcott, 2019).

Matter-start limits became particularly problematic in 2010, when almost all providers who bid were allocated 100 matter starts per office per year, leaving many too small to be viable (Harvey, 2013). This was fundamentally anti-market, since it meant some clients were 'forced off their demand curve' (Jackson & Price, 1994:p126) for their preferred provider – much like an oversubscribed school to which not all pupils who 'chose' it would be admitted. Meanwhile some lower-quality (or less popular) providers may have been kept in business by virtue of clients' inability to access a preferred provider. Since the purpose of implementing a competitive market was supposed to ensure quality services at the lowest possible cost, based on the idea of public choice, the control of matter starts appears to frustrate the system. In fact, it was intended to ration the total amount of supply, regardless of demand, in the period before cuts to scope took over as the rationing mechanism. Matter starts continued to exist in the 2018 contracts, but in far greater numbers, so that no provider should run out of matter starts, although some providers still limit capacity for other reasons, as explored in Chapter 4.

Administrative control transferred in 2013 to the Legal Aid Agency (LAA), an executive agency of the Ministry of Justice, with no responsibility to plan provision or address advice deserts. The LAA's predecessor, the LSC, had its accounts qualified by the NAO for four successive years from 2008–09 to 2011–12, leading the new Agency to adopt what a practitioner in the BAJ study described as "intensified surveillance and a zero-tolerance approach to human error". The LAA contract managers who were interviewed for the study largely agreed with that assessment. LAA contract managers explained that they manage contracts across multiple categories of law, working for a maximum of three years with any firm, "to ensure we aren't getting too pally with a particular firm". They are not legally qualified, so their monitoring is limited explicitly to financial and other compliance issues: for example, whether the file includes the required evidence of the client's means and is billed with the correct code within the prescribed time. Contract managers report to regional managers, who report upward through the hierarchy to the NAO, so individual contract managers' duties are very narrowly focused on avoiding 'errors' in payment (Partington, 2015). Some providers in the BAJ study believed this added to the general mistrust, with relationships driven by the LAA "trying to claw back money", though other practitioners emphasised that constructive relationships existed, and not all contract managers were "suspicious".

Much of the interaction between LAA and provider was moved online during this phase, with the Client and Cost Management System (CCMS) becoming mandatory for all providers from 2016. It was working extremely badly at the time of the fieldwork, yet telephone and other lines of communication had been closed off. The consequences of this are discussed in more detail in Chapter 4. The LAA, faced with cuts to its administrative budget (as opposed to the legal aid fund) also had to make savings, leading it to pilot and implement labour-saving innovations, such as allowing certain providers to grant their own funding extensions up to a certain limit, further reducing human interaction but somewhat contradicting the trend of decreasing trust.

In February 2019, the MoJ published the *Post-Implementation Review of Part 1 of LASPO* (2012), in which the government responded that the civil legal aid market was 'sustainable at present' (paragraph 52), albeit acknowledging that there were areas that needed further investigation. Much of the rest of this book calls that conclusion into question.

Why history matters

The reason this history matters is because it helps to understand the nature of the sector and system which evolved. Although this book is about legal aid, not about immigration policy, it is a core argument throughout that the whole system matters. Immigration policy and Home Office practice matter to immigration legal aid in the same way that welfare benefits law and the Department for Work and Pensions' practice would matter to a discussion of welfare benefits legal aid.

The brief exploration of context in this chapter reveals certain key themes which run throughout the book and help to explain how monopsony has led to market failure. These are: the significance of hostility as a driver of policy; the 'humans and econs' theme; the need to take a whole-system approach; and the existence of 'policy debris' as a driver of dysfunctionality.

Hostility as a policy driver

Hostility has been a driver of policy in immigration, in legal aid, and in social welfare services more broadly. The hostility towards immigration perhaps needs little elaboration, since creating a 'hostile environment' has been official Home Office policy since May 2012 (Kirkup & Winnett, 2012), resulting in the Windrush scandal, but is not new. It can be seen in the political and media discourses as long ago as the 1800s, which fed into the Aliens Act 1905 with a view to fending off Jewish refugees, and the undeniably racialised Commonwealth Immigrants Acts of the 1960s. In deportation law, it interacts with racialised discrimination in the criminal justice system. We can see it in the privileging of British ancestry, which means protecting White migration. We can see it in the further privileging of existing socio-economic advantage through the scope of migration permitted under the immigration rules. Managed migration is the commercialised end of immigration policy, a human resources tool for the destination country, cherry-picking the 'brightest and the best', as defined by a shortage occupation list and earnings or investment criteria based on host-country needs for either highly skilled or low paid work (or sometimes both at once). Migration for asylum, on the other hand, is residualised (Crouch, 2004) alongside the 'undeserving' migrant who either arrives undocumented or becomes undocumented after arrival.

The nature, extent and background of the hostility to immigration are not examined in detail in this book (for more discussion of those issues, see Gibney, 2004; Spencer, 2011; Webber, 2012; Anderson, 2015; Yeo, 2020). It will be argued, though, that this hostility often generates additional demand or need and creates dysfunctionality. As the UK slowly reckons with racism, it is important to recognise the racialised nature of its immigration laws and policies. It will require political courage to remove it.

The hostility towards lawyers, or to broad conceptions of access to justice, can be seen in both political and media comments about lefty lawyers, state-funded Rottweilers, fat cat lawyers, a legal aid gravy train, and defendants being handed large sums of legal aid, constructing both lawyer and client as abusive, particularly in cases against the government itself. In 2020, lawyers acting for people who faced unlawful forced removal to another country were condemned by the Home Secretary as 'activist lawyers' when it was the Home Office which had failed to uphold the law. The same hostility manifests in anti-judiciary sentiments expressed by government and media figures when the government loses a case in the courts. It is a persistent thread running through the book and manifests throughout the market structure, particularly in fee and auditing regimes, financial risks and high transaction costs placed on small legal businesses and charities, and in a procurement strategy (especially in immigration work) which gives little priority to the idea of ensuring full geographical coverage.

This hostility towards legal aid and lawyers can be seen as part of a broader hostility to state-run public services and welfare provision in the UK. The swing towards private sector or marketised provision of welfare can also be seen in education, healthcare and so on. This is undeniably a political and ideological movement, part of the neoliberal shift away from welfare states and towards the belief that free markets will allocate and provide more efficiently, that is more cheaply and at higher quality, than state-run services or bureaucracies – a view referred to as 'market fundamentalism' by critics such as the Nobel Prize winner Joseph Stiglitz. Neoliberalism is not discussed in any detail in the book, except to acknowledge that it is the broader ideological framework underlying the managerialism and marketisation which have shaped public service policy and delivery since the 1980s.

As explained earlier in this chapter, this trend really came to bear on legal aid in the late 1980s, since legal aid already operated somewhat as a market of private providers. In a short and highly readable discussion, De Grauwe (2017) refers to a 'pendulum' between market and state-run provision. This, he says, has swung almost entirely to the market side in recent years, but he argues that neither all-market nor all-state provision is sustainable; that a mix is always needed. This book takes as a starting point that, while legal aid should never be taken over by direct state provision, there will always be a need for some state intervention to ensure services are available in all geographical areas and categories of law. A mix will always be needed. These are choices, rather than the immutable nature of things. Despite having always operated as a quasi-market, the legal aid market will still fail if market conditions become too harsh or too dysfunctional. This unworkable harshness and dysfunctionality are all the more likely, however, when policy is driven by hostility.

'Humans and econs'

This dovetails with the second key theme, of 'humans and econs'. On the face of it, the 'hostile environment' policy declared by the Home Office in May 2012 targeted illegal migrants (Kirkup & Winnett, 2012), but practitioners perceived it as hostile to lawyers, legal aid, all migrants (including lawful ones), and even the rule of law itself.

Interviewees in the BAJ study talked about hostility from the Home Office, legal aid authorities and courts, causing "difficulty in getting a fair hearing for our clients". They expressed an "extreme sense of responsibility" for their clients where, for example, the client had a serious illness and would certainly die within a short time if removed from the UK, or was on hunger strike in detention and the barrister felt responsible for getting the case heard quickly. This gives rise to the strong identity of legal aid and refugee lawyers, which underpins a supportive professional network in which barristers, solicitors and other practitioners share expertise and support one another, even when they belong to ostensibly competing organisations.

To talk about 'the supply side of the market' and 'providers of legal aid services' sounds alien to these foundations and purposes. The changes to legal aid policy from 1998 onwards opened up the immigration legal aid sector to new entrants who did not share the same commitments, and the marketisation brought in as a result of the Carter Review later transformed the landscape in which they operate. In particular, the Carter changes treated all practitioners as rational economic actors – people who would act first and foremost in their own economic interests. Those reforms therefore aimed to ration access, control prices and interpose a competitive mechanism, which was expected to take over price-setting while maintaining quality.

This book suggests that these economic assumptions which underpin the current market structure are flawed, particularly around rational economic actors. Critiquing this idea of rational economic actors, Thaler and Sunstein (2008) distinguish between 'humans' and 'econs'. 'Econs' are rational utility maximisers, who will respond to the financial incentives placed in front of them, whereas 'humans' take into account a wider range of considerations. Chapter 7 explores the idea of a spectrum, from the most demand-responsive lawyers (humans) at one end to the most incentive-responsive (econs) at the other, and the implications of this split in the sector, the beginnings of which are discussed earlier in this chapter (see also Bevan and Fasolo, 2013). The imposition of 'econ'-like behaviour onto 'humans' engaged in a fundamentally human activity is one of the key themes of this book.

The counter-argument might be that legal aid professionals, since they are paid with public money, *should* behave as econs. The implication in this (and in market theories more broadly) is that econ-like behaviour offers better quality at lower cost (that is, better value for money) than human-like behaviour. But, as the discussion throughout the book shows, that argument is not supported by the evidence. The econ-lawyer may cost less but cost is not the same as value. A toaster costing £10 still offers poorer value for money than one costing £25 if the more expensive version lasts five years while the £10 one is broken after one year.

The £10 toaster also creates what economists call 'negative externalities', or negative consequences for wider society which are not paid for by the manufacturer of the poor-quality toaster, in the form of broken toasters in landfill sites. Externalities are an important concept in the book. They can be positive or negative. Air pollution might be a negative externality of a factory, which impacts on the local residents and is not paid for by the manufacturer or factored into the cost of the items made in the factory. Positive externalities include things like an increase in house values for homeowners living near a popular new amenity or transport hub. The book points out how low-quality legal work can generate more costs than it saves, and create negative externalities for the client and wider society.

This helps to understand why there are, in all categories of social welfare law as well as family and criminal law, practitioners and organisations that continue doing legal aid work even when they themselves argue that it is uneconomical to do so. They are, in Thaler's terms, 'misbehaving' (2015). This matters because, in discussing legal aid with policy officials, the response has often been that so long as providers keep bidding for work the terms of that work must be acceptable and, implicitly, sustainable. In reality, this book argues, the terms of doing the work create an irreconcilable conflict between providers' financial viability, quality of services and client access – an anti-market market which is only sustained by the goodwill of the humans. That, in turn, generates negative externalities for society, while often failing to meet the needs of the client or the system itself.

A whole-system perspective

The third key theme is the need for a whole-system perspective. Throughout the book, it is argued that demand and supply cannot be understood in isolation. They are products of, and factors within, a whole system and it is useless to try to reform legal aid without taking a systemic view that takes into account immigration law and policy, and the government departments which are most closely involved; in this case the Home Office and Ministry of Justice, and their subordinate agencies. The conclusion to this book (Chapter 8) offers a recent example of how a well-intended attempt to reform (in a fairly small way) the appeals system was almost derailed by the failure to take a whole-system approach.

Just as history matters in understanding the immigration legal profession, it matters in understanding the rest of the system. The forces which have shaped public services have also acted on government departments, similarly subjecting them to targets and performance management, administrative budget cuts, auditing by the NAO, and a constant process of change to delivery models. The many commentaries on changes in government discuss this in much greater depth: see, for example, Clarke and Newman, 1997 and 2012; Bevan and Fasolo, 2013; Burnham and Horton, 2012; Burton, 2013.

The Ministry of Justice has overarching responsibility for both legal aid administration and for the courts, through Her Majesty's Courts and Tribunals Service (HMCTS) which, like the LAA, is an executive agency. Policy matters and fee levels are entirely the preserve of the Ministry, and the LAA avoids trespassing into that territory, whereas the reverse is true of operational considerations. That separation is quite fiercely guarded after criticism in the Magee Review in 2010 led to the abolition of the LSC and its replacement with the LAA. There may be good reasons for this separation, but it all contributes to the fragmentation of the system and the consequent difficulty of advocating for systemic change involving multiple government departments and agencies.

Policy debris

The fourth key theme, which is introduced only briefly here, is around policy debris. This chapter has shown the main phases of the legal aid market, influenced by changes in governance and the administration of services. Wider trends in the organisation of government departments and their subordinate departments and agencies, in professional regulation, in auditing, and so on, mean that the policies acting on a system change frequently. After the Carter Review in 2006, legal aid policy was set on a pathway towards Best-Value Tendering (BVT). This substantially shaped the policy decisions around fee structure, contracting, auditing, minimum quality standards, and so on. Rightly, BVT has been abandoned as a destination (for the most part), but the debris of that policy direction is still very much in evidence and is contributing to the dysfunctionality of the system.

With these key themes and the overarching context set out, it is now time to take a close-up view of some of the organisations and practitioners who participate in the market.

3

Business of Asylum Justice
case studies

The provider base of publicly funded asylum legal services under contract to the Legal Aid Agency (LAA) consists of solicitors' firms and not-for-profit organisations of different sizes, business models and cultures. The exact number of provider offices changes constantly, usually increasing at the time that new contracts are awarded and declining throughout the contract period. In June 2020, 3,476 offices held a legal aid contract across civil, criminal and family law (down to 3,379 by December 2020). Some of these are multiple offices of the same firm, others are sole offices or practitioners; some offices offer multiple categories of law and others only one. Of these, 279 offices were authorised to offer immigration and asylum legal aid, according to the LAA's Directory of Legal Aid Providers spreadsheet (dated 17 June 2020).[1] This had fallen from a peak of 326 when the contracts were awarded in September 2018, after a low of 231 before those contracts were awarded. It compares with 1,637 offices authorised to do family legal aid work, 1,682 criminal providers, 430 for housing, and 56 for welfare benefits (which is largely outside the scope of legal aid).

These offices are not spread evenly through the country. The LAA divides England and Wales into geographical 'procurement areas', which vary in size for different categories of legal aid. For housing and debt, the country is split into 130 procurement areas, often comprising one or two local authority areas. For family law there are 108, whereas for community care there are 12 much larger procurement areas, and just 4 for welfare benefits. For immigration and asylum, the country is divided into six procurement areas which, unlike all other categories, are subdivided into 'access points'. There are 26 access points in total, varying in size from a single city to two or three counties, but some parts of the country are not access points and do not have any provision.

---

[1] See https://www.gov.uk/government/publications/directory-of-legal-aid-providers for the current iteration of this directory.

Figure 3.1 shows the distribution of asylum and immigration legal aid providers in England and Wales. The dark grey areas have no providers at all; the pale grey areas are access points with one provider each; and the white areas have more than one provider. The numbers on the map state the number of provider offices in those areas. The supply profile is somewhat more complicated: for example, not all offices with a contract actually opened any cases – a point which is discussed in more detail in Chapter 6. As can be seen, in some parts of the country, a would-be client may have to travel a long way for a face-to-face meeting with a legal representative.

As for the Immigration Bar, 531 barristers listed immigration as their main area of practice in 2019 and a further 481 derived some income from immigration work as a subsidiary area of practice, out of 16,982 barristers (excluding pupils) in practice that year (BSB, private email communication). Not all do publicly funded work. This compares with over 1,900 practitioners doing family work in 200–220 sets of chambers in 2009 (Maclean & Eekelaar, 2009). Some chambers house a dedicated immigration team, whereas others include immigration and asylum practitioners within a public law or human rights team, but individual barristers may do immigration work without a team doing similar work, so it is difficult to estimate the number of chambers involved. Geographically, specialist immigration barristers are concentrated mostly in London, with smaller groupings in Birmingham and Manchester and a dearth of practitioners elsewhere (BSB, 2016).

None of the participants in the BAJ case studies is representative of the sector as a whole, nor of any one business type (for example private firms or not-for-profits, but they offer a picture of how the policies and frameworks discussed in Chapter 2 impact on the organisations and individuals involved in doing legal aid work. The not-for-profits are identified as Centres A, B and C, with the private firms coded Firms X, Y and Z. Barristers are referred to by level of seniority and not identified further. Only the Refugee Legal Centre (RLC) is identified by name, since it is a unique case and it would be impossible to disguise its identity.

Private firms

Firm X is a London-based solicitors' firm providing private and legal aid services in various social welfare-related categories of law. It has a relatively large immigration team of over 40 legal workers, including trainees, plus an administration team. Out of these, seven legal caseworkers were interviewed, at levels from partner to trainee,

Figure 3.1: Supply map for England and Wales after September 2018 contract round

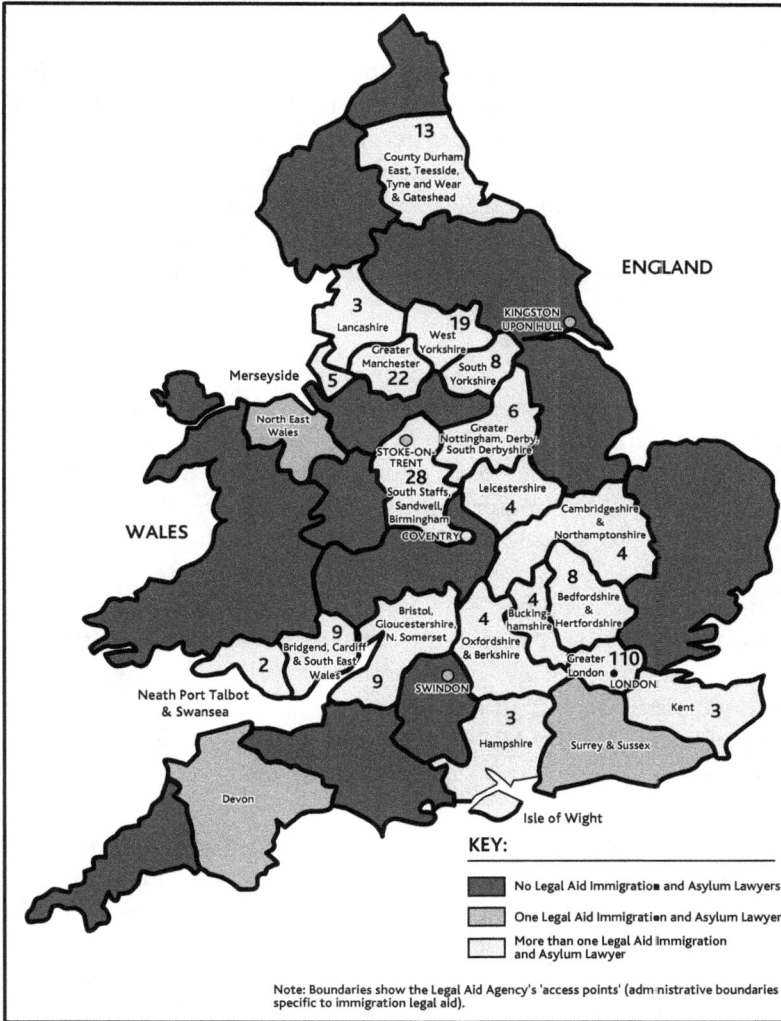

KEY:

No Legal Aid Immigration and Asylum Lawyers

One Legal Aid Immigration and Asylum Lawyer

More than one Legal Aid Immigration and Asylum Lawyer

Note: Boundaries show the Legal Aid Agency's 'access points' (administrative boundaries specific to immigration legal aid).

Source: Data from Legal Aid Agency. Map designed by Karen Hood: karenhood.myportfolio.com.

as was the partner with overall responsibility for legal aid asylum and immigration work, who combined casework and the practice-management role. The firm is identified by barristers and other solicitors' firms as 'excellent', both in terms of its casework and the fact that it bills effectively and pays promptly. Because of its reputation, it receives referrals from trafficking support organisations and local authorities, as well as effectively unlimited demand despite the presence of numerous providers in London.

Caseworkers attributed the high quality of the firm's work to ethos and commitment. As one solicitor put it, quality came from: "Not giving up when the LAA refuses funding the first time, the second time, the third time, the fourth time, to get an expert report, if that's necessary to put the case forward in the best possible way." The maintenance of quality happened both formally, through highly structured supervision systems and a weekly meeting, and informally, as ways of working were handed down from experienced staff to new trainees and caseworkers. As a trainee solicitor put it:

> 'We benefit from the fact that we've got a lot of people who've got a lot of experience and have been in some ways formed in an environment where legal aid wasn't so restrictive … that means they have a lot of experience in terms of actually what is required to do the case justice. And then they are able to pass on that experience to us, who are newer.'

This approach contrasts with another caseworker's experiences elsewhere: "In other places I've worked there's a lot more letting the case go at an earlier stage when it could go further if there was more of an emphasis on that in the organisation." This, however, was not affordable with the fixed fee and had forced the firm to abandon some of its former client base, as a partner explained:

> 'It's definitely tricky to make it work and also keeping standards up at the same time. We turn away hundreds of cases a week really. Those would be fixed-fee cases. We stopped counting but at one point it was around 500 a month. In reality what's happening is the legal aid cases are getting fewer and fewer and the private work is going up and up to make it work. It was probably only about 5 per cent of the firm's income pre-LASPO and it's now [in 2017] probably about 30 per cent, so in a very short period of time. That's been quite sad for a lot of people here who grew up doing legal aid stuff and don't really want to be private lawyers.'

Firm X also had a contract to provide legal services in detention centres. At the time of the fieldwork, this work was done on a rota system, whereby each firm with a contract for a particular detention centre provided advice surgeries four times in a week, usually one week per month. An NGO worker in a detention setting said that "everyone" wanted to see this particular firm, which had the best reputation of all the detention providers. The surgeries are divided into ten half-hour slots, paid at a fixed rate. Any work taken on through surgeries is both separate from the matter-start allocation in the contract and paid at hourly rates, which made it an important contributor to the firm's financial viability. This system changed in the 2018 contract, in that all bidders for higher allocations of matter starts could bid to do detention work. Partners in Firm X did not know, at the time of the fieldwork, how this would affect them, illustrating the constantly changing system in which the firm has to plan for financial sustainability. As a partner reflected, in relation to legal aid work and forward planning: "In terms of the business model you have, it's all very dependent on whatever they decide to do and a lot of the stuff they do is pretty random. It doesn't seem to be driven by anything particularly sensible." The point here is that, despite making a decision that legal aid provision should be market-based, the conditions created are not conducive to the operation of businesses.

Firm Y is a large non-London firm with offices in major dispersal areas. It is ranked in *Chambers and Partners* and is also identified by barristers outside London as one of the better firms. It does private and legal aid work in immigration and asylum, but also has departments in other areas of law, which are wholly privately funded. Like Firm X, a partner attributed the quality of their work to commitment, thorough and targeted supervision, as well as decisions about the business model that facilitated going beyond the fixed fee. Local context influenced that, because Firm Y benefited from a volume of new clients arriving too late in their asylum process for the firm to do work exceeding the fixed fee. This partner explained:

'The sooner you can get legal advice, the better. [But] we are seeing more people, either post-interview or even post-decision, turning up not having had a solicitor, which isn't good for them. If you're looking at it from a business perspective, we're getting paid the same amount for doing less work. Not good for the clients though.'

This seemed to happen because the workers at initial accommodation centres identified poor practice on the part of other firms in the area, whereby interpreters worked at those centres in the mornings and took new arrivals to solicitors for whom they worked in the afternoons. As the partner said:

> 'The clients were getting signed up to Legal Help and then never seeing the solicitor again and then they were being dispersed to somewhere else and would then have to go and get a new solicitor. So it appeared that there was almost this mini industry of some firms getting £413 for – often it would even be the interpreter who was filling in the Legal Help form and taking some basic instructions, if any instructions, and then the matter would be closed. One would like to think the Legal Aid Agency would look at those sorts of things, but I have no faith in them investigating anything.'

He acknowledged the impact on quality of clients' late referral to his firm and the dilemmas implicit in the private-practice business model:

> 'Sometimes we get [staff] who have moved on because they want to provide a much better service, but they can't do it within the constraints of legal aid. I know there's much less local authority or charity funding, but occasionally there's a safety net of some other things in not-for-profit organisations, whereas in a private practice you have to survive within the constraints of legal aid or else you go out of business.'

Like Firm X, the balance of Firm Y's work was shifting towards more private-client work and less legal aid, with higher-value judicial review and higher appeals playing an important role:

> 'Clearly we're doing more private immigration work, but also I think it's winning our judicial review and Court of Appeal cases. Although we're not getting paid by the Legal Aid Agency, we're getting paid by the Home Office when we win those. We can only do them if we have a legal aid contract, because we couldn't take the risk otherwise. ... We're suddenly going from £60-odd an hour to £200 an hour and that makes a big difference, so being good at judicial review and Court of Appeal work is a significant advantage.'

Although Firm Y took on a higher volume of fixed-fee cases than any other provider in the study, and found they escaped the fixed-fee scheme less often, they did find that non-asylum cases frequently ended up being paid at hourly rates:

> 'Because you're only getting £234, assuming they're a domestic violence case or something, they do take a lot of work. Doing 3 × £234 with a traumatised victim of domestic abuse when you have to spend lots of time with them to do statements and prepare, get all the evidence together, you can go "escape fee" [escape the fixed fee] on those really quite easily.'

The other important factor in its case mix was its detention-centre contract which, like Firm X, provided it with a flow of hourly rate work outside its matter-start allocation. The partner had never worked this out previously but, including its standard matter starts from all of its offices, the files it opened from detention surgeries amounted to around a sixth of its cases. The economics of this were:

> '... hit and miss. You'll have half a dozen cases that you end up claiming £40 on because you sign the client up to do a bail application and then they're moved somewhere else, or they never respond. On the other hand, you'll get a really interesting judicial review or an unlawful detention, something that's "lucrative" and can generate a decent amount of income. So it is a bit hit and miss if you're looking at it purely from the money it can bring in, but it's worthwhile because there are enough cases that you can do a significant amount of work on and make it worthwhile.'

The economics, however, were not the firm's main priority. They valued the detention work because: "I think we're good at it. I think we're better than a number of the other firms that do it already. I think we take on more cases and I think the advice we give is better." Despite its efforts to maintain financial viability, the firm had recently closed one of its offices, which was relatively expensive to run, prompted by a combination of economic challenges.

> 'We were struggling to make it financially viable. It was our office in [town] that only did immigration. Just doing it on its own, it was difficult for it to break even and then

our most experienced solicitor there, who did probably 75
per cent of the billing for that office, decided he wanted to
leave the law totally after 15 years. And we'd already been
trying to recruit other people and it had been a real struggle,
so we were never going to be able to replace him with the
right person, so we took the really disappointing decision,
because the demand there is huge and there are fewer and
fewer people available there. From a business perspective,
we should've closed it earlier, but we didn't want to, but
particularly when he handed in his notice we just thought
we can't carry on with this anymore.'

This difficulty in recruiting suitable staff arises frequently throughout
the country, but particularly for providers outside London, and becomes
chronic in areas which are already advice deserts. It affects all levels,
from accredited caseworkers through to supervising solicitors or
caseworkers. It has arisen largely since the closure of the RLC and now
appears to be one of the most significant difficulties facing providers.

Firm Z was in the process of surrendering its legal aid contract and
was studied 'opportunistically', although it did not meet the original
inclusion criteria for the study, to help understand the reasons why
firms leave the market. Both partners in the firm were interviewed.
Firm Z was by far the largest provider in its access point in a small
city, with very little competition. There was some asylum dispersal
to nearby areas, which also had limited supply. Most of its legal aid
caseload was adult asylum applicants, but it also did private work,
wholly in immigration, asylum and nationality law. Although the small
profit margins were a concern, both partners said it was the stress of
working with the LAA, including financial recoupments of payments
already made, that drove them to give up legal aid work, describing it
as "like an abusive relationship".

'You've got people doing hours and hours of work on
complex applications and you're paying them to do that and
you're getting £230 for it so … we just decided, because
of the auditing process as well, that we just didn't want to
do it anymore. And it's really sad because I really believe
in legal aid but financially and because of the audit process,
[it was] just too stressful, horrendous.'

The partners explained that both day-to-day applications to the LAA
and the auditing process created costly managerial demands and the

threat of recoupments or non-payment. On recoupment, one of the partners said:

> 'The really horrible one is contract compliance auditing. They select a number of files, say 30 that you've billed over the last twelve months, and they audit them and they'll either say, "Yes, they're fine", or they'll say, "There's a few errors, but we'll audit you again in six months", or they'll extrapolate, which means they'll say they're disallowing ten per cent of these files, in terms of the money that they pay for them. Therefore they're going to extrapolate that and … claw back ten per cent of what they paid to you in the last year. That happened to us once, the extrapolation – I think it was £103,000 they clawed back and it took a long time to bounce back from that. So that process is horrible because you're waiting, you know that there's so much in the balance.'

The requirement to self-review files was equally problematic:

> 'There's this complex coding so if you put the wrong code in you can get a contract notice. Anyway we had this audit, as a result of which they made me carry out a self-review of all the files I'd billed for the previous five years, I think it was, which was 1,200, and then I had to report back to them, so that took months to do that. And then they served us a contract notice saying you've made these mistakes, and then that triggers another audit. So they come back in and they look at a load more files and they found two minor things: an hourly rate case had been claimed as a fixed fee, and something else – I can't remember what it was. So then we got another contract notice. And then they came back again and found another little thing and gave us another one, so then because we'd had three in the same year, they then started talking about contract sanctions, which is they won't pay us for a period, they won't let us open cases, blah blah blah. And then if it happens again, they could serve us with a notice to terminate. So then we had another audit. So yes, there are errors, but you have to be there to understand the madness of it all and the approach of auditors is so inflexible.'

The consequence of all of this was that the partners had to change their managerial structure in a way which prevented one of them from doing any significant amount of casework:

> 'It's so expensive to maintain a contract because you need someone senior to work practically full-time on it without fee-earning and, given the low levels of pay, when you add it up it's just like, "What are we doing?" [My partner] was employed until we gave up the contract, four days a week, dealing with the legal aid contract [and] didn't do casework because it was a full-time job managing the contract and, when you factor that in, the cost of that person, along with the low rates of pay, when we've done the maths, it's actually something that's holding us back.'

Similar points were made by private providers in Plymouth, explaining why they had moved out of legal aid work and were unwilling to return to it, despite the unmet demand there. Auditing, the costs of contract compliance, and the threat of financial clawbacks were cited even more than rates of pay as reasons for leaving the legal aid market.

Although it had two offices, Z was a relatively small firm, particularly after making several staff redundant at the time of LASPO. Firm Y, on the other hand, was formed from a merger of a very small firm with a larger one when LASPO came into force. It seems that some law firms have opted for safety in numbers to survive in legal aid, perhaps because of the high cost of maintaining a contract, but as the next section shows, not-for-profits are mainly opting for smallness.

Not-for-profits

Between 2005 and 2018, 64 per cent of not-for-profit legal aid asylum and immigration providers left the market, falling from 105 to just 38 (Refugee Action, 2018), meaning the not-for-profits in this study are part of a small and shrinking field. They were encouraged into the market in the LSC era, as offering real choice of provider types and a high-quality, holistic service (Moorhead et al, 2003). However, the unified contract which places them on the same terms as private businesses may be fundamentally incompatible with their operating model, forcing them to abandon some of the distinctive features which made them desirable to policy makers, but still leaving them without many of the survival options available to private businesses.

Centre A is a charity in a non-London urban area. Legal services make up only a small proportion of the charity's work, and its main focus is on areas of social welfare unrelated to immigration and asylum. It does no privately paid work, so depends entirely on legal aid and charitable income. The immigration team is small, consisting of an administrative support worker and five advice staff: one full-time and one part-time solicitor, and three part-time advisers registered with the OISC. The legal teams share a practice manager, who answers to the Chief Executive of the charity. All of the practitioners in the immigration team, two recent leavers, the practice manager and Chief Executive were interviewed.

The team was identified as providing high-quality services by a range of informants, including other lawyers, NGOs and social services in the city. It is the preferred provider for the local authority when referring unaccompanied children, and has scored highly on peer review. There was only one other legal aid provider with an asylum contract remaining in the city, which informants stated did not have a reputation for high-quality services. For several years, the team had operated on a deficit budget, subsidised by its parent charity, and had been halved in size when LASPO came into force. As a senior caseworker put it: "We made a very big loss with [more] people so the rationale was that if you cut the number of people in half, you'll make half a loss. But we were making a massive loss." Another explained:

> 'Our board is actually quite sympathetic towards us and … . It's a really difficult one because they have subsidised us so much over the years and they do subsidise us now, and I think they've finally just said we're not going over this amount; anything over and above this we're not going to do.'

As a result, the team could only meet a fraction of the demand for its services, and had made a decision to prioritise the most vulnerable clients:

> 'We don't have anything written down about this. It's not necessarily a policy, but I would say we try and prioritise vulnerable people, and minors are vulnerable. Coincidentally they are more profitable in terms of hourly rate as well, so that would be another reason to take them on, but also the domestic violence cases, we try and take them on. We feel that if somebody's got an asylum claim, an adult

asylum seeker, perhaps they're more in a position to travel to London or wherever to get alternative representation.'

Even in this priority category, they could not meet all of the local need, giving rise to a dilemma expressed by several staff, whereby the quality of service for one client was pitted against providing any service at all for another. As one caseworker put it:

> 'At the moment we've got a massive [waiting] list and that's really challenging. I feel like we could do with one or two extra members of staff to be able to meet the need. Certainly over the summer we were having to turn people away and we knew they might have been going to firms which perhaps wouldn't approach their cases in the same way as us, and that was really hard, but we can't take on – I can't take on too many cases and then not be able to help that person.'

Centres B and C are London-based not-for-profits, both doing exclusively social welfare categories of law, with no private work at all, but with some related projects funded by charitable grants. Both centres were widely identified by other practitioners as exceptional providers, carrying out cutting-edge casework and litigation. Within their teams, some practitioners also work as peer reviewers or independent cost-assessors, meaning they had broad expertise in the field. Centre C had moved to accepting cases by referral only, with no walk-in clients, whereas Centre B prioritised unaccompanied children and complex cases which, in practice, also amounted to taking cases by referral only. This was a strategy for both financial survival and ensuring that complex cases could be pursued, free from some of the constraints faced by private providers.

All three organisations echoed the points made by private firms about the escalating stresses of working with the LAA, which was causing individuals to look for work outside legal aid:

> 'I've been doing this quite a long time and it's never been more stressful, because of dealing with the Legal Aid Agency. We can't plan our diaries, because ... we don't know when we're going to get decisions from them. I only do my job at [Centre C] three days a week now. I needed to move out of it. I'd quite like to leave legal aid practice actually. One of my colleagues is going on sabbatical because

she's very stressed and she's been very stressed for a long time and had issues with her health and it doesn't have to be like that and it shouldn't be. If people genuinely want a system that works, that shows fairness and adherence to human rights conventions and the Refugee Convention and other rights, then it's not difficult to change the way of working so that it enables people to live normal professional lives as well.'

The not-for-profits had experienced similar problems on audit to those described by the interviewees in private firms. Centre A was threatened with a recoupment of £180,000, which would have caused the closure of the service, which was eventually negotiated down to the centre being unpaid for "about £70,000 worth of work". The billing codes, contract specification and process of getting paid were all seen as more complex in immigration than other categories of law. As a senior caseworker explained:

'I think anybody who comes into this and looks at immigration and the spec is absolutely overwhelmed with how complicated it is. Even our IT guy, he developed our database which has to then comply with the LAA requirements, he tears his hair out at the various things to do with immigration, because you've got all the different specifications and then you've got all the different transitional arrangements, where it depends when you opened a case and what rates you get and what rules apply. It's just massively complicated.'

Recruitment was problematic, just as for private firms, but not-for-profits found the cost of training and supervising new caseworkers to be prohibitive. The Justice First Fellowships operated by the Legal Education Foundation had helped some of the centres to take on trainee solicitors, but Centre A's senior caseworker said:

'We've always recruited [OISC] level two or above. We don't have the resources to train somebody up from scratch, which is another thing we used to do at RMJ. We used to take people in off the street and train them up and that was an incredible resource for the sector that's lost now. Here, we only recruit people who are accredited already, which is becoming increasingly difficult. We've had some recruitment rounds where we haven't been able to recruit anybody. It's quite tricky. I don't know how people are actually getting qualified in the sector now because I don't know anybody who's actually training people up.'

This problem arose for centres in London, as well as outside. Centre C's solicitor explained that they needed to recruit caseworkers who already held the Law Society's level two accreditation. This was specific to immigration work and affected not-for-profits more acutely than private firms:

'We certainly need that because, without that level, you can't charge for legal aid work. It's quite an investment for people to go through that procedure to accredit. My understanding is that some employers employ paralegals and then put them through the Law Society accreditation. I'm not sure how that works really because it's very limited what people can do, charging for legal aid. I suppose providers who do private work as well can use people to do that work whilst they get up to speed with it. I hadn't really thought about that in the context of our recruitment, but that is quite difficult.'

These themes are developed throughout the book, but the focus now moves to the organisation which used to be, in effect, the epicentre of training new immigration practitioners, and to the reasons why it was unable to maintain financial viability.

Refugee Legal Centre/Refugee and Migrant Justice

The Refugee Legal Centre (RLC), later called Refugee and Migrant Justice (RMJ), offers a unique case for studying not-for-profits in the immigration legal aid market. It was the first and largest organisation specialising in asylum law and recognised widely for high-quality work, representing around 10,000 clients per year, but it suffered a catastrophic loss of financial viability as the full impact of marketisation coincided with the beginning of austerity. This section is deliberately narrative, allowing for exploration of how some of the changes outlined in the previous chapter played out within an individual organisation, drawing on some of the public services literature to understand how RLC/ RMJ reflected the wider context of the time.

Initially a unit within the UKIAS, RLC became an independent entity in 1992, with a single office in London and about 30 staff. It opened a second office in 2000 at Oakington Detention Centre, and two more in Leeds and Dover by the end of 2002 to help meet the demands created by detention and dispersal of asylum applicants. Until the extension of legal aid to asylum and immigration appeals in 1999, RLC was the only organisation receiving central government funding to represent on appeals, though JCWI, law centres and some private providers also offered free representation. In 2004, shortly after mainstream legal aid was made available, RLC moved from Home Office block-grant funding to the same LSC case-by-case funding as other providers.

This was a fundamental change to its model of delivering legal aid services, from the salaried to the 'judicare' model, creating a new set of administrative requirements. Previously, the organisation chose how to spend its block grant, but now staff had to record and bill for all time spent on each case, taking up time which had been spent formerly on direct casework. A senior manager explained:

> 'That [administrative work] was its lifeblood in terms of funding but … in a way it was a product of the ethos that the client was the most important thing and time-recording was a distraction that took you away from that. That was a huge cultural shift and it was a very difficult one for the organisation.'

With payment still on hourly rates, in some ways the effect was limited. Although it was necessary to apply for funding extensions and record the time spent, they were paid for the amount of work done. Still, caseworkers described spending two hours applying for an extension, in order to pay for an expert report which they strongly believed the case needed, then being refused by an official with no legal knowledge, and having to spend more time arguing why that refusal was wrong.

These points appear to be typical of voluntary sector organisations at this time, as grant-funding was increasingly replaced with contracts (Evans, 2016), and independence supplanted with regulation (Alcock & Scott, 2007; Stewart, 2007), which involved time and resource demands that had 'either to be absorbed … or passed on' to the provider of the service (Drakeford, 2007:p74). The need to apply 'commercial sales and business management disciplines' (Evans, 2016:p22), to essentially client-based activities, created 'mission drift' (Sommerlad & Sanderson, 2004). Even Le Grand and Bartlett, who advocate strongly for quasi-markets in public services, acknowledge that: 'Many people working in welfare services are not commercially or financially motivated and find it difficult to make the shift from considering, say, the welfare of their users to the financial state of their provider unit' (1993:p31). They recognise that the motivation to make profit is a necessary precondition for the success of a quasi-market, but it is arguably implicit in the name 'not-for-profit' that certain organisations do not possess that motivation. RLC's trajectory from grant-funded to contract-funded organisation and its difficulties in adapting to the managerial and financial demands were therefore very much of the time, in the public-service context. Organisations made up of Thaler and Sunstein's 'humans' (2008) were placed on a forced trajectory to operating as 'econs'.

Having been incorporated into the LSC's system, RLC and the Immigration Advisory Service (IAS) were given an extra two years outside the Graduated Fee scheme, which the Carter Review introduced, to prepare for the changes. RLC continued expanding throughout this period, opening eight new offices between 2006 and 2008 in areas of advice shortage. Expansion added liabilities like leases and staff and placed a heavy demand on their training and supervisory resources, which had to recruit and train non-lawyers from scratch but, as a regional manager explained, there was an expectation of some kind of mutuality: "The LSC begged us to open an office in Ipswich because it was an advice desert, and they said they would help us. Possibly RLC thought the LSC would help us out on a rainy day in exchange."

RLC sought both to reduce its costs and to diversify its income streams to cope with the pending move to fixed fees. Three main diversification strategies are available to organisations: entrepreneurship; expanding into neighbouring markets; and exploiting the emergence of new markets (Boulton et al, 2015). RLC had already expanded into non-asylum immigration work. Expanding into private markets or other areas of social welfare law would have required substantial reorganisation and required the organisation to buy in different sets of skills and knowledge. As an entrepreneurial diversification venture, RLC set up a trading arm in 2007 to provide interpreters; this was projected to bring in a significant profit to subsidise legal service provision, based on charging a booking fee in addition to the hourly rate. However, legal aid rates for interpreters were cut just as they were for lawyers, and the LSC also decided to stop paying booking fees, since it was effectively a monopsony purchaser in this market too.

Its main diversification strategy was rebranding, in 2009, as Refugee and Migrant Justice (RMJ). The rebrand aimed to reflect a broader organisational remit, using grant-funding for campaigning and policy work underpinned by the legal casework, which now included non-asylum work. The change was controversial, described by former staff as everything from "embarrassing" to "absolutely the right thing to do". The policy work brought in around £800,000 in grants before the organisation closed, making the policy director role and the campaigning work self-funding, but it was unable to keep the organisation financially afloat in the time available.

The organisation sought, at the same time, to address the pending move to fixed fees in 2009 by reducing costs per case without compromising quality. A senior manager described addressing the "micro-efficiency" of casework with a multitude of small measures designed to shave costs, each contested in terms of value and efficacy, each mediated through the culture and context of individual offices. The same dilemma arose for staff in law centres (Mayo et al, 2015; Sommerlad, 2008) and in outsourced public services more broadly, where providers' commitment to certain ideals were forced into conflict with the emerging business model (Lowe, 2016). Strategies at RMJ included recruiting assistants who would take on some of the lower skilled or administrative work at a lower rate of pay, though one such recruit describes quickly starting to take on his own casework to meet the unlimited demand from new potential clients, and becoming too busy with that to help with senior colleagues' more mundane tasks.

Alongside this micro-efficiency project were discussions around what some called "maximising the contract", by cross-subsidising fixed-fee cases with higher-paying legal aid work. In order to keep judicial review and higher appeals work in-house, the small, London-based judicial review team expanded to more offices, recruiting more solicitors. These cost more than non-lawyer caseworkers, but were entitled to do higher-value work. There was training for staff on billing effectively, including from a private solicitor who was described as "understanding the contract". Yet the many new, inexperienced caseworkers tended to under-bill, because they felt that they had taken "too long" over the work, and case-management systems designed for the hourly rate payment structure were difficult to adapt to the fixed fee and did not reflect the types of work which the LSC would now accept as billable. Clearly there were costs attached to changing the case-management system each time the fee structure changed.

The effort to reduce costs on a larger scale was hampered by decisions made under the old funding structure, including a long lease on the

Central London office which was far larger than the organisation needed: "a massive, saddling overhead, an albatross". Attempts to sublet excess space to other organisations failed. Issues of this sort limited the speed at which change was possible, although the demands on the organisation were changing rapidly.

Some former RLC staff interviewees believed that there were "too many managers", who did not bring in fees, given the case-by-case funding structure which was now in place. A senior manager who began as a caseworker counter-argued that the increased administration demanded by the case-by-case funding, regulation, contract compliance demands, and the increased size of the organisation, added to the demands on management. The same applies to diversified funding sources: the more sources, the greater the managerial burden (Hughes-Roberts, 2013). This raises the possibility that not-for-profit models are simply incompatible with the funding and contract structures created after the Carter Review, notwithstanding the government view that not-for-profits are a core part of marketised public-service provision and public choice (Moorhead et al, 2003; Hynes & Robins, 2009).

In any case, senior managers and trustees agreed unanimously that the organisation did not have the strategic financial oversight that was needed in this period for a sizeable business with multiple offices and large contracts. The former chair described how, when he arrived:

'The books showed an organisation that still appeared to be profitable and indeed it was in the technical sense profitable, [but] the accounting systems were a bit basic and particularly didn't capture satisfactorily what was happening to our cash-flow position as distinct from our profit-and-loss position.'

In other words, the trustees received feedback which (falsely) reassured them. There was no feedback providing the more alarming information about cash flow. A senior manager who joined the organisation relatively close to its closure explained:

'[P]ossibly because of the historic block-grant situation, that may have meant that the trustees didn't adequately focus on the financials and by the time there was a new batch of trustees that [did], it was almost certainly too late, because it can take a long time to change any business model [let alone] if you're doing it in the context of hanging on for survival.'

This 'lack [of] sophisticated financial and management information' is typical in the charity sector (Williams, 2011:p26), with trustees commonly not understanding the difference between profit and cash perhaps because, like the staff of the organisation, their interests lie in the humanitarian mission rather than finance. (They, too, are humans rather than econs.) The relatively sudden shift for many charities away from grant-funding and into public sector contracting, but without the ability of private companies to borrow working capital, caused a 'financial storm' across the charitable sector during a time of recession (Williams, 2011). In common with other charities, no external body was likely to recognise the risks to RMJ: as a senior manager explained, it was "funded by government contracts, has got a credible-looking board of trustees, has never failed to file its accounts", and the Charity Commission was not resourced to look beyond that.

Even retrospectively, however, interviewees were unable to identify further changes which could have been made during the transition period that would have enabled RMJ, as a multi-office legal-aid-only provider with mainly asylum cases, to survive the cash-flow demands of the switch to payment in arrears. With a two- to three-year wait for payment on cases, a senior manager said: "We calculated that the amount of working capital we would've needed ran to two or three times our actual turnover." Another manager pointed out that the civil servants responsible for procurement had failed to understand the implications of the shift from "no competition in any areas of legal aid to *all* competition", such as "the liabilities in terms of offices, leases, indemnity costs ... that charities couldn't go out and get a bank loan for £6 or £7 million for our working capital". In other words, the market was structured and administered by people who did not necessarily understand markets, and this is behind some of the dysfunction which emerged.

Despite the public-sector-wide pressure on not-for-profits to scale up services, several interviewees said that the only way anything of RMJ could have survived would have been to scale back, making most of the offices independent and closing those which could not be self-sufficient. Arguably, of course, this would not have been the same organisation which drew strength and quality from its size, took strategic litigation (or 'test cases') based on referrals from 200 caseworkers, and provided an in-depth training programme to, as a former manager described it, "take people off the street and make them lawyers".

Voluntary sector organisations across the board were encountering similar problems as private finance initiatives and payment by results created cash-flow demands which not-for-profits were unable to meet, either from their own resources or by borrowing (Burton, 2013). Policy and practice were contradictory. Ministers preferred provision by multiple small suppliers and increased voluntary sector participation in public-service quasi-markets. Yet their departments used bulk-buying power or monopsony control to drive down prices and effectively forced suppliers to scale up for economies (Burton, 2013). This was exacerbated by no-advocacy clauses in many government contracts which prevented organisations using their practical experience to inform campaigning work (Civil Exchange, 2016). This also applied to RMJ: a senior manager, when seeking rescue from the LSC before closure, was told any such rescue would be conditional on stopping their campaign work, yet this was their main alternative source of income.

In April 2009, RMJ moved onto the new system of fixed-fee payment in arrears on closure of the case, subject to a 'buffer' payment intended to ease the transition to late payment. But in January 2010, the LSC informed RMJ that it had been overpaid on the buffer system, so it would receive no buffer payment for March, and would have to make a repayment at the end of the financial year in April 2010 (Slocock, 2010). This precipitated a cash-flow crisis and managers began seeking a rescue package from the LSC. As outlined here, RMJ had a long-term relationship with the LSC, and was the second-biggest provider of legal aid services in the UK, running outreach sessions in ten immigration detention centres and around 30 prisons, as well as its own 12 offices.[2]

From early 2010, the management began taking advice from the business advisory division of a company called BDO. A management reorganisation removed the Directors of Operations and Finance to save costs, leaving only the Chief Executive and the grant-funded Policy Director. BDO's advice, however, did not differ radically from the trustees' and executive management's existing strategy, which the Chair described as trying to reduce costs, improve book-keeping, diversify income sources, "… plus acceptance of the risky strategy we were taking of seeking to persuade government at both political and LSC level to change its approach".

An LSC officer carried out an audit to check that cases were being closed properly – this being the trigger for payment under the new system – and found no significant problems with RMJ's practice

---

[2] Central London, Dover, West London, Croydon, Bedford, Ashford, Ipswich, Leeds, Birmingham, Portsmouth, Hastings, Nottingham.

(Slocock, 2010). Because the overwhelming majority of RMJ's work was asylum, its cases remained open longer than the average, but the audit confirmed that this was not due to failure to close cases promptly, meaning the cash-flow difficulties were not simply caused by internal failures.

RMJ managers had meetings with the LSC and, jointly with IAS, with Lord Bach (then the Parliamentary Under-Secretary of State for Justice) and explained the problems facing both organisations. Lord Bach is said to have given a verbal assurance that he 'would address the problem of cash flow' caused by payment in arrears, as did the opposition spokesperson (Slocock, 2010). Several law centres, which were already on the new system, had also reported difficulties (Sommerlad & Sanderson, 2013). In February 2010, the South-West London Law Centres were given a rescue grant of £235,000 to restructure, on the decision of Lord Bach (Slocock, 2010). There was ample evidence that RMJ was not the only not-for-profit struggling to cope financially with the cuts and the move to late payment.

At the same time, the procurement round which began in late 2009, for new contracts from July 2010, encouraged overbidding, partly by removing any advantage for providers which already operated in an area, and partly by requiring offices in more 'access points' within a procurement area (Harvey, 2010). This resulted in bids for far more matter starts than were available, allowing the incoming government and the LSC to announce that there was an oversupply in the market and that all other suppliers were willing and able to manage on the existing payment terms (*Guardian*, 2010).

A perfect storm of factors hampered negotiations: the calling of a general election meant Lord Bach was no longer in a position to help; the ongoing procurement exercise meant the LSC and ministers were unwilling to meet or assist RMJ; and the 'austerity machismo' of the incoming government meant cuts, rather than rescue packages, were on the political agenda (Hynes, 2012). Finally, a public campaign to save RMJ began, attracting support from figures including the Archbishop of Canterbury, but also a backlash of 'derogatory comments' from the government about RMJ's 'inefficiency' (Slocock, 2010). Ken Clarke, as Minister of Justice, told Parliament that all other providers were managing the new payment regime, despite abundant evidence from IAS, law centres and a large private firm called White Ryland, which had given up its legal aid contract, that this was untrue.

The final tipping point was the next quarter's rent becoming due. It became clear that the LSC and government were not willing to step in. There was no other adequate source of bridging funding. Instead of being, in the words of a senior manager, "too big to fail", RMJ turned out to be "too big to rescue" – at least without commitment from the LSC. The trustees decided to pay staff early, since the timing of the closure would have meant staff (as unsecured creditors) were not paid for the last month, before placing the organisation in administration on 16 June 2010. Staff recalled an impression of a very sudden failure, not preceded by any obvious changes like redundancies or office closures, which contributed to a continuing sense of not understanding. An office manager from one of the smaller offices said that despite his relatively senior position, he still did not really know what had gone wrong. A trustee referred to, "This game of poker ... that to have a chance of securing new matter starts in the contract, it was necessary to present the organisation as financially stable".

RMJ closed with a short wind-down process coordinated by a skeleton staff that attempted to place as many cases as possible with new representatives. Interviewees from all levels felt that it was the clients who suffered most from the closure, with thousands losing representation. Not all files were reallocated successfully. A former staff member remarked in 2017 that he was still seeing people, at a drop-in advice session for homeless people, whose status was unsettled partly as a result of RLC's closure and losing their legal representative. A manager explained that administration was a regulatory vacuum in which: "The safeguarding of the interests of clients was left to administrators who had never dealt with a legal organisation before." The cost to the LSC of closing the organisation was considerable, as it had to pay new representatives for taking on the cases, and much of the money it owed to RMJ for casework the organisation had already done was swallowed up by the administrators.

Understanding the closure of RMJ is particularly relevant to the history and context of the sector which influence how the participants in the market have behaved, and continue to behave, since that event. It is also important for the light it sheds on the loss of not-for profits from the immigration and overall legal aid market. The subsequent closure of IAS and several law centres casts real doubt on the continuing viability of not-for-profits in the market. Those few remaining are much smaller than RMJ and all appear to limit their capacity, or their market share, despite being recognised as offering high-quality work. It means that not-for-profits' participation in the market no longer offers a real choice of provider type.

Publicly funded Immigration Bar

There is very little published work on the publicly funded Bar. One book-length exploration of practices and attitudes across the Bar, though outdated, makes some mention of legal aid (Morison & Leith, 1992), and a new study (Goulandris, 2020) gives valuable insights into the changing character of the Bar in the intervening three decades. Those doing mainly publicly funded or social welfare work, though, have rarely been the focus of study, meaning there is limited evidence on which legal aid policy for the Bar can be based.

This case study comprised 20 barrister interviews – thirteen women and seven men – from six sets of chambers in and outside London, and four members of staff in clerking, management and administrative roles. All six sets of chambers were ranked for immigration and asylum work in the *Chambers and Partners Directory*. All but five of the barristers were also ranked individually. Barristers' seniority is expressed in years of 'call'; that is, the number of years since they were 'called to the Bar' after their academic training. It does not necessarily reflect years of post-qualifying experience. Interviewees ranged from four to almost 40 years' call. Some sets of chambers may house individual barristers who represent the Home Office and others who represent the claimant/migrant, but it is a feature of the Immigration Bar that few practitioners work for both sides. To receive work from the Home Office (via the Government Legal Department), barristers have to apply to the Attorney General's panel, so Home Office work is only offered to those who actively seek it out. All of the barristers interviewed, and all but one of the chambers involved, worked only for the migrant side.

The predominant business model remains self-employed individuals joining together as tenants in chambers. In 2019, out of nearly 17,000 barristers, 13,434 were self-employed (BSB, 2019). They mainly take referral work from solicitors and other professionals rather than working directly with members of the public. Direct access work, where members of the public instruct a barrister directly, was first permitted in 2004 and was not allowed in immigration until 2011. Legal businesses were first allowed to be non-lawyer-owned Alternative Business Structures in 2011, and the Bar Standards Board (BSB) began licensing such entities in 2015, but few sets of chambers have chosen anything other than the traditional model. Although some barristers have opted to only provide direct access work, that model would rarely accommodate asylum work, since few clients can afford to pay privately.

Barristers pay a proportion of their fee income to their chambers for the shared costs of staff, premises and other essentials. Most interviewees paid 20–22 per cent of fee income (before tax and expenses), though in some chambers, tenants pay a fixed rent plus a smaller percentage. The percentage, without a fixed rent, was generally seen by interviewees as fairer to juniors, carers or those returning from parental leave, for example, whose earnings could be lower.

Unlike solicitors' firms and not-for-profits, barristers' chambers do not have a direct contractual relationship with the LAA. Only the largest twenty chambers by 'fund-take' (receipts from the legal aid fund) have an account manager with the LAA. For tribunal work (and some other matters, though not, for example, Crown Court criminal work) the barrister bills the solicitor, who bills the LAA on their behalf, rather than the barrister receiving payment directly from the LAA. This means the relationship between barristers and the LAA is much more distant than that between LAA and providers.

None of the interviewees practised solely in legal aid asylum work; nearly all did other immigration work and most did ancillary areas of work such as age disputes, human trafficking and unlawful detention cases. Some did crossover work with other areas of law, particularly family and mental health law. Around a third also practised in unrelated areas including housing, social security, mental health, employment and discrimination, inquests, actions against the police, prison law, public international law and planning. Two interviewees also sat as part-time tribunal judges, citing a stable income as one of the main reasons. Most did some writing, training or academic teaching alongside their legal practice, and several were trustees or did other voluntary work with refugee and migrant-related charities.

The most junior barristers had little privately paid work, but almost all those over five years' call did private work which took 20–80 per cent of their time, though it often made up a larger proportion of their income. The most junior received most of their work via their clerks, rather than direct from solicitors, consistent with Flood's work on clerks (1983 & 2007). Five of the twenty undertook direct access work. Those who avoided direct access said they did not feel they had the systems in place to look after clients properly or directly. Those who did, however, cited payment in advance as an advantage:

'Obviously one of the joys of direct access is you don't do any work until you're actually paid so, unlike legal aid when you're waiting years to get paid, with direct access stuff you're getting paid straightaway. I would think roughly speaking it was probably about 20 per cent of my time [and] about 37 per cent of my income last year. I made a decision realistically, about three or four years ago, that the only way this is going to continue to be viable is if I did enough private work to allow me to continue to do asylum work, and direct access work has helped a lot with that.'

Barristers and chambers staff believed immigration and asylum work differed from other areas of law, being characterised by often urgent work and a high volume of new case law. One very junior barrister referred to "the speed with which things come at you" in immigration practice: a point echoed at all levels of seniority. Barristers reflected that urgent work arose in a different way in asylum law than in other categories, such as homelessness cases, where a senior barrister explained: "You will have paperwork and … [the client] is likely to be made homeless in two days, three days. You always have a run-up to it, unlike in immigration." The urgency in asylum work, which required the barrister to "drop everything" and work on one case, often to prevent removal to a country where the client feared torture, made the workload particularly unpredictable, adding to stress and the difficulty of combining work with family commitments.

On the other hand, hearings generally lasted less than a day, unlike criminal trials or inquests, making it potentially easier to work part-time. Both male and female interviewees with children talked about having modified their working practices in some ways to fit in with family life: working part-time; working odd hours; reducing the number of days they spent in court each week; becoming "better at saying no" to work to keep the total workload under control; reducing voluntary commitments; refusing urgent work; or doing more of their work from home. Similar strategies have been identified among female Australian barristers with children, though not (at that time) among men (Hunter & McKelvie, 1999).

Partly because of the unpredictable workload, few of the barristers interviewed had taken a systematic approach to developing their practice. Most described their practice development as fairly ad hoc or reactive, driven by the cases which came their way, rather than by seeking out a particular type of work. Being instructed in a case which became important on a current legal issue often led to more instructions in similar cases, as solicitors looked to instruct a barrister who already had experience on that issue. A barrister of over 20 years' call explained: "I'm not very good at career management. I just leave everything with the clerks or papers coming in and just put my head down. Quite literally there's been no thought about my practice or what I should be doing or whether I'm going along a path that I want to. Very reactive." However, it was recognised that 'proactive clerking' could be very effective, as another barrister explained: "I've been so busy recently, I keep meaning to have a practice-development meeting and I haven't had one, but I do think that's really important because they obviously can really steer your practice one way."

Systematic practice development, where it did occur, involved asking chambers' clerks to help find a particular type of work, asking more senior barristers to involve them as a junior or second junior in higher court cases, or speaking at training events and writing on particular legal issues in which they wanted to be recognised as experts. A junior barrister was considering booking time out of court in order to take on paperwork and particularly judicial review work, which might eventually mean she spent less time in court and potentially earned more money. This, however, felt risky in the short term because it meant forgoing the fees (however small and delayed) which she could bill for court hearings.

It is recognised across the Bar that the early years are extremely difficult, particularly for those who cannot fall back on family for financial support (Carr, 1999). This is reflected in a shrinking of the junior Bar (Rose, 2017). One junior barrister gave a vivid description of life, five years after qualifying:

> 'There is always going to be a pressure on the clerks to cover First-tier Tribunal work and if you are the second-most junior you are going to inevitably end up doing a fair proportion of that. I just did my practising certificate fee for the year and to the end of January I think I billed £41,000 and brought in £27,000 [gross before chambers and other professional expenses]. That's hard in London. So I think partly it's the financial pressure that makes you say, "Oh yeah, I'll just do that". It makes it difficult to say "No".
>
> I've moved out of my partner's flat. We were living together for a while and [partner] felt that I was bringing my work home too much, so that led to us not living together any more. I'm living with a friend, who's only charging me £350 a month rent. You can't get that anywhere in London. If I were truly on my own I wouldn't be able to afford rent and I would have to do something else, because I literally couldn't survive. The financial pressure has got to me more and more as I've got older, and the weight

of expectation from family and parents. I've had a lot of pressure from them to think about different career options in the last year.

I find it very hard not to scare new recruits, because I want them to have a realistic idea of what their day-to-day life is going to be like. I want them to know that they're going to be working at 11pm, I want them to know it's going to impact on their stress levels … to possibly impact on their relationships with their families or their partners. It's a whole body-mind-life experience being a legal aid lawyer, and they have to know it before they get into it otherwise … you don't want to give a false impression of what it's like.'

The Carter Review suggested that the perception of low incomes at the junior end was, in reality, underemployment, reflecting oversupply at the junior Bar. Yet all the barristers interviewed, even the most junior, had more demand than capacity. The idea of underemployment was alien to all of the barristers interviewed. As one, of nine years' call, said:

'I constantly feel like I'm running to keep up and constantly busy, too busy. I'm always trying to cut down unsuccessfully. The work's unpredictable. You just blink and your diary fills up … so I can have hearings in my diary which will be fine, but then I'll get paperwork on top of it, so it's trying to manage those two things.'

The uncontrollable nature of paperwork arose partly because of the system whereby immigration judges rarely give their decisions on appeals immediately. Almost invariably, the decision is 'reserved' at the end of the hearing and given in writing, without further warning, some weeks (or even months) later. If the appeal is dismissed, the applicant has only five working days to lodge an appeal to the Upper Tribunal, and can only base such an appeal on an error of law in the first judge's decision. It cannot be appealed simply on the basis that the applicant disagrees with the decision. That means it is quite complex work (which is also done at financial risk), yet it can never be factored into forward planning because of this in-built unpredictability.

The most junior were also seen as vulnerable because they tended to receive work from poorer-quality solicitors, which often demanded more preparation. They also generally received more work from poor payers and did the most travelling for court work in other cities, since they were the least confident in saying 'no' and the least informed about the reputations of the solicitors instructing them. That said, the junior barristers in the study all described feeling well supported by more senior colleagues:

> 'I'm so grateful to pretty much everyone in the immigration team who's probably had queries from me at one time or another. I've never had a situation where I've not been able to discuss a concern with somebody. Whenever I've had a situation where I've felt uncomfortable ethically, [name] has always been a very wise and level-headed and kind source of advice and support. And when I do trafficking stuff, [name] has been there the whole time and has been very encouraging and has also been very active in getting me involved with the team, so that I feel an integrated part of the team. I felt very touched. I felt almost like she'd taken me under her wing to make me part of the team when I first joined and that was very much appreciated. And I've had so much support from everyone that's been absolutely amazing. I can't imagine being anywhere else because of that.'

Most of the barristers interviewed had been in one or two sets of chambers in their career so far. Several had been in three and one had been in six. The main reasons for moving were chambers folding, chambers merging with another set whose ethos the barrister did not share, not being taken on after pupillage, or wanting to move into a different area of law. Although there are specialist immigration barristers working as sole practitioners, sometimes in areas where there are no chambers with immigration teams, they appear to be experienced barristers with an established client base who have moved out of chambers for various reasons. It is not a viable model for a very junior barrister and there are only 609 sole practitioners across the whole English and Welsh Bar (BSB, 2019).

Business models were not unchanging, however. Within the publicly funded Bar there was a recent experiment in setting up alternatives to the physical chambers model. Tooks Chambers – formerly one of the main immigration sets – closed in late 2013 stating that, since 90 per cent of its work was publicly funded, legal aid cuts made it impossible to continue. Some members joined the larger Garden Court Chambers, whereas others set up the virtual Mansfield Chambers, with minimal physical office and conferencing space and barristers effectively working from home (Baksi, 2013). Another prominent immigration set, Renaissance Chambers, closed in early 2014, also citing legal aid cuts, and its 13-strong immigration team joined Mansfield Chambers. However, Mansfield's immigration team left en masse for the traditional building-based Goldsmiths in November 2015, finding the virtual model incompatible with the resources needed to bill and chase fees in immigration (Smith, 2015). The remaining Mansfield Chambers merged with 1 Gray's Inn Square in late 2016. It remains to be seen how the COVID-19 pandemic will impact on barristers' attitudes and practices around the use of physical office space.

Several sets of chambers had appointed directors or chief executives, who took over some of the roles held traditionally by a senior barrister as head of chambers, reflecting the increased administrative demands on heads of chambers. One set of chambers began employing paralegals and researchers to assist the barristers, which was a significant change to its business model with a view to facilitating direct public access work. Some had discussed whether junior advocates (barristers or otherwise) could be employed to meet demand for lower-level work without compromising those individuals' ability to make a living. In reality, the small profit margins in asylum legal aid work make it inherently unappealing as a business proposition for any but the most committed, regardless of business structures.

Those small profit margins are discussed in more detail in Chapter 4, which shows that barristers are underpaid for legal aid work in terms of the number of hours paid for, compared with the number of hours they work. They therefore make a choice to subsidise this underpaid work from other earnings (apart from the most junior practitioners) rather than abandon the underpaid work in favour of higher earnings available from private work. This is in spite of the fact that the legal aid work is often the most stressful because of short time scales and the extreme or traumatic nature of many cases. Other barristers who only do private work remain in legal aid chambers, paying high management contributions which keep those chambers financially viable. The overall picture from the barristers and chambers in the BAJ study is of a small number of individuals who are very committed to the individual clients and client group that they represent.

This description differs from that in some other literature on the Bar in England and Wales: for example, that barristers are difficult to research, 'closed to outsiders' (Rogers, 2010; see also Flood, 1983), and 'represent a pocket of self-righteousness, arrogance, smugness and professional isolationism of the most extreme type' (Harris & Piercy, 1998). This is said to lead to resistance to marketing, new business models, or new ways of working like direct-access (Flood & Whyte, 2009), which leave the Bar stuck in the past and unable to innovate. The difference may arise because legal aid work is done mainly in the 'outsider' sets which some authors refer to (Abel, 1986; Rogers, 2012), which chose to locate outside the Inns of Court and break with some of the more restrictive traditions. Equally it may reflect gradual and ongoing changes in the demographics of the Bar since the 1970s (Boon, 2014).

Barristers expressed a shared identity with the broader publicly funded Bar, which primarily encompasses crime, family and social welfare areas of law, and a shared professional identity with other immigration practitioners, regardless of qualification, particularly via ILPA and online forums like the Refugee Legal Group. There is a 'collegiate' approach, with barristers in ostensibly rival chambers, and practitioners across the sector, supporting each other with advice and sharing of arguments. As a barrister of 13 years' call stated:

> 'The immigration sector probably is very supportive.
> We all know who the enemy is and we all rally around.
> I suspect that in some other sectors it's not quite the same.
> It's a way of channelling people's experiences into a wider
> policy-making sector. It's also about helping to foster this
> sense of common endeavour which we do have, I think,
> in immigration.'

This collegiality appears different in character from that described in Boon's (2014) discussion of collegiality at the Bar, less ritualistic, less based on physical proximity, linked more to the client group and less to the branch of the legal profession, and derived more from the commitment discussed in Chapter 2.

Conclusion

This and the previous chapter have begun to explore the interactions and interconnections between individual organisations and practitioners and the environment in which they operate, affected by immigration law and policy, legal aid policy, professional regulatory structures, court procedures and so on. The micro-level focus on the people and organisations which make up the supply side of the market begins to demonstrate the playing-out of the key themes outlined at the end of the previous chapter.

The following four chapters develop the argument that financial viability is difficult to reconcile with quality in the current fee and audit regimes, meaning that providers have to carefully mediate demand and supply to ensure their own survival, such that quality can only be maintained at the expense of client access. This conflict, which can be seen in all of the case studies in this chapter, seems the direct opposite of what marketisation was supposed to achieve. Indeed, some argue that welfare services were not marketised at all, but were instead commercialised, in a process which actually distorts the market (Crouch, 2004). The state outsources services which are commercially viable for the private sector to provide. There is a residue of services which the private sector is not interested in providing, used by people who are poor and less effective at demanding improvement (Crouch, 2004). Econs, who respond to financial incentives, are willing to provide commercially viable services, together with residualised ones at a poor quality. Humans maintain quality in the residualised sub-sector, but cannot meet the demand. This distorts the very idea of a market, even as market-based procurement remains the notional core of the policy.

4

Broken swings and rusty roundabouts

Since 2007, and the implementation of proposals from Lord Carter's review of legal aid (Carter, 2006), most immigration and asylum application and appeals work is paid for on a system of fixed fees. The premise of the fixed, or standard, fee is that providers are paid a sum which represents the average cost of a case. Some cases will cost more and some less, but overall the payments should roughly equal the work done – the 'swings and roundabouts' principle. The fee varies depending on the type and stage of the case, and is set out in regulations (secondary legislation) which are updated periodically. Cases which cost three times the fixed fee will 'escape' the fixed fee and be paid at hourly rates, which also vary according to the type and stage of work.

Even before the Carter Review and the LASPO Act (2012), which reduced fees further, Moorhead noted the discrepancy between the government view that the legal aid scheme was generous and practitioners' arguments that it was a 'toxic job' and they could barely survive on legal aid rates (2004:p186). He pointed out the lack of robust data on the operation of firms and not-for-profits working in legal aid, the relationship between legal aid and commercial practice, and how legal aid practices responded to economic changes. He also discussed the increased bureaucracy and surveillance and the passing of administrative costs to the providers even before the fixed fee and the most recent cuts were implemented, which made those cuts more difficult to manage. Still less is known about how barristers manage these issues.

This chapter explores in more detail the economics of immigration legal aid businesses and practitioners, arguing that there are five main threats to financial viability in the market-based system:

1) The fixed-fee scheme causes significant financial losses.
2) A great deal of financial risk has been placed on practitioners.
3) Delays or lag between doing the work and getting paid cause severe cash-flow difficulties.

4) The transaction costs of doing legal aid work are too high and have not been factored into the price paid for the work.
5) Economies of scale are not available, or had already been maximised before the fixed-fee scheme was implemented.

Most of these factors apply to barristers as well as solicitors and caseworkers. Barristers do not need a contract with the LAA to do legal aid work, which seems to expose them to lower transaction costs. In other respects, though, they face similar difficulties to solicitors' firms and advice centres, especially around payment delays. Aged debt – money which is owed to them for more than six months – causes particularly acute problems. Since the majority of barristers are self-employed within sets of chambers, financial viability of practice is considered at individual level, as well as for the practice team and chambers as a whole.

Fixed fees and the escape threshold

The swings and roundabouts principle was not working for any of the organisations in the Business of Asylum Justice (BAJ) study (see Chapter 3 for an introduction to the organisations quoted here). The fixed fee pays for an amount of work which all interviewees argued was insufficient to provide a quality service in the vast majority of cases. A partner in Firm X explained:

> 'It's the fixed fee of £413 [at Legal Help stage], and our average cost per case for cases that don't reach the escape-fee [triple] threshold is between £800 and £900, just for our time. So that's one of the reasons why we're just doing less of that work. We're basically getting paid £25 an hour for that. We've worked out that our average costs per case are twice the fixed fee, pretty much.'

Firm X's early strategy was to attempt to get most cases paid at escape fee, via careful recording and justification of all time spent on cases, but it found that fewer than 50 per cent of cases actually did escape. Practitioners emphasised that they did not, and probably could not, "bump it up", but just did "what's needed". In contrast, some caseworkers talked about "self-censorship", where they would under-record the time taken, feeling that a more experienced person would have done the work faster, or in the expectation that the LAA would reduce it on assessment.

Table 4.1: Hourly rates for barristers in First-tier Tribunal appeals if escaping the fixed fee (until June 2020)

Hourly rates (escape-fee cases: appeal stage)	London	Non-London
Preparation and attendance	£57.83	£54.09
Travel and waiting	£28.62	£27.81
Advocacy	£65.79	£65.79

Source: Civil Legal Aid (Remuneration) Regulations 2013 SI/2013/422.

Practitioners in the QALSS interviews likewise said cases commonly cost two to two-and-a half times the fixed fee. Centre A's practice manager said there were "very few" cases which cost less than the fixed fee: most cost significantly more, but did not reach the escape threshold to move onto hourly rates. One caseworker provided examples of her cheapest cases, which cost around £60 over the standard fee, meaning she could never make up the losses on one case by being paid extra on another. Another explained that she could only make savings by taking on eligible cases other than asylum applications or appeals:

> 'The only time I have cases that come in below the standard fee is where someone is applying for indefinite leave to remain, having [previously] received five years' humanitarian protection or refugee status. That is still considered an asylum new matter start and so the fixed fee is payable, but it's a much more straightforward application. The only way you can have a bit of sanity in your life is if you take on some of those.'

The inadequacy of the standard fee affects barristers as well. The gross fee for presenting an asylum appeal is £302.[1] All barristers at all levels of seniority said that this does not cover the amount of work they do, even on a straightforward case. The amount of work covered by the fixed fee can be estimated by comparison with the hourly rate payable in cases which escape the fixed-fee scheme, as shown in Table 4.1.

The standard fee would cover, for example: three hours of preparation, *including* a discussion with the client before court, plus one-and-a-half hours' travel and waiting, and an 80-minute hearing, amounting to £303.92. However, barristers said that this would be

---

[1] Civil Legal Aid (Remuneration) Regulations 2013 SI/2013/422.

Table 4.2: Illustrative fees for a barrister on hourly rates in a straightforward case

Typical time spent	Illustrative fee on hourly rates
Preparation and attendance (four hours)	£260.23
Travel and waiting (two hours)	£57.24
Advocacy (two hours)	£131.58
Total	£449.05

Source: Civil Legal Aid (Remuneration) Regulations 2013 SI/ 2013/ 422.

an exceptionally short time in all three sections. As a minimum, they would spend three to five hours on preparation in a case which presented no special legal or factual challenges, *plus* half an hour in conference with the client at court before the hearing. Travelling and waiting would rarely be less than two hours and hearings generally lasted at least two hours as well. On hourly rates, this would be paid as shown in Table 4.2.

So even the most straightforward asylum case, as described by practitioners, would cost 50 per cent more on hourly rates than is covered by the standard fee. In the costing example in Table 4.2 of the simplest case, assuming four hours' preparation, including the client conference, the barrister would receive £302.00 gross and pay at least 20 per cent as a management fee to chambers, leaving £241.60. At that bare minimum of eight hours' work, the barrister would receive £30.02 per hour before tax, travel costs and all other business expenses, such as insurance, practising certificate and continuing professional development.

However, barristers said it was not unusual to add another three hours of waiting, because the case was last on the judge's list (all hearings are listed for 10am) or the interpreter had not arrived; an hour of travel because the court was further away; an hour in the hearing because the Home Office representative had a long cross-examination or the judge had questions for the appellant or there was another witness as well as the appellant; another two or three hours of preparation because the case was a little more complicated, or there was more evidence to read, or a long list of reasons for refusal, each needing to be addressed specifically. They argued that the real payment per hour on the fixed fee soon became untenable. A solicitor gave an example of this: "There was one case we were looking at: this barrister had done a really great skeleton argument and we worked out his hourly rate on fixed fee – I think he was getting something like £6 an hour, so less than the minimum wage."

For barristers, there is even less opportunity to influence whether the case escapes the fixed-fee scheme, as they depend on the instructing solicitor or caseworker to bill the case as an escape-fee file. Where caseworkers are poorly supervised or firms have a business model which relies on standardising work, using low-qualified staff or capping work at the standard-fee level, tasks are shifted to the barrister. The barrister does more work with less chance of getting hourly rates because the caseworker's own work is unlikely to escape the fixed-fee scheme. One barrister (under ten years' call) described the unpredictability of this:

'I'm just looking at [the system] now. I've just been paid for two cases which [escaped the fixed fee]. One I got £1,475 for and that was a complicated child asylum: it was in Harmondsworth [detention centre], so a little bit of extra travel. That's five times [the fixed fee] and I didn't spend an exceptional amount of time on that. I've definitely done £302 cases where I've spent the same amount of time, but for this one I got nearly £1,500. And there's another one here, I got £952, that also [escaped the fixed fee]. I would say that, yes, I spent a lot of time on that but it wasn't a case that was particularly more complicated than others. So I would say on a £302 case, on average, I do about £800 worth of work if it was going to be billed on an hourly rate.'

As a result, many barristers did not spend time on detailed billing of cases which would be paid the fixed fee. As one (under ten years' call) described it:

'I really noticed it when I first started. I could see my colleagues working on things for hours and hours and billing two to three hours' prep for an asylum appeal. I don't know if it was a pressure to seem like they were really quick or not taking the mick. I don't always bill the hours I put in, because it does just feel like a lot sometimes, but I've been surprised at how little people put – considerably less than they have worked. They certainly knew they'd spent all day on this case.'

There was an awareness that this under-billing meant the LAA might not have accurate information about how long barristers really spent on cases. One (under ten years' call) argued that:

'We have to bill how long it actually takes because otherwise no one's going to know how long it takes. I think that there should be a sector-wide push for people to make sure that they're inputting realistic figures into their billing. It's not a good plan to say it took me five hours to draft those grounds when no one could possibly draft them in five hours.'

Part of the reason that the fixed fee and escape threshold cause such problems is that they are not based on data about actual costs of asylum cases, but rather on other categories of law and on guesswork about expected services in a routine case (Trude, 2009). Trude points out that these estimates fail to take into account, for example, the information-gathering process needed to fill in a form, as opposed to merely the time spent filling it in; no allowance is made for the extra time taken when using an interpreter, which Asylum Aid (2010) found effectively halves the time available. Lawyer interviewees explain that it takes longer to take instructions when a client is distressed, as they frequently are when describing their experiences or when suffering from depression. Similarly, clients need things explained to them repeatedly, because the system is complex and they struggle to retain information. They do not fit into simplistic expectations of how long tasks might take in a routine case.

Even once the work is done, it is far from straightforward to actually receive the hourly rate payments. Files must be sent to the LAA with a bill detailing each individual item of work, unlike billing fixed-fee files. Assessors disallow payment for certain tasks or part of the time claimed if they deem them unnecessary or excessive. The provider then has a right to appeal the assessment. Disputes are decided by an independent funding and costs adjudicator, who is paid by the LAA at (currently) £52 per hour,[2] roughly similar to the London hourly rate for legal help on immigration cases escaping the fixed fee.

Quite apart from wanting to be paid for the work they had already done, providers are compelled to appeal against reductions (or downward assessments) to avoid breaching their legal aid contracts. The contract includes a KPI whereby, after appeals, aggregate reductions must total no more than 10 per cent of the money billed (Standard Civil Contract, KPI1).[3] Appealing reductions is yet another time-consuming

---

[2] https://www.gov.uk/guidance/apply-to-legal-aid-appeals-panel.

[3] https://www.gov.uk/government/publications/standard-civil-contract-2018.

task, and the time spent appealing is unpaid, even if the money for the original work is reinstated.

Escape-fee billing attracts scrutiny compared with files billed at fixed fee, which are only inspected if they are selected for audit. The accounts of practitioners of the process of billing and assessment help to explain why some organisations avoid it, as a junior solicitor explained:

> 'I think billing is the thing I really struggle with the most. Sometimes there's so much to do, I'm sometimes just flinging papers in the file. They're tightening up all the time – we're supposed to go through and make sure every single attendance note is there in order and it matches our billing ledger and whatnot, and I often find I've missed half-an-hour's recording here, or I've missed printing out that email there. It just takes me ages to make sure that's all in there. And I've had escape case files that have been returned for silly things – you know, I haven't printed out a copy of the statement I worked on that day, or properly written an attendance note about exactly what I did, so it's about just heading that off before it goes off for assessment.'

Assessment was described as "arbitrary", with some LAA officials taking a "broad view" whereas others went through every item. This made escape files difficult to bill because it was hard to know how much extra time to spend justifying each piece of work, which might be unnecessary. One solicitor explained that some files came back from assessment with long lists of "knock-offs" while others "come back with no errors, and I don't think I work on files in a different way, so that feels a bit random".

Another solicitor characterised the assessments as an attempt to standardise reasonableness, combined with a sometimes careless approach by LAA caseworkers regarding their own guidance:

> 'They then wrongly apply their guidance, so one bit of their guidance says that drafting a normal document will take about 1–2 units a page, so 6–12 minutes. That's the assumption if you're just transcribing or writing something very straightforward, but complex documents will take longer. But then they misquote this to say that this paragraph says that a document takes 12 minutes per page. It's like, well that's not what your guidance says, but I'll have to go through that and raise that.'

Aside from this carelessness, the solicitor described the behaviour of a small minority of officials "who like to invent new issues":

> 'There's one person who thinks he's a bit cutting-edge and will try and raise an issue that's not there; like when you apply for a costs extension on a particular case. So he said, well I can see from the history of the case, at this point in the past, eight years ago, at a previous Legal Help stage that happened in your case, you should've opened a new matter at that point. Therefore none of this work is payable.'

Several workers explained that they tended to get "most of" the money reinstated on appeal, meaning it was worth doing from a financial perspective, though it took away from client time. Appealing could be difficult, though, because asylum cases tended to be long-running. As a solicitor put it:

> 'I've had cases come back to me that I did three years ago, where I'm now having to justify the work that I did on them because they're only just being assessed for escape fee. I do remember, but it's the minutiae of exactly why I did a certain thing and then it's also taking up time that I want to be using to progress cases now.'

This was all the more difficult when the person who did the work had left before the file was assessed, which was not unusual in long-running cases, leaving another worker to try to justify that person's work without direct knowledge of it.

More recently, a solicitor explained that changes in the LAA itself had shifted assessors' focus:

> 'There used to be times when you'd get 5–6 pages of reductions and they'd say this 12-minute letter is going to be six minutes and this 18-minute letter is going to be six minutes, and they'd focus on loads of really small things. They don't tend to go for the small things now because they don't have time, so they'll mainly go for big chunks of work.'

Another solicitor explained that she had adopted a strategy of "protecting" her work by breaking down the larger chunks of time into component parts, though this was time-consuming.

'[In] your typical, complex, messy, fresh claim case, where you have to spend hours doing certain tasks, drafting representations, going through evidence – cases that are quite prep-heavy – they will just go for all your six hours, five hours, four hours, and say, "Well, where's the output? What did you produce? There are only so many pages, so we know mathematically how many units you can have per page and we don't think you've justified this time." And even on appeal, probably a cautious assessor will cut it down. Five hours: the LAA gave me two hours and the assessor gave me three hours, but we spent *five* hours, we did the work. So you learn from that, you have to protect your work against that, so you spent five hours and you'll go through and say okay, I spent thirty minutes doing that, forty minutes doing that, and your work is protected if you do it like that, so it's quite frustrating.'

Earlier studies noted changes in the way solicitors billed work after the introduction of new fee structures (Cape & Moorhead, 2005; Tata & Stephen, 2006; Fenn, Gray & Rickman, 2007; Stephen, Fazio & Tata, 2008). This account may shed light on why billing practices change: not to 'manipulate' new rules, as Goriely (2002) put it, but to protect work which was necessary and justifiable from being unpaid.

To avoid more serious losses, a solicitor in Firm X explained that they tried to make a conscious decision about how much work over the fixed fee to do at a particular stage and to avoid being just below the escape threshold for the stage. These were not calculations that the solicitor wanted to make, but she felt obliged to do so to protect the firm from losses. Workers are compelled into apparently self-interested types of behaviour because they work within structures which were built around the expectation that they *would be* self-interested (Caulkin, 2016:p24). 'Ethical indeterminacy' describes the idea that, when faced with two courses of action of equal benefit to the client, lawyers will advise on (or take) the course most financially beneficial to themselves (Tata, 2007). The participants in the BAJ study appear to take financial benefit into account only when there is a threat to the organisation's financial survival.

In this way, the imposition of contractual incentives and bureaucratic structures that *assume* lawyers are rational utility maximisers has the effect of forcing them to *behave* as such (Self, 1993). They are compelled to behave more like Thaler and Sunstein's 'econs' (2008). This is probably the reason why Fenn et al (2007) found that solicitors' travelling and waiting time increased when fixed fees were introduced for preparation and advocacy, but with travel and waiting paid separately. Rather than deliberately travelling further to court or waiting longer to be heard, they simply had to start recording and billing that time.

For barristers, a practice manager described serious "financial leakage", such that billing had represented only about 70 per cent of work done on non-fixed-fee cases. Billing software was beginning to be used in all chambers in the research, though not all individual barristers were yet using it. Those using it said it had certainly led to them billing more for cases, since it made it easier to bill each piece of work immediately it was done. They said the fixed fee and rate cuts meant it had become important to bill for even small items of work, such as a few minutes spent emailing the solicitor about the case, which previously they would not have bothered to bill for. A barrister of over thirty years' experience believed that the government had failed to recognise how much free labour it had received from legal aid lawyers over many years. There is likely to be a continuing process of barristers' bills increasing, assisted by technology, to reflect the actual work they do on cases (even if they will only receive the fixed fee in some), echoing a similar process which began earlier for solicitors, as falling rates force publicly funded barristers to pay more attention to getting paid than previously.

Practitioners believed some firms avoided billing at escape fee to avoid these long and potentially unrewarding assessment processes, choosing instead to keep their work within the fixed fee and receive payment more quickly. Indeed, two practitioners had been expressly told, when interviewed by another firm, that "we don't get expert reports or go to escape fee; we keep within the fixed fee". That firm was offered by several interviewees, particularly barristers, as an example of one which prepared cases poorly, "went through the motions" even in work such as bail applications where it would be paid hourly rates, and paid late. This is part of a growing body of evidence that some providers cap their work at the fixed-fee level, regardless of whether that is compatible with quality (see also Chapter 7).

Another oddity in the system is that, although the hourly rate is higher for London than non-London cases, the fixed fee is the same everywhere. Yet the hourly rate (rather than a total number of hours and minutes) is the reference point by which providers can calculate whether they have reached the escape threshold. That means practitioners working outside London are less likely to reach the escape threshold in any given case than those working in London. This was apparently unintended, since no rationale appears to have been given for the difference.

Despite practitioners' efforts to find workarounds, only two strategies effectively mitigated the risk of underpayment: doing fewer fixed-fee cases, or capping the work done at the level of guaranteed payment. The former strategy maintains quality but limits clients' access; the latter maintains clients' access but to a service which would only rarely meet the needs of the case. In economic terms, the fixed fee represents a purchaser with monopsony power in the market imposing a price which does not reflect the unit cost of doing the work. In the same way, it has been able to shift risk onto providers.

Risk

The fixed fee, with the implicit risk of underpayment, is part of a larger process of shifting risk onto legal aid lawyers (Rickman et al, 1999). In judicial review (JR) and higher court appeals work, there is an explicit risk of non-payment. Onward appeals to the Upper Tribunal were placed at risk in 2005, so that lawyers were not paid unless they succeeded at permission stage. That risk was initially mitigated by an uplift in the fees if they succeeded, but the uplift was removed by the LASPO Act, from 2013. The next year, judicial review funding was also placed at risk. (Judicial review is an application to the High Court for review of the lawfulness of decisions by a public authority, such as the Home Office, when there is no right of appeal.) The combined effect of these funding rules is that legal aid lawyers have to do a significant amount of their work without knowing whether or not they will be paid for it.

Financially, judicial review functions as both a risk and a subsidy: a risk because all work is unpaid unless and until permission is granted;[4] but a subsidy because, if the application succeeds, the applicant's legal costs are normally paid by the opponent at *inter partes* (private) rates, which are much higher than the legal aid rate. For not-for-profits, which had no private work, *inter partes* fees were their main source of self-generated (as opposed to charitable) subsidy. Centre C had done a detailed analysis for the purpose of deciding whether to continue with judicial review work, and concluded that the amount they won in *inter*

---

[4] Civil Legal Aid (Remuneration) (Amendment) (No. 3) Regulations 2014, which were quashed and replaced with Civil Legal Aid (Remuneration) (Amendment) Regulations 2015.

partes costs outweighed the losses on cases where they were unpaid. Firm X, by contrast, had avoided analysing figures because it believed the work was too important to drop, but was considering reserving it to more senior workers. This only applies to organisations employing solicitors, because accredited caseworkers cannot conduct judicial review work (which means some access points have no immigration providers able to do judicial review cases).

Success or failure at permission stage is a particularly flimsy basis for placing all financial risk on the lawyers, since such decisions are unpredictable. The barristers interviewed said they did usually win and get paid "in the end", but that this involved a large amount of work at risk, particularly if permission was refused on the papers and they had to appear in an oral permission hearing. A barrister described how in one case: "We didn't get permission in the Administrative Court because we got a commercial judge, who really just didn't get [the legal test], and in the end we got permission from the Court of Appeal, but by this point there's just a huge amount of work that's at risk". This was not a matter of the barrister's inexperience: another barrister of over 20 years' call confirmed that: "It's the ones where you've put a lot of work in, it's a really good point and it gets rejected and it's just because you got Mr Justice [Name] or someone being difficult". Genn (1993) concluded, albeit in the context of appeals rather than judicial review, that the identity of the judge in asylum appeals did have a significant, independent effect on the prospects of success. This was a larger difference in immigration than in any other specialist tribunal.

This system may affect clients' access to judicial review and higher appeals. Some lawyers thought they made exactly the same merits decisions as they did before the funding changed. A partner in a legal aid firm said, "I'm gambling with my own money", so felt freer to take on borderline cases. Others said they were more cautious about the amount of work they did at pre-permission stage, rather than about whether they took the case at all. A few felt they were "self-censoring" when they were less confident. Where workers had billing targets to meet, however, the risk could be insurmountable. A solicitor in a not-for-profit explained:

'Here it's a bit different because we're a charity but, for example, at [previous private firm] it was a big hit because it's obviously on your targets. If you've billed that amount and then you can't claim it, that's all the work you've done that's not reflected in your monthly targets, so it was very stressful. [If you didn't meet the monthly target] you were told off big time. You had loads of meetings and it was a lot of pressure for not doing it, so I think that meant that people started not doing JRs if they didn't see clearly that they were going to get permission.'

Most barristers said they tried not to let the risk affect their judgement on whether to proceed with a judicial review claim, but some thought their consideration of the merits had become stricter. It meant that borderline or complex cases were at most risk of being unrepresented. A barrister who had been "really badly stung" by being unpaid for work admitted to being "even more cautious" about merits testing, and others acknowledged that they "wouldn't need many unpaid cases" before they would stop doing judicial review work.

As a result, the identity of the solicitor was particularly important: barristers preferred work from solicitors whose own "merits filters" were known to be "robust". A senior barrister explained that, "I get briefed by solicitors that are quite good at public law, so they generally have identified quite a solid point in the first place". Several barristers cited a particular large legal aid firm whose work they tried to avoid because low-qualified caseworkers sent "an email with 45 attachments and 'please advise'". By not volunteering for work from those firms, they protected themselves from doing many hours of unpaid work on weak cases. The likely consequence is that, far from numerous unmeritorious applications wasting court time (though those undoubtedly are generated by certain private firms), people whose cases have real merit are going unrepresented, hidden behind weaker cases where supervision has been inadequate.

The importance of *inter partes* fees from judicial review also affected the economics of staff ratios. Accredited caseworkers cannot make applications in judicial review cases. That work has to be conducted by solicitors, so although a caseworker may be cheaper to employ, a solicitor can do higher-value work. When judicial review work was funded per hour regardless of outcome, Moorhead (1998) discussed the possibility that solicitors, being over-trained for lower-level work, might be tempted to cherry-pick certificated work which used their skills and was better paid. Centre A had chosen to take on a solicitor to replace a caseworker and was benefiting from being able to do more of its judicial review work in-house, rather than referring clients out. Firm X had unintentionally found itself "top-heavy", with more solicitors than caseworkers in each of its teams. The providers in this study did seek to ensure they could do judicial review work, despite the costs and risks, both as an essential service for clients and as part of the economic make-up of the work mix, though only where there was legal merit. Recent case law has exposed the problem of certain non-legal aid firms making judicial review claims with little merit (*R [on the application of Sathivel and Others] v SSHD*;[5] Hyde, 2018a, 2018b, 2018c; Seelhoff, 2018), for which they charge high fees. The restrictions on legal aid funding either make no difference to this or drive desperate people to pay for unscrupulous or less skilful lawyers. These cases and lawyers, however, receive inordinate publicity for the small proportion of applications which they represent – while government criticism has been directed at those who make successful (and therefore meritorious) challenges.

As well as threatening lawyers' financial viability, therefore, the shifting of risk onto providers creates a risk to supply, so that there is already a real prospect of individuals with meritorious cases being unable to find lawyers willing to take the risk on their cases. Combined with the risks of underpayment in fixed-fee cases and the uncertainty over what they would be paid after escape-fee assessments, practitioners and organisations are forced to accept significant financial risk, which is avoidable only by limiting client access through turning away at-risk cases. But still further risk shifts from the LAA onto providers via payment delays, as the next section explains.

Payment lag and cash-flow crisis

The basic rule of the legal aid fee regime is that providers are paid in arrears when cases close, with limited exceptions. That means any delays in progressing and closing cases have an impact on cash flow, since they delay billing and payment. Home Office processing times for asylum applications or fresh claims determine the time that Legal Help (application) files remain open. Tribunal processing times determine the wait for payment in appeal cases. Providers have to pay interpreters' and expert witnesses' invoices, or clients' travel costs, several months before they can claim the cost of those disbursements.

Although winning *inter partes* costs at private rates on judicial review makes a vital contribution to financial survival, actually receiving payment can take a long time. Where the bill is below £10,000 (generally representing a case that was settled without a full hearing), the process was said to be reasonably quick. When higher sums are involved, both sides usually outsource billing to costs lawyers, who can

---

[5] [2018] EWHC 913 (Admin).

also charge the paying party for their time in billing and negotiating. In these situations, it is common to receive an offer to pay around half of the bill and have to negotiate.

Although negotiation over final bills is a normal part of litigation, lawyers are dissuaded from challenging low offers because the receiving party pays the costs of assessment unless they beat the paying party's offer by at least 20 per cent across the solicitor's and barrister's bill. It means the actual payment (to both solicitors and barristers) is usually about 20–30 per cent lower than the bill. A Home Office litigation manager argued that claimant lawyers' bills are sometimes "ridiculous", meaning that in his view they needed to be disputed, to protect public money. He had no legal experience or qualification, however, and did not know whether these "ridiculous" bills might simply reflect very complex cases. Either way, the barrier to independent assessment of costs is arguably too high, since it enables the paying party (the Home Office) to routinely discount payments it owes to lawyers without justifying its assertions that the work was excessive, or could have been done by a lower grade of lawyer.

These lengthy negotiations deepen cash-flow problems: barristers said it was not unusual to wait two years or more to receive these costs. One explained:

> 'We just got a costs assessment in a case [where] I drafted the grounds [five years ago] and we finally just got an order from the court in terms of costs assessment. [The Home Office] seem to have got this firm of costs solicitors based in Peterborough who are not terribly good, but will quibble over absolutely everything and force you to respond to every one of their little quibbles so that takes up more time. It's quite normal now to be waiting years to get costs.'

Another barrister had just been paid for work done fourteen years earlier, while a third believed that the long delay was a deliberate tactic to reduce the eventual payment:

> 'I don't monitor it but [it takes] a long, long time. And then increasingly they're arguing over what you've billed and all that takes time and cleverly, by the time it comes round to that time, you just want the money, you can't be bothered to engage in a debate about why it took you however many hours it took you to do your extremely skilled work, and

why you had to review the bundle six months after you last worked on it, for not a very long amount of time. I think the delay in it really affects how much I'm willing to fight those points.'

Several of the barristers interviewed had been unaware, until the interview, of how high their aged debt was, or how significant a proportion was made up of *inter partes* fee debt from the Home Office, as opposed to other work. One (ten years' call) had aged debt of £189,000, of which £96,000 had been outstanding for over 19 months. Another, also of ten years' call, said:

> 'Just having a quick look at my aged debt … There are cases where I've been waiting in excess of three years to get paid and that's difficult because it's a cash-flow problem that you have. Just looking back, there are some things for which I haven't been paid for four years; some things that are in my three-year column – I'm just trying to see if there's any kind of pattern. It's legally aided stuff that's a delay in being paid, legally aided JR work, so Court of Appeal, judicial review, which was successful *inter partes*.'

This did appear to be specific to immigration and asylum work. A senior manager and a head of finance both described aged debt as a 'massive problem', with payment delays 'worse in civil than in crime' and *inter partes* debts owed by the Home Office especially high. It meant that the debt owed to that chambers' immigration team was as high as the team's collective income. A barrister who also undertook inquest work reflected that payments were more prompt for that work, both from the LAA and from other government departments:

> 'In an inquest, once a solicitor bills the LAA for their own work and counsel's work, the LAA pay me directly into chambers' account, whereas the problem in immigration is that the solicitors are being paid by the LAA and then [some are] not passing the money on. There's no need for an intermediary with legal aid. The Home Office is shit at paying *inter partes* costs but, for example, I just got costs in a claim against the Met [police] and they just paid it. And the MoJ is really quick with [a damages] claim arising from an inquest.'

Junior barristers without a backlog of cases to tide them over described having to take on external work because they could not pay their rent, despite working full-time at the Bar. Even for more senior barristers, the payment delays and discounting of fees means that the sum billed – and therefore their tax bill – is inflated compared with what will eventually be received. One senior barrister (over 25 years' call) explained how this left too little money to live on as the main earner of a family in London:

> 'My tax bill this year was, I think, £14,000 less than my net profit. I had a massive tax bill because I've got £100,000 aged debt. Obviously my tax bill's going to be huge, only I haven't actually had that money to pay it so it's a vast amount.'

For self-employed barristers, these payment delays cause acute cash-flow problems at both individual and chambers levels which threaten their continued participation in legal aid work and certainly compel them to reduce their legal aid work as a percentage of their overall time. Where other businesses might use bank loans for working capital, this was difficult both for individuals and for chambers because, as a senior manager put it, banks "don't like self-employed professionals" despite the fact that the government debt is "gold-plated" in the sense that the debtor will not go bankrupt or disappear.

Delays also flow from the way in which the higher courts manage their workload. This is a fairly complex point, but is an important illustration of how the interactions between different parts of the system cause a cash-flow problem. When the High Court or Court of Appeal receives several appeals or applications on a similar issue, like the safety of returns to a particular country, their practice has been to stay all cases behind one or more test cases, instead of making a permission decision on each one. Under the old system, lawyers could claim a payment on account, of 75 per cent of the total bill to date, twelve months after starting the case. Now that there is no bill until permission is determined (because payment is at risk), lawyers no longer receive payment on account in these cases, which may cause a very significant cash-flow problem, as a senior barrister explained:

> 'Historically, for 20 years, we would have payments on account every week. We still get payments on account ... once we've got permission, [but] permission can take several months. Often things get stacked up behind the test case.

> I had a number of other cases behind [a test case] for a year or so, but there was no permission on them because the court, of its own volition, just stayed everything … because it means less [work] for them.'

Often the stayed cases will never receive a permission decision, because the decision on the test cases will determine all the other cases. At that stage, once the case closes, lawyers can usually claim payment whatever the outcome, because the claim was arguable when it was lodged (though only because there was a successful judicial review of the original payment regulations).[6] Sometimes, however, the client loses contact with them during the period of delay and they are compelled to withdraw the application. In other words, taking into account the discussion of risk in the previous section, the cutting-edge cases that develop the law present the greatest risk.

Transaction costs

The economist Oliver Williamson (1975) developed the idea of transaction costs, to understand the costs of running or participating in markets. These include bidding for work, drafting and negotiating contracts, compliance monitoring and reporting, as opposed to the production costs of providing a service or manufacturing items. Williamson (2000) argued that, for a market to be successful, transaction costs should be minimised, but that zero-cost transactions were impossible. There is a heightened risk of market failure when 'prices lie' because they ignore transaction costs (Bozeman, 2002; Bozeman & Johnson, 2015).

The Carter Review of legal aid (2006) did consider transaction costs to some extent, predicting that awarding fewer and larger contracts would lower transaction costs for the LSC. This may have been an overoptimistic view: marketisation tends towards increasing transaction costs in public services (Haynes, 2012), meaning that a choice has to be made about where those costs should fall. But as Whitfield (2007) pointed out, there has been little discussion of the transaction costs in the legal aid market before or after Carter.

The starting point then is that some transaction costs are inevitable in the marketised system, but should be both minimised and factored

---

[6] *R (on the application of Ben Hoare Bell and Others) v The Lord Chancellor* [2015] EWHC 523 (Admin).

into pricing if the market is to be sustainable. In the context of legal aid work, transaction costs include the costs of bidding for and managing the contracts, compliance with contract terms and buying or operating office systems essential for legal aid work. The staff costs, and case-related expenses and disbursements, like interpreter and expert witness costs, are production costs. The core office costs, costs of professional regulation and professional indemnity insurance are overheads rather than transaction costs, but it is useful to bear in mind that a not-for-profit provider without private clients also has to pay for these expenses from its legal aid income or any grant-funding it can obtain.

Compared with some other public-service markets (welfare to work: Bennett, 2017; mental-health services: Rees et al, 2017), the process of bidding for legal aid contracts is not especially onerous, though providers said earlier rounds of contracting were more difficult. Contractual prerequisites, however, can be costly. Providers must first obtain the SQM or Lexcel accreditation for any categories of law in which they want legal aid contracts. Providers did not object to the SQM itself, but did criticise the time and resource investment needed to comply with its requirements, particularly the impact of this on not-for-profit providers (Sommerlad & Sanderson, 2009).

Unlike all other categories of legal aid, individual immigration advisers must also be accredited through a scheme run by the Law Society (Ling & Pugh, 2017). No legal aid funds can be claimed for work carried out by a person who is not accredited; the contract specifies the level of work which may be carried out by those holding different levels of accreditation.[7] Interviewees felt the accreditation course was reasonably rigorous legally, though it did not necessarily address the "soft skills" needed to deal with a case effectively and its effects on quality had never been evaluated. The bigger concern was the expense of accreditation, which made it difficult to recruit suitably qualified caseworkers and expensive to train them from scratch. All organisations bear training costs, but the requirement for specific additional accreditations to do immigration legal aid work make this a transaction cost rather than a production cost.

The most significant transaction costs to providers arose from contract compliance and management obligations. There is an extensive compliance-auditing regime, described by both providers and LAA officials as "zero tolerance". Requirements to apply in advance for some kinds of funding, as well as the appeals against assessments, as

---

[7] Standard Civil Contract Specification 2013, paragraph 8.15.

discussed in the previous section, lead to a "low-level back and forth", as interviewees described it, between providers and the LAA that adds greatly to the costs on both sides of managing contracts. For example, solicitors were frustrated that they still had to apply for funding before starting a judicial review, despite the work being at risk. Only the court fee, disbursements and any applications for interim relief are covered unless permission is granted, therefore the application process was seen as wasting both lawyers' and LAA time for no apparent policy reason. One solicitor explained that she was given a default costs limit of £1,350, regardless of the costs she applied for, after which she had to apply to amend the scope of the funding certificate, though she would be paid nothing unless she obtained permission. Lawyers argued that they should be given delegated powers over funding for at-risk work, saving costs and effort for both sides.

At the time of the main BAJ fieldwork in 2016–17, the most significant transaction costs to providers were caused by the online Client and Cost Management System (CCMS). CCMS has been mandatory since 1 April 2016 for all funding applications, case-specific communications between providers and the LAA and some billing, causing severe stress to providers across civil legal aid because there were serious problems with its functionality . Interviewees described forms which would not accept most forms of punctuation, so they could not enter an email address or copy and paste a legal argument; forms which gave no means of entering a particular piece of information; slowness; instability such that users lost their connection to the system mid-session; inability to access previously submitted information; lawyer-users seeing different information from LAA-users; a message system which was inefficient because of the time it took for responses to appear; no means of notifying the LAA that an application was urgent; and so on.

The additional unpaid time in which providers were not doing casework because of CCMS and the frustration and stress of dealing with it emerged as the most significant problems for providers at the time of the fieldwork, and a real threat to survival for some who felt they were already "on the brink" because of the fee cuts. This is reflected in the minutes of bi-monthly Civil Contracts Consultative Group meetings and practitioner organisations across legal aid. A solicitor with 17 years' experience in a not-for-profit explained that:

'A paper application for a legal aid certificate [used to] take an hour, maximum two if it was a complicated case but now ... you have to set aside a day.

In the past if you did an emergency application, it was slightly repetitive, but now if you obtain an emergency certificate, you have to resubmit the entire application to get a substantive certificate. It doesn't copy anything through. I've got a case where I applied for a public funding certificate two years ago and I've long won the judicial review and my client has got indefinite leave to remain, but I cannot get it through CCMS because it fell out between emergency and substantive, and they've … revoked his certificate. I've got an order that says the other side will pay my costs but I can't bill them because they'll refuse to pay anything if I didn't have a substantive legal aid certificate. The humans at the LAA know that, the immigration team at the LAA understand that, but they can't make the computer understand it at all, so I just keep getting letters saying, "We're going to revoke your certificate", "We've revoked your certificate". It's just crazy.

Or you might have a sponsor in the UK who's a refugee, and then a wife and five children abroad, and if you have to get a public funding certificate [to apply for family reunion] for the wife and five children, you have to do it six times. And even though it's been computerised, it won't copy all of the information across, so you have to do six applications using the same information.'

A replacement for CCMS was being tested by December 2019 (Fouzder, 2019), but providers felt that the decision to make CCMS mandatory in 2016, when it was known to have major problems, showed a disdain for their time and viability. Given the tight financial margins, providers felt they were ill-equipped to bear the additional costs of dealing with CCMS. Although the LAA had allowed for the possibility of exgratia payments for time lost to CCMS on application, this required providers to spend yet more time applying for such payments and providing evidence, with no clear criteria for when they would be granted.

Barristers had far less administration to deal with in legal aid work, not being contracted to the LAA, but were also frustrated by the "waste of time" in having to undertake detailed billing first at legal aid rates (at risk) as the case proceeded, and then at *inter partes* rates when the case succeeded. Billing requires a detailed breakdown of the work done and allows for the barrister to request a percentage 'enhancement' on the normal rate, to reflect the expertise, skill or speed with which the work was undertaken. Yet enhancements will only become relevant if the case ultimately fails (so does not get *inter partes* costs) but still qualifies under one of the exemptions for payment from the LAA. Some said they did not bother billing at enhanced rates, taking the view that they would be paid at *inter partes* rates or not at all, but others "always" did so and felt that this was an essential part of ensuring that the LAA understood the amount and quality of work needed to bring cases to court. The main exception was injunction or other interim relief work, which is payable regardless of permission, so all barristers billed enhancements for this work. Some said they always billed (and usually received) the maximum possible enhancement (100 per cent) to reflect the stress and urgency of the work, suggesting it would be more efficient to simply specify a higher rate for emergency interim relief work.

This complex billing placed additional demands on barristers' clerks and finance staff, as a senior clerk explained:

> 'The billing procedure that our fees clerks have to go through is really time-consuming. Just to give you an example, there were four barristers in chambers that were involved in [a case] in the High Court. We got costs on that, so the fees clerks had to bill all their work first of all at legal aid rates, produce those fee notes to the solicitors, and then we had to do *inter partes* costs fee notes. We had to produce two sets of fee notes for these four barristers, and you can imagine the [amount of] work that was put into the cases in the first place. Between two, sometimes three staff all working on these fee notes, it took them nearly ten days! The administration surrounding the billing process has got so complicated.'

The difficulties of managing the legal aid contract had compelled all of the case-study providers to either employ a practice manager or divert a fee-earner into that role, which increased the transaction costs, but was seen as essential to avoid catastrophic clawbacks, an issue earlier identified by Sommerlad and Sanderson (2009) for civil legal aid providers. One well-regarded firm went into administration after financial irregularities emerged. A former staff member believed it happened because there were insufficient management resources to deal with the contract, but that sufficient resources could not be afforded given the cash-flow issues.

All providers agreed that the price for legal aid work did not cover the costs of managing the contracts. The funder placed many of the transaction costs onto providers, but had not factored those costs into prices, so those costs could only be covered by privately paying clients, by grants and charitable funding, or by shifting more capacity into judicial review work in the expectation of winning costs at a higher rate.

Economies of scale

Standard market models, and the architects of competition in the public sector, assume that efficient providers can achieve economies of scale, which will reduce price without damaging quality. This assumption is narrated in the Carter Review, which predicted "an increase in the average size of firms through growth and mergers, rationalisation and harmonisation of the way separate services are delivered", with "fixed pricing ... reward[ing] efficiency and suppliers who can deliver increased volumes of work" (2006:p3). The review projected significant increases in profit for larger firms. For not-for-profits, Carter suggested many "may need to increase the number of clients they help for the funding they receive, so that their productivity compares with private practitioners" (2006:p106–7), again rewarding "efficiency" by generating a surplus to support the organisation's wider work. Yet Mayson's analysis (2007) on behalf of the Legal Services Board concluded that not all legal services were scalable, particularly in complex areas of social welfare law.

Assumptions about economies of scale demand close examination in the context of specialist professional services. In the manufacture of goods, it is a relatively simple equation: the more the company makes of a particular item, the lower the cost per unit, at least up to a certain point, after which diseconomies of scale may occur. The economies arise because the production costs are divided by more items, as are the internal function costs like accounting and IT, and the company can buy raw materials in bulk and benefit from labour specialisation. Buying of raw materials is a minor consideration in legal services, but the sharing of internal function costs, specialisation of labour and lowering production costs merit attention.

Sharing internal function costs, like billing software and obtaining the SQM, among more fee earners does offer savings. A partner in a large firm explained that his small, niche firm had merged with a much larger one at the time of LASPO for precisely that reason. Some sets of chambers had merged with others to share staffing and facilities between more barristers, and for diversity and "safety in numbers". Even so, practice managers described a constant tension whereby the more barristers a set of chambers accommodated, the more staff they needed to provide clerking, billing and administrative support.

Economies of labour specialisation were part of the Legal Aid Board's policy focus in the 1990s. The franchising system, and later contracting, compelled providers to specialise, deliberately excluding generalist solicitors and allowing for the inclusion of specialist non-lawyer providers. There was an expectation that specialisation would save on costs, because an expert would be more efficient than a dabbler. Economies of specialisation are consistent with quality because there is strong evidence that specialisation and experience correlate strongly with quality, more so than qualification type (Genn & Genn, 1989; McConville et al, 1994; Kritzer, 1999). Experienced staff cost more than inexperienced ones, but supervision costs should be lower for the same level of quality. Meanwhile the system for referral to independent barristers offers economies of labour specialisation because (at least in theory) it allows all clients access to niche expertise and skilled advocacy without needing that level of specialism in every organisation. These economies of specialisation were probably maximised, however, around 2000 when the franchise became mandatory.

The more complicated issue is whether economies of scale can be obtained by lowering production costs, or costs per case, without lowering quality below an acceptable level or creating diseconomies of scale. Quality is a contested concept but fortunately there is already a reasonable level of consensus as to what amounts to quality within asylum or immigration casework, encapsulated in the LAA's own peer-review criteria (2017), which were validated in the block contracting pilot (Moorhead et al, 2003) and subsequent work (Sherr & Paterson, 2008) which tested quality and cost under different contracting models. Here, quality is a spectrum from Excellence to Failure in Performance, covering communication with the client, appropriateness and comprehensiveness of advice, prompt and effective fact-finding and information-gathering, and effective tactics, referrals to other organisations and use of interpreters.

The peer-review criteria are underpinned by strong evidence that high-quality services are those which focus on the specifics of the case (Sherr at al, 1994; Sherr & Paterson, 2008; Trude & Gibbs, 2010), and that time spent on asylum casework correlates positively with quality. Gibbs and Hughes-Roberts (2012) were unable to identify a point where that correlation ceased. The block contracting pilot provides good empirical evidence on this point, as it compared the cost and the quality of work produced under different contract models and incentive structures, according to transaction criteria and various other measures

(Sherr et al, 1994). The contracting models that enabled caseworkers to spend as much time as needed produced the highest-quality work, whereas the model which most resembled price-competitive tendering produced the worst (Moorhead et al, 2003). That research supports the argument that there is a positive correlation between time/cost and quality.

Every case is fact-specific. Caseworkers in the BAJ study felt there was some scope for standardisation in administrative procedures, but very little in casework. The applicant's witness statement needs to be detailed, setting out as precisely as possible the facts of their case, because that is what the Home Office requires. It is an inherently individual (and time-consuming) process. Written representations need to set out the precise law applicable to the case, rather than simply stating *all* asylum law without application to the facts. An experienced solicitor gave examples of a former colleague in a large firm who attempted to exploit economies of scale with standardisation:

> 'This [colleague] had an extremely standard attendance note he used to put on all his Eritrean cases and it was all about military draft. And I remember getting a case at [appeal stage] and ... he had quite a detailed account of being a border guard and being asked to shoot, and dropping the gun and then running. There was more to it than the normal and none of that was in the instructions. It was just a very standard attendance note.
>
> [A]nother ... guy used to draw cartoons. He was a political cartoonist and he was in national service teaching in one of the schools and he used to draw these cartoons, which again is quite interesting. None of this was in the instructions when I got the case; you wouldn't have known. .... And the exact same attendance note, just about draft. He apparently did an hour's research here about draft, which is exactly the same hour he did on this other case. And some of these could've been grants actually. But that's obviously very inefficient, for somebody actually to put the hours in to get a grant at Legal Help stage.'

We can compare this solicitor's point about what was considered "inefficient" in practice to the Carter Review's prediction that fixed fees would reward "efficient" providers exploiting the economies of scale. In financial terms, the fixed fee rewarded this caseworker's "efficient" work, notwithstanding that it did not meet the needs of the client or the Home Office and in fact led to the need for an appeal, at the cost of another fixed fee for the appeal stage.

Country background evidence, which is often central to asylum cases, likewise needs to be tailored to the case: the position in Kandahar province rather than the whole of Afghanistan; the position of Christian converts rather than that of all Christians in a country; the position for divorced women rather than everything published on women in a particular country. Multiple examples of this kind were offered where standardisation was associated with poor quality, and none where it gave rise to good-quality work.

It is possible to exploit economies of scale by taking on large numbers of fixed-fee cases and doing no more work than is paid for. There is evidence that some providers do cap their work per case at the amount they will be paid for. But, in the majority of cases, that amount of work is not commensurate with the demands of the case, meaning there is an inevitable tension between quality and financial viability. Firms which use a lot of standardisation are often referred to as 'sausage machines' (Bridges et al, 1975), churning out large amounts of poor-quality products that look identical, regardless of their actual content.

For barristers, a chambers practice manager suggested that they needed to consider whether they could do the work for the £300 they would be paid, rather than doing £600 worth of work, by standardising procedures to exploit economies of scale. Barrister interviewees, however, agreed unanimously that an asylum appeal could not be done adequately within the standard fee. They said that they did the work the case needed, regardless of what they were being paid. Economies of scale could only manifest when doing a very high volume of work on a particular country or case type. One explained that preparation took "anything between three hours and ten hours". A case could only be prepared in three hours if it was: "Say a very formulaic Iranian Christian case that I've done hundreds of times before, which is very simple and [the client's] credibility isn't disputed, where I've already got a [written argument] which sets out all the case law." Yet referring back to the section on fixed fees in this chapter, this bare minimum three hours' preparation, including the client conference at court, was the *maximum* time the fixed fee would cover, based on the hourly rate fixed by law.

The unpredictability of legal aid work and future market conditions made it difficult to plan for efficiency or economies, either at organisation level or on a case-by-case basis. Case-by-case, Firm Y found that it was impossible to predict whether it would be more cost-efficient to instruct a barrister for a Tribunal hearing or send their own caseworker, because it depended entirely on how long they waited to go into court. The not-for-profits in the study had opted to scale down rather than up in response to the cuts and there was a sense that it was safer to be smaller and more agile. RMJ's large size made it more difficult to respond to changing fee and contract regimes. Centre A's director believed that there were only *dis*economies of scale: annual losses which could be reduced proportionally by capping the number of staff and the number of cases taken on. Even administrative support was kept minimal, and the trustees were reluctant to invest in more without a business case showing that administrative workers were likely to save more than they cost, given the complex contract-management demands discussed in the previous section.

The BAJ study did not identify any clear correlation between size and quality. In 2007, the House of Commons Constitutional Affairs Select Committee noted the government's intention to have fewer and larger firms providing legal aid services, but likewise noted 'the absence of a robust link' between quality and either size or efficiency (2007:p86). Interviewees in larger teams felt that a critical mass of knowledge and expertise meant there was strength in depth, with most specialisms covered by someone and "always someone to ask", provided that there is "a good team dynamic". For smaller teams, the wide and supportive professional network replaced this in-house support, whereas a small and cohesive team allowed for effective information sharing and ad hoc supervision. In larger organisations there was a risk of poor work going undetected if supervision structures were not robust enough.

The only real advantage of size emerging in this research was that, at the time of the fieldwork (until September 2018), only relatively large providers could take on detention-centre contracts. Detention work provided a steady flow of hourly-paid work, outside the restriction of matter starts, which helped with financial viability. Since September 2018, detention work has been available even to very small providers, to the apparent detriment of detained clients, who find providers do not always have capacity to take on all cases (BID, 2019).

Importantly, it does appear that firms cannot operate at large scale without some inexperienced staff and they cannot therefore provide quality at that scale without thorough supervision (see Sommerlad, 2016). At RLC/RMJ, quality was maintained, but the cost of supervising new staff was high. One particular large firm was much criticised by interviewees for delegating complex work to cheaper and less experienced workers, without adequate supervision in place to mitigate this. A solicitor who had worked in both a large and a small firm explained that in the latter, the level-one (lowest qualified) staff "were working under very close supervision doing specific tasks rather than running whole cases". In the large firm, there was a split whereby level one staff did asylum applications, often very badly, and passed them to level two staff for appeals. Equally, some smaller firms have been severely criticised by the courts for failing to adequately supervise the work of paralegals.[8] It appears that business model, commitment, training and supervision influence quality more than size.

The evidence suggests that economies of scale on a per-case basis are at best minimal and present a significant risk to quality. Where individual firms exploit economies of scale by using inexperienced staff with inadequate supervision, it creates a diseconomy at system level because they add no value and often generate failure demand (see Chapter 5).

Conclusion

An LAA official accepted that the margins for firms they managed were tight, but nevertheless argued that the fees must be adequate because providers continued to bid to do the work. The official, however, implicitly acknowledged the doubtful effectiveness of both economies of scale and the swings and roundabouts principle:

> 'I would be surprised if you could make it work without private work, unless the organisation was very small. If you were wholly reliant on legal aid income, you would have to do more certified and detention work. I don't think any of mine are solely legal aid – they're doing less and less, and doing more private work. That is concerning for people who might be eligible.'

The result of the low rate for fixed-fee cases and the high escape threshold is that high-quality lawyers lose money on standard-fee cases. Transaction costs, particularly around contract compliance, are too high. Solicitors in not-for-profits said that unpaid administration wipes out any balance from the rare cases which cost less than the fixed fee, and would still do so even if all of their fixed-fee cases did balance out.

---

[8] For example, *R (on the application of Okondu & Anor) v Secretary of State for the Home Department (wasted costs; SRA referrals; Hamid) IJR* [2014] UKUT 377 (IAC); *R (On the Application Of Akram & Anor) v Secretary of State for the Home Department* [2015] EWHC 1359 (Admin); *Hamid* [2012] EWCA 3070 (Admin).

Delays in case progression and in payment, combined with the shifting of risk onto practitioners, create extreme precariousness around cash flow, which can only be addressed by doing less legal aid work and replacing it with other income-generating work. Assumptions about economies of scale are simply flawed.

This combination of factors means that prices in this sector lie, because they have been set by a monopsony purchaser who has not taken relevant factors into account. This is probably unintentional, but it creates a threat to supply (at least at the high-quality end of the spectrum) for First-tier Tribunal appeals work and for those with standard-fee cases, as lawyers reconcile quality with financial viability by reducing client access. For RMJ, as detailed in the previous chapter, the attempt to maintain both quality and client access resulted in catastrophic loss of financial viability. Other providers have chosen to reconcile financial viability and client access by reducing quality. The evidence strongly suggests that it is impossible to reconcile all three.

But it is not irreparable: transaction costs could be reduced to the benefit of all and factored into prices; delays could be reduced by changing the payment structure; risk could be redistributed, especially if preferential terms were applied to more trusted providers. If the fixed fee cannot be abandoned, then the escape threshold could be reduced. These themes are picked up again in Chapters 6 and 7.

5

New framework for demand

What drives demand? What drives supply? How can the two be made to match in a way that safeguards rights, dignity and the rule of law, and secures, as far as possible, value for money? The answers to these questions should form the bedrock of all legal aid policy and influence the design of asylum procedures. Without understanding demand, it is impossible to operationalise a market that protects availability and quality of services. Yet there is no clear framework for making sense of demand and supply in social welfare legal aid which, as Moorhead (2004) put it, is an obstacle to the development of solutions.

To address this problem, two main arguments are made here:

- There are different kinds of demand. Any aspect or instance of demand for asylum legal services can be placed into a four-square matrix, which allows for exploration of the drivers of each type of demand and their impacts on cost.
- The failure to build the market around demand in immigration legal aid has led to systems of payment and auditing which are poorly aligned with the drivers and consequences of demand, creating obstacles to high-quality provision responsive to that demand.

What do we already know about demand? Legal aid received little academic or policy attention until the early 1990s, when the managerialisation of public services was well underway and politicians began to view legal aid spending as out of control. Costs certainly rose significantly in this period and there was a drive to explain this. Much of the academic focus was on 'devising sophisticated models based on simplistic and untested assumptions about how lawyers behave' (Goriely, 1998:p14). One such model, the theory of 'supplier-induced demand' (SID), had real influence on legal aid policy making which continues to be felt today.

The theory suggests that lawyers supply excessive services when a third party is paying for the work, particularly when there is competition between lawyers for private clients, or other sources of income are reduced (Gray, 1994; Bevan, Holland & Partington, 1994; Bevan, 1996; Gray, Rickman & Fenn, 1999). The premise was that both the number of cases and the costs per case were increasing, and that this was likely down to professionals manipulating the payment system (see Wall, 1996), or characterising all problems as legal and claiming public money to solve them (Abel, 1986, 2003). It was assumed to be a problem with legal aid and lawyers, rather than a problem with law, policy or procedure. This fitted the developing managerial ideology of the 1980s and 1990s (outlined in Chapter 2) and the Lord Chancellor of the time considered it a 'compelling' analysis (Goriely, 1998:p14). It came to underpin the significant legal aid changes in the Access to Justice Act 1999 and, later, the imposition of fixed fees for legal aid work.

The idea that suppliers induce demand for legal aid has been discredited in academic circles. Goriely (2002) concludes there is no evidence for what she calls 'strong SID', whereby lawyers would supply services that clients neither wanted nor needed, for their own financial benefit. She suggests there is evidence for a weak version whereby lawyers supply services when the marginal (per case) returns from doing so exceed the marginal costs; in other words, they provide a service if they can make a profit from doing so. This does not reflect the evidence from the practitioners and organisations in the BAJ study. In any event, it tells us little about the drivers of demand, only about businesses' decisions on which demand to meet.

International comparisons of justice systems show clearly that system factors are primarily responsible for increasing costs of supply (type of justice system; number of crimes prosecuted and their seriousness; level of demand for divorce), though contractual incentives might also play some role (Bowles & Perry, 2009). More analysis has focused on drivers of demand for criminal legal aid than for civil work (Zander, 2000). We know that a tiny number of high-cost cases take up a disproportionate share of the criminal legal aid budget. The adversarial trial system and greater use of imprisonment contribute to significantly higher criminal legal aid costs in Scotland than the Netherlands, whose lowest courts do not even have a power to imprison defendants (Goriely, 1998). Other identified system factors driving criminal legal aid costs include delays and the inputs required from lawyers (Cape & Moorhead, 2005), procedural complexity and the knock-on effects of other, more ideological, policies like toughness on crime (Wall, 1996). Policy, however, has not been reshaped to reflect this understanding of system-factor impact. In other words, there is policy debris from the discredited belief in supplier-induced demand.

There is scant evidence relating directly to the economics of immigration work, even though it was one of the main sources of overall cost inflation in the early 2000s. Sir Henry Brooke, in his review of the history of legal aid, attributes that inflation to the increasing complexity of immigration law in the 1990s (see Chapter 2), the inclusion of asylum appeals in the scope of legal aid from 1999, and the growth in numbers of people seeking asylum in 1997–2003. In social welfare legal aid more broadly, including asylum, Paterson (2011) and Brooke (2017) cite government bodies' poor decision-making or poor compliance with their legal obligations as drivers of need.

Problem clusters were another important development in the comprehension of demand: one issue, like loss of employment, often gave rise to others around housing, debt and welfare benefits (Pleasence et al, 2004). That meant social welfare legal needs were often clustered and it would be advantageous to make sure legal services were joined up to meet demand. Community Legal Advice Networks and Centres (CLANs and CLACs) were established to act as a one-stop venue or outreach service for advice, funded jointly by the LSC and local authorities. These were to be closer to the salaried model of legal aid provision, to ensure holistic supply coverage across England and Wales.

Evaluations suggest they failed because: local authorities had different funding priorities from the LSC and were therefore not willing to contribute enough to the funding of legal services; other local organisations were opposed; and because of 'a crude and divisive tendering process with little respect for the providers' (Brooke, 2017:p27) – perhaps reflecting the continuing theme of hostility towards legal professionals. The tendering process resulted in private and other not-for-profit organisations being squeezed out of legal aid provision, instead of consolidating resources. Just six CLACs and one CLAN opened between 2007 and 2010. This followed the abandonment in 2005 of Community Legal Service Partnerships, an earlier attempt by the newly formed LSC in 2000 to research and rebalance need and supply at local level. As Brooke (2017) summarises, the partnerships failed because of lack of resources (even before the 2008 financial crash), leadership and clarity of purpose. The availability of social welfare legal advice remained patchy.

Since 2013, when the LSC was abolished, data collection on civil legal need has been mainly through periodic legal needs surveys. The LAA does not research demand. It receives certain information about supply (for example, how many cases have been opened, the time taken on those files, the costs of work and disbursements), but no information about unmet demand.

Two stories

Two case examples are used throughout this chapter to help explain the framework for demand and supply (names changed).

Ana's story

Ana is a Vietnamese national. Vietnam is the country of origin for a large number of victims of human trafficking and has very poor state protection against trafficking and retrafficking. Ana was convicted of cannabis cultivation, a strong indicator of trafficking, and deported from the UK. She was retrafficked from Vietnam to another Asian country, before arriving in the UK again. The Home Office accepted that Ana had twice been trafficked from Vietnam but nevertheless concluded that she was not a victim of trafficking 'for the purposes of the trafficking convention', because she was (possibly) not trafficked into the UK on the second occasion. That decision was unlawful: the courts had already decided there is no such distinction in law (*R (Atamewan) v SSHD*).[1]

Being recognised as a victim of trafficking is separate from an asylum application, but the person may also qualify for asylum if there is a real risk of harm (including retrafficking) on return to the country of origin, so the trafficking decision was critical to the asylum application as well. There is no right of appeal against a negative trafficking decision, only judicial review. Ana's solicitor wrote to the Home Office, as required by the judicial review Pre-Action Protocol. The Home Office did respond to this pre-action correspondence, but maintained its flawed trafficking decision.

Ana's lawyers applied for judicial review. The solicitor had to lodge a claim form and a bundle containing all the evidence and to instruct a barrister to draft grounds for review. The Government Legal Department took over conduct of the case as legal representative to the Home Office and responded on its behalf. It conceded this case at the earliest opportunity, in the Acknowledgement of Service, recognising correctly that the decision was legally indefensible and agreeing that the Home Office would withdraw the decision and pay the applicant's legal costs at *inter partes* (private) rates. Meanwhile, Ana's asylum application still awaited a decision.

---

[1] [2013] EWHC 2727 (Admin).

Bella's story

Bella's case was a pure asylum claim. Her application had been running for nearly two years. The case was particularly strong in that it was closely related to those of two other women who feared the same man, and whose asylum appeals had been allowed 18 months earlier. Bella gave evidence in those women's appeals and her evidence was believed by the appeal judge. Yet the Home Office failed to make a decision on Bella's case within six months and had therefore classified it as 'complex', despite the clear evidential support. Bella also had a minor child and an adult child with a serious disability and was, as her caseworker said, "understandably at breaking point" as the family depended on asylum support, which did not provide the extra care her disabled child needed. The caseworker felt frustrated at being unable to reach a resolution, which would enable Bella's husband to join her under the refugee family reunion rules.

The caseworker sent a pre-action letter threatening judicial review of the delay. As a result, the Home Office committed to making a decision within the next six months. That response meant it was not viable, in terms of cost, timing and prospects of success, to proceed with judicial review at that point, since the most likely outcome of a judicial review would also have been an undertaking (albeit in a court order) to make a decision within a similar period. It meant, however, that there was nothing more the caseworker could do to speed up the decision for another half-year.

Four types of demand

Demand for legal aid services arises in two main stages: **potential-client demand** from people who would like the lawyer to take on their case; and **in-case demand** from existing clients for services on their open cases. In the stories, Ana and Bella represented potential-client demand when they initially approached their representatives. They represented in-case demand once they had open files, even when this involved starting a new judicial review matter alongside the asylum application or appeal.

It also arises in two main types: **value demand**, for what the service is supposed to do; and **failure demand**, which is work required because the value demand has not been met or the purpose of the system has not been achieved (Seddon, 2003). Failure demand arises either when an actor in the system fails to do their job properly, or when a system is

Figure 5.1: Demand matrix

	VALUE DEMAND	FAILURE DEMAND
POTENTIAL CLIENTS	Potential client Value demand	Potential client Failure demand
EXISTING CLIENTS	In-case Value demand	In-case Failure demand

badly set up or becomes distorted by, for example, performance targets and measures (Seddon, 2008).

Breaking down demand in this way helps to develop a more nuanced understanding of the drivers of demand. All demand for asylum or immigration legal aid services can be placed in one of the four matrix squares in Figure 5.1. The dividing line between potential-client and in-case demand is represented by the horizontal line. The distinction between value and failure demand is less sharp, recognising that there are likely to be 'grey areas'. This is represented by the blurred vertical line in the matrix, indicating *borderline* demand.

Potential-client demand

The primary driver of potential-client demand for asylum legal advice is the arrival of people wishing to claim asylum. The number of people seeking asylum rises sharply during times of global conflict – the wars in Syria, South Sudan, Iraq, Afghanistan, the Balkans – or political, ethnic or religious oppression, as shown on the Home Office's quarterly statistical releases.[2] (See also Sturge, 2020.) The nature of the asylum system means that all of these are likely to require advice and representation for applications and, if refused, for appeals.

---

[2] Available at: https://www.gov.uk/government/collections/immigration-statistics-quarterly-release.

Not all asylum applicants are newly arrived: they can make fresh asylum claims, with new evidence, any time (sometimes many years) after a first application has been refused and any appeal rights are exhausted.[3] Fresh claims may lead to a grant of asylum, a fresh right of appeal, or to certification as unfounded. The latter can only be challenged by judicial review.[4] Clearly, then, demand for judicial review can be driven by this decision-making.

Demand for fresh claims work rises when country guidance case law changes so that asylum claims are more likely to succeed. For example, most Zimbabweans had been refused asylum in the years up to 2008, when the courts had held that most faced no real risk of persecution. Since there were no diplomatic connections through which to enforce removals to Zimbabwe, many were still in the UK, living in limbo without the right to work, but afraid to return. Numerous others had entered the UK with work or study visas, affording them limited leave to remain in the UK. Then, in 2008, the new country guidance case of *RN Zimbabwe* meant that most Zimbabweans who had been outside that country for more than three years qualified for asylum, whether or not they had applied for it previously, generating a sudden spike in demand both for first-time claims and for fresh claims from Zimbabwean nationals already in the UK.[5] For any nationality, the individual's circumstances may change during this limbo period, for example, because of a religious conversion, same-sex relationship, or political activity against the home country government while in the UK, which would put them at risk on return, again creating demand for work on a fresh asylum claim.

The geographical patterns of potential-client demand are shaped substantially by the government's practice, since 2000, of dispersing asylum applicants to areas of the country where housing is cheap and readily available (Robinson et al, 2003). In Scotland, there was barely an immigration legal aid sector at all until people seeking asylum began being accommodated in Glasgow. Unaccompanied children, by contrast, were accommodated wherever they first came to official attention, until the National Transfer Scheme was created in 2016,

---

[3] Immigration Rules, paragraph 353, and see *ZT Kosovo v Secretary of State for the Home Department* [2009] UKHL 6.

[4] Data on fresh claims are difficult to access because statistics have been 'temporarily discontinued from January 2019 due to data issues'. Home Office, *User Guide to Home Office Statistics*, February 2020.

[5] *RN (Returnees) Zimbabwe* CG [2008] UKAIT 00083.

which meant that some areas of the UK, particularly Kent and Croydon, received the majority of unaccompanied children (Wilding, 2017).

Immigration detention also drives the volume and geographical patterning of potential-client demand. Contracted firms provide advice surgeries on a rota for each centre. All detainees have a right to be represented in an application to an immigration judge for bail. Detainees may also have a viable claim for unlawful detention. Legal aid remains available for detention cases, though it might not be available for the detainee's substantive immigration case, such as an appeal against deportation.

Some legal need never manifests as potential-client demand; for instance, in regions where there are no providers or when word goes around that help is not available (Thomas, 2016). This was reflected in the comments of providers and barristers who said they had no record of the number of cases turned away by receptionists or clerks owing to lack of capacity, but believed that still others did not come at all because the news travelled that they would not take on new cases. As a caseworker put it, despite being in an area with limited provision: "Word gets out that we're not really taking on referrals. There are people that come into reception and call all the time, but we're not inundated because ... word gets out and people don't bother coming to us because we're too busy". All interviewees described having more potential-client demand than capacity, with no real competition for clients, meaning they had to make decisions about which demand to meet. The drivers of potential-client demand at market level, though, are external to providers and outside their control.

In-case demand

In-case demand means all of the services which must, should or could be provided on an open case, whether directly to the client or to any other body involved. Deciding how best to run a case – what evidence will help the client; which legal authorities assist or sabotage the case; what support the client needs; which legal points to argue and which not; and how to balance those decisions with financial or other resource considerations – is very much a matter of judgement, based on experience, knowledge and tactical skill. There are genuine differences in view between practitioners about how best to progress a case. What practitioners call basic client care may look like overworking or a 'Mother Teresa complex' to the funder (Sommerlad, 2008:p189), particularly when the funder does not have direct experience of practice.

Barristers characterised their work as essentially reactive or responsive to in-case demand: "doing what needs doing" (often regardless of what they will be paid for doing). Like solicitors, they described a general mental framework for deciding what needs doing, depending on the type of case and the time available, exercising their judgement in deciding which steps to take. Best practice might be impractical; for example, using a telephone interpreter was "not ideal", but might be "the most workable solution". All practitioners in the study identified detailed witness statements as essential, but reported that some other providers produced very brief statements which did not always deal with the real issues in the case – an assertion which was supported by the file reviews in the QALSS research (Migration Work et al, 2016).

In Bella's case, the in-case demand included taking detailed instructions from her and compiling a detailed witness statement, both about her fear in her home country and about her child's disability, since that would be relevant to the question of whether they could relocate safely in the home country. Medical evidence was needed to support that, as was country background evidence demonstrating that the country was not willing or able to protect Bella adequately. It also included obtaining evidence from the other two women who feared the same man: if available, this could be the witness statements they made for their own appeals and, later (after Bella's application was first made) the judge's determination of those. In-case demand includes preparing the client for their asylum interview, reading back that interview with the help of an interpreter, correcting any errors or confusion in the interview record, submitting evidence which has been requested by the interviewer, and making representations as to why the application should be granted.

In-case demand also comprises services to the funder relating directly to the case, which generally means billing and submitting the file for audit. Certain steps might be required as part of this, even though they are not best practice in terms of client care, like obtaining robust evidence of means at the outset, even if that distorts the lawyer-client relationship.

> 'You have to put that almost first. Over the years that I've worked in this area, it's really become the main thing that we have to look at to stay alive, whereas in the past I'd see the person and I'd say right, please bring that to me later, because I'd trust that they would do that. I find it uncomfortable because the beginning of the appointment is all about the financial circumstances when you're talking to someone

that's an asylum seeker: "Do you own any property? Have you got any savings?" … It's a difficult approach.'

In-case demand is unpredictable and barristers, in particular, described a lack of control once a case is accepted, where work is (or becomes) urgent, such as an attempt to prevent the client's imminent removal from the UK if they fear for their safety. For solicitors doing detention work, taking on a case in the former fast-track procedure entailed intensive in-case demand over a limited period of time in which all other work was sidelined. Some practitioners, male and female, adapted their practices to avoid the risk of urgent work because the in-case demand was incompatible with family commitments. One explained that they filtered out emergency work at the potential-client stage because: "I just can't sustain that kind of practice with young children. With emergency litigation … you may just have to stay in chambers till midnight to do something for the next day." Another had shifted the focus of their practice to achieve the same thing:

> 'Once you take it on it's quite all-consuming until it's over, so very urgent JRs I've tended to say I'm just not in a position to give enough time to. [But] false imprisonment cases, I've not been turning away because they're much easier to manage. Most of the time they come in with very long deadlines … so generally it's easier to fit those into a working week.'

Both legal complexity and the extreme adversarialism of immigration and asylum law escalate in-case demand. Asylum and immigration work involves a greater volume of new statute law and policy material, generating ever more new case law and a faster pace of change, than perhaps any other area of law. Its specialist tribunal is characterised by greater complexity and technicality than other tribunals (Thomas, 2016). As a barrister of 22 years' call expressed it:

> '[In many areas of law] they have virtually no case law, whereas we've got such a churn of judgements coming through that I need almost to be able to talk to someone else or a couple of people, just to say, have I missed something? …. And in the other areas I do, there's just not this churn.'

For example, a review by the author of all unlawful detention cases reported in 2017 shows that each one demanded extensive reference to rules, precedent and policy material, including Detention Centre Rules, Detention Service Orders, the process guidance in respect of Detention Centre Rule 35, the Immigration Rules, various chapters of the Enforcement Instructions and Guidance (a Home Office policy document) and the Home Office Policy on Assessment Care in Detention and Teamwork (regarding food refusal). In respect of each provision, the parties had to present relevant personal evidence, including claimants' medical records, detention reviews, Home Office computerised records, medical reports prepared under Rule 35 and the Home Office's responses to those reports.

These are essential to demonstrate how the claimant's personal circumstances relate to the, often fine, distinctions in the policies and case law. Painstaking line-by-line review of medical notes and Home Office records may be required. In some cases, where the detainee had first served a prison sentence, the evidence included standard prison and probation records. Where detention had been lengthy, it might include multiple witness statements about the possibility of voluntary or enforced return to the claimant's country of origin at different points in their detention. The evidential requirements created by the complex framework of law and policy, combined with the finer distinctions derived from the growing body of case law, undoubtedly drive up in-case demand.

Not all in-case demand becomes supply, because a practitioner may decide not to provide every service, or may fail to recognise some possible actions. Take, for example, the caseworker described in Chapter 4, recording one hour of generic country background research on the issue of forced military service, "which is exactly the same hour" he did on multiple other Eritrean cases. The cases described – the political cartoonist and the border guard who abandoned his post – had unique features which were not mentioned in the files at all. The in-case demand was for detailed witness statements, gathering the evidence which was available to the clients (published material, statements from other witnesses) and country background research specific to these men's cases, but this was not reflected in the services supplied.

The LAA attempted to standardise the in-case demand for country background research, by specifying that one hour was the length of time that would usually be necessary. This obscures the difference between cases, and means that the lawyer might, depending which assessor audits the file at the end, experience higher (unfunded) in-case demand when justifying why the research took longer than the presumed standard time.

It appears that in some firms, caseworkers see these standards, and the fixed fee itself, as a limit or cap on in-case supply. One solicitor interviewee had left a firm which capped work in this way, and two caseworker interviewees were told in job interviews that the prospective employer did not work beyond the fixed fee. An MoJ official who was interviewed for the QALSS research noted that suppliers had to report the actual time spent on the case, even when claiming the fixed fee: he said that "most come in within the fixed fee". He saw this as evidence that the fixed fee was sufficient. It would also mean that case demands were quite uniform. It is at least equally consistent with the inference that some suppliers cap their work at the amount they will be paid for – in short, responding to the financial incentive rather than to demand.

Value demand

Value demand is a demand for the intended purpose of the system (Seddon, 2003). Seddon offers two examples: in the planning system, the value demand is for a decision on whether or not a new development should be permitted; in the housing benefit system, there are two value demands, namely for decisions on initial claims for benefits and for recording changes of circumstances (Seddon, 2008). Applying that to the asylum system, there is one core value demand of the Home Office: to make a (lawful and fair) decision on the request for protection from persecution, indiscriminate violence or other serious harm. Different parts of the system have different roles, therefore each application for asylum creates several different value demands. The value demand on legal practitioners, from the client perspective, is for advice and representation at the relevant stage of the proceedings. The value demands on the LAA are to facilitate provision of that service and to account for their use of public money.

As with in-case demand, there is a subjective element – professional judgement – which makes it difficult to identify value demand. Every appeal has a winner and a loser but this does not mean one side necessarily misjudged the merits: there is a broad grey area where either result is possible, bearing in mind the difficulties in predicting success. For that reason, the designation of failure demand should be applied only when the law and facts are very clear and not in borderline instances.

Failure demand

Failure demand is any additional demand generated either by the system being badly set up or by an actor or body within the system failing to fulfil its function. In the planning system, Seddon found that many applications were refused in order to meet processing time targets, when they might otherwise have been allowed with modifications or conditions. As a result, 20–30 per cent of planning offices' work became 'rework' (2003:p9). Similarly, in one sample of housing benefit applications, 40 per cent of claims were nil-qualified and had to be restarted, meaning claims reported as lasting 28 days had taken up to 98 days from claimants' perspectives, sometimes because they were asked to show documents they had already submitted. The service was poor from the service-user's perspective, but met its processing time targets (Seddon, 2008). Failure demand, therefore, is the waste work generated by bad system design, as well as individual decision-making. Seddon argues that applying the concept of failure demand can help to understand which aspects of the system are badly designed.

In the demand matrix (Figure 5.1), the concept of failure demand accommodates and examines both substantive decision-making and procedural or system factors, in all parts of the system. All interviewees in the BAJ study gave examples of failure demand within the asylum system. These involved the Home Office and LAA, less commonly the tribunal or courts, and sometimes other lawyers, which are discussed in the following subsections.

Failure demand from Home Office

The Home Office's function is to operate the asylum procedure and make protection and other immigration decisions. This includes participating in appeals or other court procedures where they have refused an application. It also has functions around detention, support and accommodation for people seeking asylum, and removal from the UK, but those functions are not considered in detail here.

The National Audit Office (NAO, 2004, 2009), the Independent Chief Inspector of Borders and Immigration (ICIBI, 2017), the House of Commons Public Accounts Committee (2020) and academics (Thomas, 2005, 2015a, 2015b; Mullen, 2016) have all criticised the Home Office for delays and flawed decision-making. The Chief Inspector's report noted that 25 per cent of decisions were below 'satisfactory' on the Home Office's own internal quality assurance procedures, with some indication that quality worsened as the six-month decision target approached (ICIBI, 2017).

In demand terms, leaving aside distress to the applicant, a poor-quality asylum refusal generates demand for a solicitor or caseworker to lodge and prepare an appeal and either present the appeal themselves or instruct a barrister. It creates a demand for the tribunal to process and hear the appeal, for the Home Office Presenting Officers Unit to process and present the appeal, and for the LAA to either process a fixed-fee bill or assess an escape-fee claim.

With Ana's case, the flawed trafficking decision created failure demand for judicial review work by Ana's lawyers, creating failure demand for the Home Office to respond to pre-action correspondence, for the Government Legal Department to conduct litigation on the Home Office's behalf, for the Administrative Division of the High Court to process the claim and Home Office response, and for the LAA to carry out administrative work in granting funding to Ana and her lawyers, even though the costs were eventually paid by the Home Office. The delays in making asylum decisions on both Ana's and Bella's cases created failure demand for their lawyers to keep updating them and explaining the delays. In Bella's case, it also created failure demand for the lawyers to challenge the delay by way of judicial review pre-action work, which required the Home Office to respond with an undertaking to make the decision which constituted the original value demand.

A larger-scale example arose in 2015 when the Home Office began refusing Eritrean asylum claims based on a report from the Danish Immigration Service. It asserted that conditions had improved in Eritrea such that there was no longer a risk to returnees (*Economist*, 2015; Lyons, 2016). The report had already been discredited in Denmark before the Home Office began relying on it. The grant rate for Eritrean asylum applicants fell from 86 per cent (year to March 2015) to 42 per cent (year to March 2016). This generated numerous appeals, of which 85 per cent succeeded, before the Upper Tribunal heard and published a new country guideline case concluding that the Danish report was inaccurate and the risk to Eritrean returnees remained high. Had the report not already been discredited, these appeals might have been value demand arising from borderline cases but, in the circumstances, they amount to failure demand, falling on the applicants' lawyers, the Tribunal, the Home Office's own presenting officers (who argue the appeals on its behalf in the Tribunal), and the LAA, which funded the appeals.

Even after successful appeals, though, Home Office decisions can still generate failure demand, as described by a senior barrister:

> '[The Appellant] was aged 99 and had a prognosis of twelve months. Not a single penny was cost to the public purse and [the Home Office] refused him. We won on appeal within five minutes and [the Home Office] gave him six months' leave! So the family had to do a further application.'

Though the lawyers were privately paid, the appeal generated work at public expense for the tribunal. The Home Office, also at public expense, had to process not only the appeal but also the further application for leave to remain, despite the lack of any prospect of a material change of circumstances. Immigration policy and individual decision-maker error interacted to create yet further failure demand, as the same barrister explained:

> 'He'd had a carer for 20-odd years. The Home Office unlawfully treated her application as invalid and we had to straightaway judicially review it because it would mean that he was committing a criminal offence in employing her! She couldn't be living in the house that they were both living in because she'd become an over-stayer, so this hostile environment is distorting everything now.'

The abandonment of pragmatic approaches to granting leave and the introduction of draconian policies criminalising landlords, employers and migrants, combined with the flawed decision to treat this carer's application as unlawful, created failure demand which eventually fell on the Administrative Court, the Government Legal Department and, above all, the client's family (and their lawyers). This can be seen throughout what became known as the Windrush cases, whereby people who migrated to the UK as British subjects from the colonies, often as young children, and had never needed documentary proof of their status were suddenly excluded from services, employment and rental housing as a result of hostile environment policies. Some were wrongly detained or even forcibly removed from the UK, while many lost their jobs, and there were examples of people being unable to get cancer treatment on the National Health Service because they could not prove their entitlement, despite many decades of residence in the UK. The hostile environment policies of the Home Office, combined with the withdrawal of legal aid for most immigration matters, created this failure demand which has included a (so-far flawed) compensation scheme.

Practitioners accused the Home Office of frequent 'dysfunctional litigation behaviour', complaints which are supported by an analysis of all unlawful detention judicial review cases reported in 2017.[6] Judges severely criticised the Home Office for its litigation behaviour in 6

---

[6] Identified by searches on Bailii, Westlaw, Lawtel and Electronic Immigration Network.

of the 55 cases – almost 11 per cent of the sample. This included late or non-filing of a defence, evidence or skeleton argument;[7] arriving at the hearing unprepared to proceed;[8] an 'enduring casualness' about multiple applications for extensions of time without good reason;[9] or misrepresenting the facts which were said to justify detention.[10] A judge's comments summarise how this generates failure demand:

> '[T]he Secretary of State's failure to get an early grip on proceedings and to give the Government Legal Department sufficient instructions to enable them to make complete and accurate disclosure of all relevant matters in a timely way has made dealing with this case far more complex and costly than it would have been if there had been proper record-keeping, and consequently full and accurate disclosure at an earlier date, and a properly informed (and factually accurate) response to the pre-action letter.'[11]

As in Ana's case, this point about flawed responses to the pre-action letter means that judicial review applications have to be made even when the legal position is clear, if the Home Office refuses to acknowledge it.

This is not to suggest that claimant lawyers always conduct litigation appropriately. Examples of claimant lawyers' litigation failings are discussed further on, and indeed there was criticism of claimant lawyers in one of the reported 2017 detention cases, albeit for less serious failings. Generally, however, where the claimant's representative fails to comply with directions in the ways described, the claim is struck out at an earlier stage, or otherwise dealt with through the court's case-management powers. By contrast, the normal sanctions imposed on private litigants are rarely applied to the Home Office; it is usually permitted to participate in hearings even if it repeatedly fails to comply with directions, because of the public importance of the issues raised and the public money at stake in damages.

This means the courts' case-management powers, which should reduce failure demand, are largely ineffective against the Home

---

[7] *R (on the application of Liban) v SSHD* [2017] EWHC 2551 (Admin).

[8] *R (on the application of Iqbal) v SSHD* [2017] EWHC 79 (Admin).

[9] *R (on the application of Ademiluyi) v SSHD* [2017] EWHC 935 (Admin), paragraph 23.

[10] *R (on the application of OA) v SSHD* [2017] EWHC 486 (Admin).

[11] *R (on the application of Omed Abid) v SSHD* [2017] EWHC 1962 (Admin), paragraph 5.

Office. The same applies at tribunal level, where directions to disclose information or produce original documents at court were said to be frequently ignored, causing hearings to be adjourned. In one example, a caseworker described how a hearing had been adjourned on three successive occasions because of the Home Office's repeated failure to disclose information. The tribunal has even less effective case-management powers than the higher courts to prevent this behaviour.

The evidence thus supports the argument that poor-quality decision-making, delays and poor litigation conduct pull demand into the system, not only for lawyers' work, but also for services from the Government Legal Department and the courts and tribunals.

Failure demand from Legal Aid Agency

The LAA's role is to operationalise the legal duty on the Lord Chancellor to secure the availability of legal aid for people who are entitled to it. In relation to the asylum system, this means maintaining a network of providers and facilitating them doing the work and receiving payment. Failure demand is generated through the LAA's administrative procedures, primarily through the imposition of inefficient practices and poor-quality decision-making, criticised by practitioners as a 'culture of refusal'. Chapter 4 discussed how the zero-tolerance auditing of providers' work generates a time-consuming and unpaid "low-level back and forth", whereas the mandatory use of the online Client and Cost Management System (CCMS) is an element of enforced inefficiency.

Practitioners argued that these inefficient systems also created waste work for the LAA. The requirement to apply in advance for funding in at-risk cases, where there is minimal cost to the legal aid fund unless the case succeeds, duplicates the work for the lawyer and demands the involvement of an LAA official. A partner in a private firm explained that there is no way, on CCMS, to alert the LAA to cases which are urgent, meaning they had to involve a senior manager in each of these cases.

> 'It's a bit of a mad system where you have to lodge the application on CCMS then you have to phone up [senior manager] to say this one's urgent, because they haven't really got a system of working out which ones are urgent. Someone has to click on each case at their end to actually work out which ones are the urgent ones. So it's completely bonkers, it's just a poorly designed system ....'

A solicitor in a not-for-profit had likewise resorted to direct emails to a senior manager, who she happened to know from a previous job. This manager had on a few occasions granted an emergency certificate or an extension via email, whereas when the solicitor had sent messages through CCMS, as she should, she said, "I think I've maybe had a reply once".

This was all the more frustrating because, despite the prior application process, they would not be paid unless the court granted permission for the case to proceed, meaning there is no risk to the legal aid fund. Yet before 2013, when providers were paid for judicial review work regardless of whether they got permission, they had devolved powers to issue their own funding certificates, subject to their own assessment of the merits.

The transition from emergency to regular funding could be similarly problematic. The emergency certificate allows work to start on urgent cases, but providers are not paid for work carried out once this expires. Frustration appears mutual, as a solicitor in a not-for profit described:

> 'I had an emergency [certificate] that ran out and then I was calling every day to the LAA and I was told off every day saying why are you calling me, I can't do your application if you're calling me. And I said I do understand that, but what do you want me to do? My emergency ran out on Friday and you're not even looking at it. If there's another way, let me know and I'll do it, but I don't know what else I can do.'

These examples fit Seddon's idea of failure demand coming from compliance with badly designed systems. The LAA appears to recognise this to some extent and is seeking to save administrative costs. Most of the providers researched had been given the power in 2016 to self-grant extensions to existing funding, which reduced the time they spent applying and sometimes re-applying for extensions; for example, to obtain an expert report.

Nevertheless, legal aid lawyers across all categories of civil and criminal law continued to express frustration over what they described as a culture of refusal within the LAA (Bowcott, 2019). Housing lawyers in the case of *Samuels v Birmingham* described a '32-month battle to secure legal aid' (Mullings, 2020), eventually securing a landmark decision in the Supreme Court in the substantive case. Another housing lawyer, Derek Bernardi (@derekbarnardi) regularly tweets about cases where legal aid has been refused by an LAA official, simply quoting the defendant's arguments (in the decision which was under challenge) without further explanation. These refusal decisions are made despite written advice from an experienced barrister explaining why the defendant's arguments were flawed, resulting in months of additional and unpaid work to have legal aid granted. To one of these tweets, another lawyer responded that funding for one of his clients was delayed, though she was well within the earnings threshold, because there was a £6 deposit in her bank account for which she was unable to remember the source.

In immigration, similarly, a barrister interviewee gave an example where permission to appeal had been granted by the Court of Appeal. This meant the case had sufficient prospects of success and there would be a full hearing unless the Home Office conceded the case. The work would eventually be paid either from the legal aid fund at legal aid rates or by the Home Office at *inter partes* rates. Yet the LAA continued to refuse funding for the appeal on the basis that it did not have at least a 50 per cent prospect of success at the final hearing; an approach which was clearly flawed. The barrister argued that, "For them to refuse funding in a case where the Court of Appeal is saying it's arguable that the Upper Tribunal has screwed up, that's really wilfully difficult". Continuing unfunded, in the hope of success, is rarely an option since the client is at risk of being ordered to pay the other side's costs if they lose the case without the protection of legal aid.

At least some of the systemic and the individual factors generating failure demand from the LAA can be seen as manifestations of mistrust. It is clear from the accounts of both LAA officials and lawyers that this emanates particularly from the time when the LAA's predecessor, the LSC, had its accounts qualified for four successive years and was criticised by the National Audit Office. There is very little in the way of earned autonomy – greater trust for those who display competence and integrity – and all providers are treated as risky. This pulls demand into the system with limited benefit to the public purse.

Failure demand from lawyers

The BAJ study focused on lawyers peer-identified as providing good-quality services. All these participants identified failure demand generated through poor-quality work by other lawyers. Practitioners cited inadequate or even damaging work on the initial asylum claim, creating a demand for "repair work" on an appeal, or for a fresh claim based on evidence which could have been obtained for the initial claim. They suggested this was often caused by "sausage factory" providers delegating casework to the lowest paid and qualified staff and effectively co-opting (often junior) barristers into a supervisory role.

A series of cases in the higher courts demonstrated the failure demand created by a small number of poor-quality firms persistently submitting 'late, meritless applications by people who face removal or deportation [which] are an intolerable waste of public money, a great strain on the resources of this court and an abuse of a service this court offers'.[12] The firms criticised in these cases (referred to as *Hamid* cases, after the first case) were not legal aid ones, but their model of delegating complex work to under-qualified and under-supervised staff, which led to some of the court's criticisms, is replicated in some legal aid firms and implicated in much of the poor-quality representation.

Some practitioners who sit as immigration judges commented on the poor quality of some legal representation, meaning the judge has to struggle to understand the case. As one barrister–judge put it: "More than 50 per cent of what I get is not fit for purpose in terms of grounds and arguments. People get the law wrong, they don't understand it; they miss the point." Home Office presenting officers were also said to be often poor quality. As the barrister–judge said, "You do get some good ones but you also get some coming through that just aren't well trained", cross-examining at length on irrelevant issues, prolonging hearings or making the legal and factual points harder for the judge to discern.

Good-quality representation, on either side, was considered invaluable. It is harder for judges (that is, it increases in-case demand on judges) when appellants are unrepresented. One part-time judge interviewed had adjourned every case in a recent day's court list because the appellants were unrepresented and crucial pieces of evidence were missing. The judge (who is paid a fee per case) was not paid for any of the adjourned cases, meaning the costs of non-representation were shifted onto the judge personally and to the tribunal system more broadly, which incurred the cost of the adjourned hearing. In economics, this can be seen as a 'negative externality' falling on the judge, in circumstances where (expected) market efficiencies appear to have replaced a value-based approach to justice.

Poor-quality work has a ripple effect in terms of demand: a solicitor gave the example of families who do not have leave to remain because they received poor legal advice earlier in the process and, as a result, become homeless and in need of representation for housing

---

[12] *R (Hamid) v Secretary of State for the Home Department* [2012] EWHC 3070 (Admin).

proceedings. An asylum applicant whose appeal is dismissed becomes a liar, in the eyes of the system (Bauder, 2014), so that any future applications for leave to remain or for release from detention are pre-tainted by the earlier inability to prove their case. This makes the case more complex, increasing its in-case demand at later stages.

Those lawyers who produce excellent work, accurately identify the merits of cases, are strategic and supervise junior staff thoroughly, rarely generate failure demand. That reduces the burden on judges at all levels, on the courts, opponents, regulators, and so on. Paying for poor quality, on the other hand, ends up generating extra demand. Yet there is no differentiation in the legal aid contract, neither in auditing and risk management nor in funding, between the treatment of the highest and lowest quality lawyers.

Failure demand from system incompatibilities

It is equally important to consider the system as a whole, not merely the sum of the parts. The value demand on the system as a whole is to produce fair and humane outcomes for people seeking international protection, while offering good value for public money – both of which are fiercely contested and hard to define. The asylum justice system is a complex, multiparty system including lawyers, the Ministry of Justice, LAA and HM Courts and Tribunals Service, the Home Office, privately run detention centres, and so on, which have to interact. Some failure demand arises because the parts of the system are not well aligned or compatible with one another.

By way of example, asylum decision-making and representation are complicated by the fact that most decisions depend not on points of law but on credibility: that is, whether or not the applicant is believed. Yet as Thomas (2006) points out, most of the Home Office's information-gathering happens in the asylum interview, where most applicants are unrepresented because legal aid does not cover a lawyer's attendance, and where applicants commonly experience problems with Home Office interpreters or feel intimidated. Some Home Office decision-makers are good or experienced interviewers, knowledgeable about country evidence, traumatic memory, or the application of the benefit of the doubt, but many are not (Taylor, 2016). At the same time, Home Office decision-makers are arguably handicapped by making decisions without the expert evidence which may later sway the tribunal (Thomas, 2005, 2011). Legal aid will not fund the obtaining of country and medical expert evidence *before* an asylum refusal, however, on the basis that it may not be needed. This is in stark contrast to the early advice procedure which was piloted in 2006–12 and eventually abandoned, which suggested that a more collaborative approach to evidence-gathering throughout the applications and appeals processes would potentially save time and distress, though financial savings were less clear (Lane et al, 2013).

Robert Thomas (2015a), one of the main writers on tribunal justice, shows how politically motivated reforms aimed at cost-reduction have often targeted the wrong parts of the system. For example, when immigration appeal rights were limited, partly to save money, would-be appeals were recycled as more expensive judicial review cases (Bridges et al, 2000) because Home Office decision-making was not improved first. When (as a result) the number of immigration judicial reviews in the High Court became overwhelming, jurisdiction was shifted to the Upper Tribunal. The Upper Tribunal, Thomas notes, was given no extra resources to deal with the new caseload. There was a sharp increase in applications dismissed at the first stage as 'totally without merit', meaning they could not be renewed to an oral hearing. He argues that the increase reflected 'system manageability' rather than the actual merit of the cases, at the expense of applicants who had no other remedy for wrong decisions (Thomas, 2015b).

As an alternative, imagine a non-detained, fast-track decision process operating a presumption that refugee status would be granted for all nationals of countries which had an asylum grant rate of, say, 70 per cent or higher. For the year to June 2019, these included Libya (95 per cent), Syria (89 per cent), Sudan (89 per cent), Eritrea (88 per cent) and Iran (70 per cent) (Walsh, 2019). These made up over one fifth of applications in 2018. At present, there is no consistent triaging system in place in the Home Office whereby these applicants can be identified and given positive decisions quickly, channelling back into the main asylum procedure only those cases that are genuinely more complex. It could remove around 20 per cent of the decision caseload, saving distress for applicants, and time and resources for the Home Office. It would enable legal aid providers to focus their resources on cases where legal advice was necessary, reduce the costs associated with delay and allow newly recognised refugees to move on more quickly into communities and out of asylum accommodation. It could dramatically reduce in-case demand without limiting access to justice.

Advocating a whole-system view of demand in the asylum system is not necessarily unorthodox: even the Carter Review (2006) emphasised the need to look at police, prosecutors and judiciary as well as legal aid, for the causes of rising costs. On this basis Carter argued that fair pricing, which recognised that other parts of the system also drove up costs, was essential for maintaining a supplier base. There is no evidence that pricing or policy on legal aid are, in fact, informed by a detailed understanding of the drivers of demand and this lack of systemic thinking or alignment continues to generate failure demand.

Cost consequences of demand

All demand has resource implications, but failure demand appears to cause three main cost consequences:

- Escalated cost: when an existing cost (the cost of the value demand) is increased, such as when a lawyer or the Home Office has to do more work, or the Upper Tribunal has to process an onward appeal which should not have been necessary.
- Generated cost: when an entirely new cost is generated when it should not have been needed – for example, because a judicial review is required.
- Shifted cost: when a cost which would have been incurred anyway falls on a different organisation or individual, or when one party incurs the cost of failure demand created by another.

Cost consequences can be added into the demand matrix (Figure 5.2), offering a framework for analysis of the drivers of both demand and cost in the system. These are essentially what economists refer to as 'externalities': costs (or benefits), which fall on a party other than

Figure 5.2: Demand matrix with cost consequences

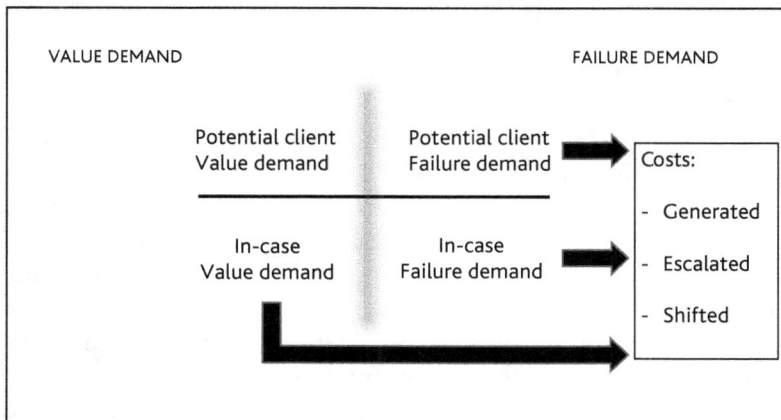

the one which generated them. Negative externalities of an airport, for example, might include air pollution, noise and heavy traffic, the costs of which fall on surrounding communities, local government and health authorities rather than on the producers. It would be an impossibly huge task to analyse all demand and externalities in the asylum system, but the exercise of breaking down demand and cost consequences in individual cases can help us to understand what works and does not, and where better outcomes and value could be achieved.

Returning to Ana's case, it is now possible to break down the demand types and cost consequences at each stage (see Table 5.1). The work on her asylum application is funded by the Legal Help fixed fee of £413, unless the case costs at least triple that amount, excluding the disbursements (costs paid to third parties such as interpreters). As shown in Table 5.1, the case was not expected to reach that threshold, so the solicitor expected to be paid for only about two-fifths of the work done and to make a loss of £607. In this scenario, the cost of some of the value demand is *shifted* from the LAA to the provider. The Home Office's delays in deciding her asylum application created in-case failure demand which *escalated* the costs and *shifted* them from the Home Office onto the provider.

The Home Office's seriously flawed trafficking decision created failure demand, since the law was already clear on the matter. This *generated* new costs. The solicitor's pre-action work cost £300, which would be paid on hourly rates by the LAA, meaning the costs were *shifted* from the Home Office to the LAA.

The costs of the judicial review application were also failure demand costs caused by the Home Office's flawed response to pre-action correspondence, but the consequences here were more complex because more parties were involved. As billed, before negotiation, the costs were around £1,500 for the provider's profit costs, £270 in disbursements and around £2,000 for counsel's fees, for a total of £3,770 (see Table 5.1). As discussed in Chapter 4, the actual payment is commonly 70–75 per cent of the costs billed. The lawyers' costs were both *generated* and paid by the Home Office, but other generated costs were *shifted* onto the other parties in the system. The Government Legal Department incurred costs in conducting the litigation on behalf of the Home Office; the High Court incurred costs in processing the case; the LAA incurred some administrative costs, through the initial funding application, albeit partly due to its own system design which requires providers to apply even for funding which is at risk.

Bella's case looks quite similar on a breakdown of costs (see Table 5.2), yet it was, on the face of it, a much simpler case with

Table 5.1: Demand and costs in an asylum and trafficking case (Ana's story)

Stage	Cost	Demand type	Costs destination/s
Asylum application	£1,020 profit cost + £498 disbursements: £1,518 total	In-case value demand for provider's services; some failure demand caused by Home Office in failing to recognise trafficking, prolonging the process.	LAA pays provider (£413 + £498 disbursements). Provider sustains loss of £607. Escalated and shifted costs.
Judicial review pre-action	£300	Failure demand caused by Home Office for provider's services; also for Home Office's own services and LAA's administrative work.	LAA pays £300. Generated costs.
Judicial review application	£3,770 full cost; final payment likely £2,600–£2,850	Failure demand caused by Home Office for work by lawyers, Government Legal Department, LAA (administration only) and Administrative Court.	Home Office pays costs it generated for lawyers. Other parties absorb the generated costs.

Table 5.2: Demand and costs in delayed asylum application (Bella's story)

Stage	Cost	Demand type	Costs destination/s
Asylum application	£1,033 profit costs; £500 disbursements.	Value demand for provider's services. Failure demand caused by Home Office delays and extra work required.	LAA pays provider £413 + £500. Provider loses £620. Escalated costs.
Judicial review pre-action	£165	Failure demand caused by Home Office.	LAA. Generated costs.

strong evidence and no collateral trafficking issue. As Bella's caseworker explained: "This is an example of a case which, because of the linked cases, could have been resolved very quickly and we wouldn't have lost out on it financially". She explained that delays always escalate costs because providers cannot simply shelve a delayed case: they have to keep the client informed and chase the Home Office, even if the delay is not yet severe enough for a judicial review application. This is all the more important with "vulnerable or anxious clients", who need things "re-explained" several times because they struggle to take in or retain information.

In contrast, in this caseworker's two lowest-cost cases, the Home Office granted asylum at the application stage in five and seven months, respectively, costing £472 and £471 in profit costs, plus £256 and £258 in disbursements. That meant the provider lost (only) £59 and £58, respectively, in those cases (in-case value-demand costs partially *shifted* from the LAA to the provider).

In Tables 5.1 and 5.2, the provider organisation stood to lose around one-and-a-half times as much as they would receive. They said it was neither possible nor appropriate to "bump up" the amount of work they did to try to reach the escape threshold. The fixed fee means that value-demand costs are shifted regularly from the LAA to the provider, because the level of service required exceeds the price the LAA pays for it. It also means that all of the escalated costs of failure demand caused by delay fall on the provider and not on the LAA. The fixed fee is an attempt to standardise the cost of the value demand, but where providers respond to the actual demand and do work above that notional standard cost, they incur financial risks and losses. This is a direct consequence of the LAA's monopsony power, since it is able to fix a price below the full marginal cost of meeting the in-case value demand.

This is not to suggest that failure demand and its cost consequences are all one-way. As explained previously, it can come from any part of the system, but the government bodies in the system are not funded on a fixed fee per case. They do not face the sort of financial precariousness that providers do. Although they are accountable for their own spending via the NAO and Parliamentary committees, they face little accountability for costs they generate for non-public organisations.

Demand- and incentive-responsiveness

Most of the criteria for quality, which are identified and validated in the LAA's peer-review criteria (see Sherr & Paterson, 2008), require responsiveness to individual and specific features of in-case demand. There is a causal correlation between quality and responsiveness to in-case demand, but the incentives in the contract, fee and auditing regimes pull towards standardisation. The incentives are poorly aligned to the patterns of in-case demand in asylum legal work, creating a conflict for practitioners and provider organisations between financial viability and meeting demand. Having offered a framework for understanding demand, the chapter now argues for aligning the incentives with that demand as closely as possible.

There has been extensive work on 'incentives' in publicly funded legal services (Kritzer, 2002, 2009; Fenn et al, 2007) – a term which Sandel (2012) notes barely appeared in academic literature until the 1980s – but this idea of misalignment goes somewhat beyond the observation that there are perverse incentives in the contract and payment regimes. The funding structure both incentivises minimising work time, which is linked with lower quality, and also creates obstacles to quality which the auditing structure does nothing to balance, especially since there is no reward for high peer-review scores in terms of earned autonomy or preferential treatment.

Some practitioners and organisations orient their supply around in-case demand – they "do what needs doing" on the case, underpinned by legal knowledge and skills ensured through training and supervision. Others orientate their supply around incentives, doing the work they will be paid for. Again, this reflects Thaler and Sunstein's distinction between humans and econs, but they operate within a system which presumes all participants are econs. This is why neither system factors nor contractual incentives can fully explain demand and supply in legal aid, because the system and contract apply equally to all participants in the market. They can be seen as the boundaries of what is possible within the system, but cannot explain the differences between providers and their levels of responsiveness to in-case demand.

There is a spectrum of providers, from those who are the most *demand-responsive* to those who are the most *incentive-responsive*. This idea enables us to move away from talking about scrupulous and unscrupulous providers, while understanding that those providers who are most responsive to in-case demand offer the highest quality of work, but also face the greatest financial difficulty. Those who respond to the financial incentives – by work capping and standardising – are better able to survive in the system and increase their market share, but offer lower quality work (see also Chapter 7).

It is helpful to visualise this with a Venn diagram (see Figure 5.3), with one oval representing in-case demand and the other representing incentives (including financial, audit and any other incentives). Where incentives are closely aligned with in-case demand, the ovals overlap to a greater extent. The overlap is the space in which providers are able to do good-quality work which responds to demand without risking financial viability. Where incentives are poorly aligned with in-case demand, there is little or no overlap between the two ovals, representing greater conflict between financial viability and meeting in-case demand. Outside the overlap, providers either work unpaid

Figure 5.3: Visualisation of spectrum from demand-responsiveness to incentive-responsiveness

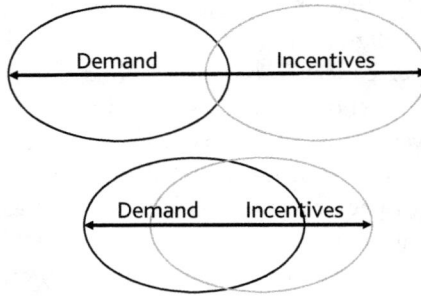

or at excessive risk (demand-responsive end) or maintain financial viability, but fail to meet in-case demand, providing an inadequate service (incentive-responsive end).

The combined diameter of the circles represents the length of the spectrum, from the most demand-responsive (on the left arrow head in these diagrams) to the most incentive-responsive (on the right arrow head). The longer the spectrum, and the smaller the overlap, the more difficult it is to maintain both demand-responsiveness (strongly correlated with quality) and financial viability. The financial incentives of a fixed-fee scheme may align with meeting a high volume of potential-client demand, in the sense of taking on many cases, but it is difficult to argue that the demand is met meaningfully where the provider fails to respond adequately to the in-case demand of those clients.

All of this means a demand-responsive provider (a 'human') is far less likely to generate failure demand than an incentive-responsive provider (an 'econ'), but the contracting, auditing and fee regimes give no advantage whatsoever to the demand-responsive provider. This turns on its head any suggestion that 'econs' offer better value for money and that 'humans' should behave more like them. The Carter Review envisaged a higher peer-review threshold to obtain a legal aid contract – a minimum of level two, with quality control delegated to professional regulators and the LAA trusting its providers. Instead the LAA awards contracts to firms achieving level three (threshold competence) on peer review, and treats all providers as equally risky. That generates failure demand.

Failure demand could therefore be reduced by differentiating between providers, affording greater trust to providers who achieve levels one or two on peer review, who are by definition the more demand-responsive providers. This would reduce the transaction costs and could be organised to minimise risk and payment delays, potentially enabling the demand-responsive providers to expand or at least to maintain their market share. Those limitations on market share or capacity, and their impact on potential clients, are the focus of Chapter 6.

6

Droughts and deserts

Mariam was subjected to serious violence by her husband in a country which offers women little protection from family violence. She borrowed money secretly from a relative to flee to the UK with her daughter Zainab, after her first daughter was forced into marriage against her will by Mariam's husband. She suffers from depression, anxiety and post-traumatic stress disorder (PTSD) as a result of her experiences. With her daughter, she was accommodated in Suffolk, in the East of England region.

As Figure 3.1 shows, no legal aid advice is available in Suffolk, nor in the counties to the north and south, although all of those counties accommodate dispersed asylum applicants. Those to the west appear to be well supplied, with five providers having received contracts in September 2018 in the closest access point, Cambridgeshire and Northamptonshire. One of them either lost or surrendered its contract within the first year, leaving four in Figure 3.1, and another did not open any cases in the year. All but one of those providers is in Northampton, to the far west of that access point, over two hours by car and three by train from Ipswich. The total number of cases opened in that access point that year was just 49. Eventually, Mariam found a solicitor in Bedfordshire, also over two hours away by train – a daunting journey for a woman suffering with anxiety and PTSD, and barely able to speak English.

Worse, her solicitor turned out to be of the 'minimalist' variety and she lost her appeal, despite country background evidence that women in her home country are often subjected to serious domestic abuse and forced marriage. No evidence was taken from Mariam's daughter Zainab, who was old enough to give a statement and (it later turned out) recalled seeing her father assault her mother and her older sister being taken from the family against her will to marry. No medical evidence was obtained, either of the scarring from the violence or the psychological effects. Evidence of Mariam's mental state would have been particularly important, because she found it difficult to give a coherent account of her older daughter's disappearance and her own escape from their home country, a fact fully explained by the effects of her PTSD and depression, which are well documented for women subjected to domestic abuse. Instead, that lack of coherence led to the judge deciding she was not to be believed about her escape or about any part of her case.

After this, Zainab's school got involved and supported her to talk to the police about her own fear of forced marriage. The police took the matter seriously, interviewed Zainab at school and concluded that she was at risk, as was Mariam from further violence. They put Mariam in touch with the safeguarding hub, which helped her to access psychiatric support. A social worker for the local authority began supporting the family, which is not always possible because of local government funding cuts. With all of this support, Mariam was able to make a fresh application for asylum. Again, the solicitor failed to take a statement from Zainab, now clearly old enough to give evidence.

When the Home Office refused her application, paying little attention to the police's concerns for both Mariam and Zainab, the solicitor dropped them, on the basis that the appeal had limited prospects of success. In large part, this was because Mariam struggled to answer their questions. Yet that was precisely the conclusion of the psychiatric evidence: she was so traumatised that her memories were fragmented, she was unable to concentrate and could only give evidence in court with significant support.

The rules of legal aid do allow another provider to make their own assessment of the merits, grant legal aid, and take over client representation. The problem was that, with a hearing coming up, living in an area of advice desert, Mariam had little prospect of finding a new solicitor within reach who would be willing to take on a case which demanded expert, careful, painstaking work with such a vulnerable client. Looking at Figure 3.1, it is clear that there are swathes of England and Wales which are without even nominal supply. The focus now moves to an exploration of why, despite robust demand, supply becomes constricted and does not increase.

Survival strategies and client access

There are two main ways demonstrated in the BAJ and QALSS research in which legal aid lawyers attempt to maintain both quality and financial viability:

- They rely on subsidy and cross-subsidy to make up losses (the 'Robin Hood model').
- They make prioritisation decisions about which demand they will meet, to minimise their losses, while also reducing the overall

amount of legal aid work they do, to cap their losses at the amount they can raise in subsidy.

The combined effect of those strategies is to reduce client access. These providers can take on fewer clients or a narrower range of case types. They reduce their responsiveness to potential-client demand in order to maintain responsiveness to in-case demand.

The language of 'advice deserts' has become familiar. These are regions, like the East of England, where there is no advice at all in a category of law, or where there is only one provider, as seen when we plot providers by place on a map. 'Advice droughts' are harder to identify because there *appears* to be provision. There are providers within the geographical area, who are permitted to open more cases (matter starts), but in practice they are unavailable to would-be clients because their capacity is limited as a result of these survival strategies. This describes the Cambridgeshire and Northamptonshire access point, neighbouring the East of England advice desert where Mariam and Zainab were living. Capacity appeared to have increased from one to five providers in September 2018, but only three of these ever carried out any work under the contract (with one withdrawing altogether recently) and the increase in supply was negligible, from 41 cases in the year to August 2017, to 49 in the following year. This does not reflect a lack of demand, since the East of England includes several areas which accommodate dispersed asylum seekers.

Reliance on subsidy

There are four main sources of subsidy: charity and other grants (for not-for-profits); private work (for barristers and private firms); judicial review and higher appeals work, which win costs at *inter partes* rates; and, to a much lesser extent, other areas of law that are higher or more promptly paid.

Subsidy or investment from the wider charity enabled Centre A's immigration team to continue operating at a loss, otherwise it would have had to stop providing legal aid services altogether (see Chapter 3 for case study details). Its legal advice services made a loss of more than £400,000 in the year to March 2016, following losses of between £200,000 and £400,000 in each of the previous three years. LASPO cut the pay rate for all work, and removed non-asylum immigration work from the scope of legal aid. Since those cases were usually quicker to close, the lag between work and payment was expected to (and did) increase, worsening the cash-flow position – a difficulty also faced by providers in other legal aid areas of law such as housing and family. Shortly after LASPO came into force in April 2013, Centre A's advice teams in all areas of law were reduced by 50 per cent, and salaries reduced, with a view to capping the total losses.

Centres B and C both received grants from charitable foundations and local government. Local government grant making had long been an important source of funding, but was shrinking dramatically as austerity affected local authorities' funds. Although these grants previously targeted issues not covered by legal aid, Centre C's manager said he was now "open" with grant makers that the money was needed to top up legal aid. The grants enabled "risk-taking" and involvement in complex cases, which many private firms were said to be understandably reluctant to take on because of the risk of losses. Grants were essential under a fixed-fee regime, as a centre manager explained:

> 'We do a lot of welfare benefit work as well and the difference is, with those [non-legal aid] contracts, you can cover your overheads, whereas with a contract with the Legal Aid Agency it just doesn't. If you're getting the fixed fee, you don't cover your overhead costs. So with housing, if you put it into our budget, it doesn't even cover one person's salary. But it's not just that. You've got your management costs, your office costs that go along with that. So you'd have to earn an awful lot of money to be able to cover all that.'

All of the not-for-profits, however, found that grants brought their own transaction costs. Each stream of funding demands expensive and separate management to demonstrate proper use of the money, detailing which clients were helped on the non-legal aid funding, meaning a layer of middle management was needed for the "juggling act" of demonstrating precisely which money covered what work. As not-for-profit providers explained, grants and contracts are not purely subsidies.

In Firms X and Y, attracting privately paying clients was a key element of cross-subsidy, as these clients were usually asked for payments on account in advance of any work being done, meaning firms doing private-client work could sustain cash flow (subject to demand) through private income. Legal staff in Firm X had high individual billing targets which were easier to meet by doing more private work though, as several caseworkers said, they found most private work boring compared to asylum and trafficking cases. Although providers over a certain size can opt for a Standard Monthly Payment, which is reconciled at the end of the financial year, a partner explained that this created the risk of a large repayment demand at the end of the year:

'It's nice having a Standard Monthly Payment so you know what you're going to get each month but we stopped ages ago, because we ended up in a bit of a pickle. It was after the last tender because we used to have only one office with a legal aid contract in immigration and asylum. Suddenly to be able to get all the matter starts we had to have [more] offices. One of the offices was still getting a large Standard Monthly Payment, but obviously the claims for that office dropped because they were now spread among [several] offices. We ended up owing huge amounts of money to the Legal Aid Agency, which was my fault because there were other things going on and I didn't quite get a handle on it, so now all our contracts are Pay-As-You-Go.'

For barristers, the overall picture was one of chambers, and immigration teams in particular, being heavily subsidised by small numbers of high earners, most of whom no longer did any legal aid work themselves. At chambers level, one manager explained that the average break-even figure had been calculated at around £153,000 gross per barrister. Only a very small proportion of the barristers in that chambers were reaching the break-even figure, meaning that chambers as a whole depended significantly on those few individuals. These high earners were doing almost exclusively private work. This pattern had existed in another chambers, which closed shortly after the LASPO cuts when a small number of high earners decided to move elsewhere, leaving them in a "precarious" position. Another set of chambers was coming to terms with the en-masse departure of a high-earning team in another area of law whose work was entirely private. Ultimately this means that a small number of high earners choose to subsidise the publicly funded Bar, perhaps out of commitment to legal aid, since most could pay a lower management fee elsewhere. This is not a sustainable model for training and supply of barristers to ensure that publicly funded advocacy work can be covered.

For individual barristers, privately paid work was the main source of subsidy, whether through direct public access or via solicitors, though this was least available to the most junior lawyers. Winning *inter partes* costs against the Home Office was also an important source of cross-subsidy, as discussed in Chapter 4, but the payment delays caused cash-flow problems, whereas private fees tended to be paid more promptly.

Some also sought out non-practising work like teaching, writing or judging, which displaced some legal aid work.

This applies not only to the asylum and immigration Bar but to all publicly funded categories of law. Immigration teams are better placed than some others, such as housing or welfare benefits, to attract privately paid work, meaning other teams may be subsidised by immigration practitioners. Barristers in different chambers said that the Hillsborough inquests, which involved numerous barristers and brought in regular payments over a two-year period, had cushioned the impact of the LASPO cuts for the whole of those chambers, but the full impact was beginning to show since the inquests had ended.

As might be expected, there are often internal politics around this subsidy. A partner in one firm said he was fortunate that another partner, who only did a limited amount of legal aid work, nevertheless understood the complexities of legal aid, accepted that "I'll never bill as much" as the other partners, and helped to justify the existence of his department to other partners in the firm. The high demand from clients boosted turnover without any marketing effort, even if profit was limited. In Firm X, which lacked non-immigration private-income streams, there were concerns that attracting more private clients might split the team, for reasons of specialism, into those bringing in a lot of private-client money and those continuing to do lower-paid legal aid work, losing some of the sense of shared purpose – a concern shared by many of the barristers in the study.

Centre A's practice manager explained that the financial aspects of the legal aid contract were "completely different from" the finances of the wider charity and its other contracts, meaning that legal aid often appeared to suck up funds which could have been used elsewhere. The director emphasised the importance of framing this as "investment in our charitable objectives" rather than subsidy. Neither immigration nor legal casework was Centre A's core purpose, and the director felt that the trustees had been "tested" repeatedly on their commitment to legal advice within the charity. At times particular trustees had been hostile to it or sceptical of its place within the organisation, which meant members of the advice team had sometimes felt resentful, insecure or undervalued, and that senior managers did not really understand what the legal advice staff did or how their work was paid for.

This understanding gap seemed to have been mitigated somewhat by the appointment of the practice manager. She was in a position to explain the intricacies of the payment systems and contract to the trustees in a similar way to the partner in Firm Y, who understood legal aid work despite not doing it personally. It may be that having someone in this role is key to easing the internal politics of subsidy in any organisation that is not focused wholly or mainly on legal aid work. The political position (if nothing else) was easier in law centres, where legal work was the core purpose and there were (in most) no private clients.

Barristers and staff likewise felt there was some tension between financial demands and ethos, in those chambers where legal aid, vulnerable clients and work with a political edge had been the historical priority. The twin pressures to do privately paid work and keep high earners in-house were seen as a threat to team and chambers cohesiveness. Discussions about finances could leave part-timers and lower earners feeling less valued, as a junior barrister with family commitments explained:

> 'For example, if [name] left chambers that would immediately massively reduce the income of chambers and anything that might lead to that outcome would cause people to be very twitchy. So in reality, the people who are big earners and bring in a lot of money, their word counts for an awful lot. We may not be viable if it weren't for those people. The way the legal aid landscape has changed, it's not viable any more to be only doing that very low-end fixed-fee asylum appeals or magistrates' court work. I think we've seen that recently in terms of discussions about low earners, which is not meant to alienate anyone, but I think does.'

A manager acknowledged this problem, suggesting there was some degree of "split" between those doing almost exclusively private work and those maintaining mainly legal aid practices:

> 'There's always this conflict: one group that is only focused on the public, the other that is focused on the big money and those in the middle that want a bit of both. They rub along but basically they don't talk about it because if they do they might upset someone.'

The only chambers where barristers said there was no concern about low earners was a large set whose work was mainly private, with a fairly small number of legal aid practitioners whose lower earnings were not seen as any sort of threat to the organisation's overall financial security. Ultimately, all of this suggests that increasingly, the specialist publicly funded Bar is heavily subsidised by colleagues who do not do legal aid work, so that its foundations are therefore increasingly fragile and dependent on goodwill.

It is implicit in all of this that there are limits to subsidy. For the private firms, and for barristers, it was the amount which could be raised from private clients. For Centres B and C, the limit was what they could raise in grants, whereas for Centre A it was the budget set for investment from the wider charity. The practice manager explained (in 2017) that their decisions about how much work to bid for in the September 2018 tender, and in which categories of law, would be shaped by the caveat that they could not increase their existing operating losses.

Limits to subsidy translate into limits to legal aid capacity: each practitioner and organisation limited its legal aid work in order to cap its losses at the amount it could raise from other income sources. In effect, they reduced or limited their legal aid market share. This strays from the traditional assumption that providers are rational economic actors, who will choose to provide services when the marginal returns are greater than the marginal costs. Instead these organisations provide services until the overall losses from doing so reach an agreed maximum. It may also be time-limited: where private practitioners "subsidise the system", there is a risk that they will eventually decide to stop doing so.

Prioritisation decisions and minimisation of loss

The strategies of minimising losses by limiting overall legal aid capacity and prioritising certain case types are so closely related that it makes sense to examine them together. Solicitor and caseworker organisations do this in a different way from barristers, so they are discussed separately.

Solicitors and caseworkers

For all of the organisations in the BAJ study, demand outstripped supply and they had made prioritisation decisions about which demand to meet, aimed at focusing capacity on the most vulnerable, while maintaining financial viability and a high quality of work, and mitigating risk, including audit risk. This enabled practitioners and organisations to reconcile quality and financial survival, but had consequences for clients' ability to access services.

As discussed in Chapter 3, Centre A focused its reduced capacity on the most vulnerable clients, primarily children, victims of domestic violence, trafficking victims and those with additional difficulties, such as disabilities which made it difficult for them to travel further for legal advice. The focus on unaccompanied children has a positive effect in the sense that these are paid at hourly rates rather than by fixed fee. Therefore, although there is some risk of downward assessment for work, the team is generally paid for the work done. A reduced number of clients is implicit in this strategy. Part of representing a child asylum seeker is accompanying them to the Home Office interview, which is likely to take the entire working day. Other aspects of representing children also take more time, which inevitably means they can take fewer cases in total. They avoided fixed-fee cases except for particularly vulnerable clients who were unable to travel further afield. Centre B made an explicit decision to take cases only by referral from other organisations, ensuring their limited capacity was reserved for the more complex cases which needed their expertise, but which would certainly escape the fixed fee, if not already in an hourly rate category. Firm X similarly prioritised detention, trafficking, children and other vulnerable cases, expressly seeking hourly rate work and avoiding fixed-fee cases where possible.

Without planning to, Firm X had become "top-heavy" in its ratio of solicitors to caseworkers. Although that increased the wage bill, it meant there were more workers able to do higher-value judicial review work, though it was reconsidering this in light of the introduction of at-risk funding. Centre A had deliberately chosen to replace a departing caseworker with a solicitor, who cost the centre more but was able to keep existing clients' judicial review work in-house and bring in the higher fees which that generated. This is not a strategy available to all providers, since OISC-regulated organisations cannot do any judicial review work.

At the time of the fieldwork, detention-centre work was an important part of some firms' financial strategies. Only around eight firms held contracts to do Detention Duty Advice surgeries, which were arranged on a rota basis. Each firm spent a week on the rota at the centre for which it had a contract, offering ten half-hour advice slots each day for four or five days. They were paid a fixed fee for the day's surgery, but any cases taken on from the surgeries (subject to means and merits tests) were funded at hourly rates. The time and cost of travel to detention centres were capped and not paid in full, but losses on the surgeries were compensated by a steady stream of hourly rate work. This was a crucial part of the financial survival strategy for two of the firms in the BAJ study. The detention contracts changed in September 2018, so that a much larger number of firms were doing detention work, with far fewer rota weeks each. Most importantly, this caused serious concerns around the new representatives' knowledge and experience in detention work (and detained clients still had no choice of provider), but it also removed an important source of hourly rate work for those providers. For Firm X, the move displaced more legal aid work directly in favour of private work.

Only Firm Y, which was located in an asylum-seeker dispersal area, took any volume of first-time asylum claims. They took on all initial asylum clients who came through the door until their matter starts were used up. They often had little time to incur costs before a decision was made, because clients tended to reach them midway through the application process (having been moved on from initial accommodation centres). That made it financially viable to take on fixed-fee cases, though they acknowledged that clients received a limited service at application stage as a result. At the time of the fieldwork, they had already used all of their annual allocation of matter starts for the main office and had received the automatic 50 per cent uplift, less than six months into the contract year. They referred people wanting to make fresh claims to their free drop-in sessions, where they could "triage" those with a real chance of success and advise clients of what they would need to obtain, to avoid using a matter start on what might be a hopeless case.

Firm X tried to use matter starts strategically, to maximise the return on each one, but described having to keep some in reserve for existing clients who needed a new matter opened, which might happen because the Home Office withdrew a decision, bringing the matter to a close, but then issued a new refusal. Firm X had more than 1,500 matter starts per year before the LASPO Act removed non-asylum work from the scope of legal aid, but afterwards received the standard 100 matter starts per office. It created additional offices but, even given the guarantee of a 50 per cent uplift on the matter starts at each office, it had to turn away large numbers of would-be clients because of the shortage of matter starts. In effect, this meant letting it be known that it did not take on any new cases except those which were referred by other organisations. Detention work was separate from the matter-start limits, adding to its vital importance in the financial survival of firms like X. That said, a partner doubted whether they would take on more fixed-fee cases even if they had unlimited matter starts, since those cases were not financially viable.

Since the 2018 contract, matter starts no longer play the same role in prioritisation decisions. Providers were allocated as many matter starts as they asked for and (rightly) no client should now be prevented from accessing a preferred provider on the basis of it having run out of matter starts. Although it is positive that matter start allocations probably no longer feed into providers' prioritisation decisions and no longer distort the market, it is difficult to discern any remaining purpose to allocating matter starts (as opposed to counting the number of matter starts actually used), as they create a misleading impression of surplus capacity in the market (see final section of this chapter).

Local context matters. Centre A's prioritisation decision was influenced by the prevalence of unaccompanied children within the procurement area and the lack of alternative provision. Firm Y's decisions were shaped by dispersal to the area, whereas reasonable proximity to detention centres was relevant for Firms X and Y. Other elements of local context which shape demand include the existence of certain migrant communities within the area and the proximity to ports, transport hubs and a dispersal area. The London-based providers clearly had greater local competition, but a smaller proportion of first-time asylum applicants, since they were mostly dispersed out of London.

Is this prioritisation of higher-paid hourly rates work tantamount to cherry-picking or cream-skimming more profitable cases for the organisation's own economic benefit (called 'adverse selection' by economists)? All of the providers, having excess demand, had to ration supply, or prioritise some potential clients over others. This 'prioritisation of clients by relative vulnerability' occurs in other services throughout and beyond advice work as demand increases and funding is cut (Evans, 2017:p24). The LAA's decision to create a more favourable funding scheme for those case categories is based on precisely the same reasoning. The fixed fee is premised on the assumption that providers will be paid for approximately the amount of work they actually do, because cheaper and more expensive cases should balance out (although, as has been shown in Chapter Four, they do not). On that basis, seeking to do more complex work cannot be characterised as cherry-picking because the provider should still expect to be paid for the approximate number of hours worked, at the same hourly rate. The bigger concern is that complex cases may go without representation because some firms cherry-pick the simple cases and drop those involving clients like Mariam, because they cannot be done adequately within the fixed fee.

These prioritisation decisions do appear to help providers reconcile quality with financial viability, maintaining the standard of work they considered necessary while limiting the financial losses to the organisation. But they also mean that a potential client with a fixed-fee case has limited chance of being represented by a high-quality, or demand-responsive, provider.

Barristers

Up to the point where they were at capacity, barristers said they took on any work that came in specifically for them and any work which their clerks booked in for them. Several pointed out that they were required to do so by the 'cab-rank rule' – whereby they must accept any case offered to them, so long as the fee is adequate and they have sufficient time and expertise.

Turning away work, however, could be difficult. Particularly at the most junior end, several said they found it hard to turn work away, partly because of the feeling that, "If you say no to something, you'll never get instructed again", and partly because, "When you're very junior it feels harder to say no because of the impression that you're not committed enough". Those with young children tended to limit their work time more than others and several said that family commitments made it easier to say no to work.

Even when they felt "at capacity", some would sometimes still take on more work if the case was for a solicitor they particularly liked, or for a particularly vulnerable client – much as solicitors prioritised by relative vulnerability. One, for example, always took on trafficking cases if possible because she felt there were very few barristers who specialised in trafficking work. Others had crafted a niche of demand, such as trafficking, family crossover or unlawful detention work, or asylum relating to a particular country, so that they did relatively little of the more generalist asylum work. In this way, barristers sometimes came to craft working partnerships with particular solicitors whose work was of high quality.

At chambers level, though, prioritisation was more in evidence, with clerks saying they tended to offer only the most junior counsel for fixed-fee cases, reserving more experienced barristers for better-paying work. Barristers acknowledged that they were unaware of how much, or what kind of, work was turned away. As they gained experience and contacts, barristers tended to receive more of their work through a few regular solicitors and less via their clerks, so they became less available for work from other firms. They also became less willing to travel to more distant tribunal hearing centres because travel costs were no longer paid on legal aid, meaning the train fare might exceed the net fee for going to court. That means that client access to specialist barristers might be limited by their case-funding type and by which hearing centre their appeal was assigned to.

Beyond the questions of client vulnerability and financial survival, barristers described another dilemma specific to their position at the end of the 'supply chain' (BSB, 2016), which impacts on clients' access to barristers' services. Where they receive poorly prepared cases, barristers have to put more work in to present the case. As one barrister (over 20 years' call) explained:

> 'I do feel that if you're a legal aid lawyer, you should be doing all that work [to repair the damage], but it is hard. And then with certain firms, it's all too little too late so you feel very compromised because you're not a magician, you can't reverse things when they're at that late stage – if a medical report should've been got or something. They're just a damage-limitation job sometimes.'

Another firm was named by five separate interviewees who refused to take its work because doing that work took up more time and effort by the barrister. One, with over 20 years' experience, explained that: "By the time you get it, you can't always do the work that needed to be done, it's just too late and so you're compromised, and your client's compromised."

Another (over 25 years' call) highlighted the problems caused by some firms' delegation of work to inexperienced staff with inadequate supervision, who then send poorly prepared work to barristers:

> 'I think you really feel like you have to supervise them as well. I've had cases where they don't tell you what you need to know, and how do you know you need to know something unless they tell you? They're just not really competent enough to be doing the work.'

Many barristers said their attitude to rescuing cases had changed with experience. One of the most junior barristers felt "you can add more value" where the case is badly prepared. Another reflected that, in her early days, she was more likely to work "till one in the morning" assembling relevant background evidence and trying to make good the gaps in preparation. This does not seem to be an attrition of idealism, like Lipsky's 'street-level' public service workers (1980), who become less concerned about helping people over time, and more focused on making their own workload manageable. Rather, barristers believed they developed, through experience, a more nuanced view of the impact that they could have in any given case and of where to focus their efforts:

'I think maybe now I'm a bit more realistic about the kind of difference that might make, so maybe I spend less time on them than I did when I felt it was almost purely my responsibility to win the case, whatever the solicitor and whatever the judge. I don't think that's how it works.'

But more importantly, even where they could have a positive impact in an individual case, this might have the unintended negative consequence of "prop[ping] up incompetent firms who have cases saved by counsel and really I think that they should go out of business". Working for some firms amounted to "propping up the really deficient solicitor who's basically sabotaging the client's case because they're not good enough". A barrister referred to a particular solicitor who had instructed her in the past, who had recently been criticised by the High Court for having "not even read the procedure rules":

'I refuse to work for him because you're facilitating his negligence and incompetence. [In one case] having come out of court and done what I could, got an adjournment and given the client an advice, you know, I'm bound to tell you I think you'd be better off represented by someone else, I told [the solicitor] this and told him I'm cc-ing my letter to the Law Society. It's that bad. ... It's really, really significant stuff ... and he's still there. So no, these really poor firms, I think we should refuse to enable them.'

This was not always clear-cut, as a junior barrister explained: "It's not easy to decide where the balance lies. I just think there are certain cases where you feel you can fix it and certain cases where you feel you're part of the problem." They could "fix it" where the solicitor was willing to work with them to rescue the case or to learn lessons for future cases, where they "want to improve but they're not sure how to so they're quite grateful for that feedback". Although it took more work to give feedback to a solicitor and try to help them improve, which was more properly the responsibility of the solicitor's supervisor, barristers said they were willing to work with solicitors who made the effort to improve "because the client's life is at risk". On the other hand, they would turn down work from those who continued sending badly prepared cases. But it was difficult and stressful to have too many such cases, both in terms of the time they took up and because they did not feel they had the skills to supervise or manage the competence of another person: "How do you nicely tell someone that they've done a really shit job? I just hated the whole thing so I try and avoid it at all costs." This was all the more common in private work. Barristers also named private firms whose work they refused to take, particularly where the firm took clients' money for a poor job or an application which could not succeed, and did not appear willing or able to learn from the barrister's feedback.

All of this suggests that immigration barristers' relationship with the cab-rank rule is more nuanced than either the Code of Conduct or the rule's critics suggest (Flood & Hviid, 2013). All those in this study represented claimants, not the government, which somewhat departs from the cab-rank rule, though they would have to proactively apply to be on the Attorney General's panel in order to receive government work. Within that context, they treated the rule as absolute in respect of individual or 'lay' clients, but not in respect of certain solicitors or professional clients. Since those cases took longer to prepare, barristers argued they could legitimately be turned away, despite the cab-rank rule, on the grounds of inadequate time to prepare, inadequate remuneration for the amount of work or even the barrister not having the competence to take on work where the solicitor had prepared it badly.

Barristers avoided unwanted work simply by not volunteering for cases offered to the team by the clerks through a general email, or less often by telling their clerks they would not do that firm's work anymore. Clerks also filtered the work offered, turning away unwelcome solicitors by telling them nobody was available, rather than saying the firm's work was not acceptable. The firms which prepared poorly were often also guilty of poor payment so that, as one clerk put it: "The barristers are having to do all the work for them, as well as being compromised at court and then they're not going to get paid for it."

The combined effect of these prioritisation decisions made by lawyers is this: clients whose cases will be funded on the fixed fee have less chance of being taken on by a high-quality solicitor or caseworker, who is responsive to the in-case demand. As a result, they have less chance of being represented by a specialist barrister, especially if their appeal is to be heard at a tribunal far from London, Birmingham or Manchester. It means there is an advice drought for adults with first-time asylum applications and appeals: services appear to be available but, in reality, are either inaccessible to many clients or are provided at a quality level which fails to meet the client's needs. Yet those prioritisations emerged as a vital part of the strategy for maintaining both quality and financial viability for every practitioner and organisation in the BAJ study, by minimising the financial losses per case as far as possible, helping to cap overall financial losses at the amount which could be raised in subsidy.

Emergence of droughts and deserts

The precise number of providers changes over time. Figure 3.1 provides a snapshot of one moment, but it offers a framework for examining the complexity of patterns of supply. This helps to illustrate how and why deserts and droughts occur.

One such pattern is that, nationally, the number of offices providing legal aid services tends to peak when new contracts are awarded and then decline throughout the contract period. There were 380 providers holding franchises with the LSC in 2004 (Langdon-Down, 2006). By the time the Carter Review was published in 2006, this had fallen by 40 per cent to 234 (Langdon-Down, 2006), dropping further to 204 in 2007. There was a roughly 25 per cent increase to 257 when the unified contract was tendered for the first time in 2007. The number of providers then declined fairly gradually, to 242 in the three years to the 2010 contract round.

The number spiked at the time of the 2013 contract round, at 413,[1] but began falling rapidly as the LASPO Act took effect. By the time of the next contract round in September 2018, there were 231 offices – a loss of 44 per cent over five years. The number of offices rose again to 325 in the 2018 contract round – albeit there were still six access points which received only one or no compliant bids, and other areas which were not referred to as access points at all.

The spike-and-decline pattern continued. Already, 15 providers had been lost by mid-January 2019, offset partly by the award of four new contracts in the East and West Lancashire advice desert following a retender. By mid-September 2019, a year into the contracts, there were 291 providers (nearly 11 per cent loss); in March 2020, 285 remained (12.5 per cent loss) and by August of that year there were 277. There are no 'exit interviews' or statistics on providers' reasons for surrendering contracts.

Another 24 offices still had contracts as of September 2019 (8.25 per cent of the provider base at that time), but had not reported doing any matter starts since the contracts began. By October 2020, two years into the contracts, 15 offices (5.4 per cent of the remaining provider base) had not opened any matter starts.[2] These dormant contracts were spread throughout England and Wales, but included offices which were

---

[1] Freedom of Information (FOI) response, Legal Aid Agency's published spreadsheets and responses to Parliamentary Questions by Richard Burgon MP (available at: https://members.parliament.uk/member/4493/writtenquestions?page=32).

[2] FOI response 200909021 from Legal Aid Agency, 7 October 2020

one of only two or three providers in their access point or even, in one case, the sole provider in its access point. Half (eight) of the access points with six providers or fewer had at least one inactive provider in 2019. The LAA has no data on the reasons for these contracts being unused and there is no indication on its spreadsheets of contracts or providers which are dormant. Because nearly one in twelve contracts were dormant for at least the first 14 months of the contracts, the shortage of advice may simply be unseen by the LAA.

Three main possibilities appear to arise:

- The LAA awarded far too many contracts in 2013 and 2018 (which is not an adequate explanation, given the number of advice deserts and droughts).
- It gave contracts to providers which could not in fact perform those contracts.
- It gave contracts on terms on which providers could not survive.

In any of those cases, unnecessary transaction costs are generated throughout the granting, management and termination of the contract. There is an urgent need for more information on why providers leave the market or remain dormant: how many have contracts terminated for failing on peer review? How many are terminated for other reasons? Why do providers close offices or withdraw from legal aid? What prevents dormant providers from taking on cases? This information should be used to make appropriate changes to procurement procedures and contract terms if these are confirmed as causing wasted transaction costs.

From Figure 3.1 and the accounts of support workers and practitioners, it appears there are two kinds of drought: type-based droughts and place-based droughts. A **type-based drought** is a shortage of advice for certain types of case. It arises where the provider has made prioritisation decisions for survival or maintenance of quality, and is therefore unable to take on certain kinds of cases. An advice drought then affects some clients, most commonly first-time adult asylum applicants. It can also arise where providers within an area are unable to do judicial review and higher appeals work, or where there is no provider with expertise on a niche issue like trafficking, so a client appears to be receiving advice, but has no prospect of receiving the kind of advice they need. A worker in a support organisation said:

> 'I had a trafficking case and he needed advice specifically on trafficking, but most firms were not taking someone who

137

had a trafficking case if they hadn't made an asylum claim. How would he know whether or not to apply for asylum without advice? But we don't want to make it worse by making the wrong application.'

Similarly, as in Mariam's case at the beginning of this chapter, there may be no providers within an access point who are willing to pursue complex appeals that require work in excess of the fixed fee.

Exceptional Case Funding (ECF) is subject to a high risk of type-based drought. This is a funding type designed for cases which are generally outside the scope of legal aid, but where there is a risk of a breach of fundamental rights if advice or representation is not provided. It is obtained via an application to the LAA. Support organisations which obtain ECF for clients report serious difficulties in finding legal aid providers once funding is secured. Some providers have stopped doing ECF work because of the low fees and the complexity of cases. People who should receive ECF are "falling through the gaps" because of support organisations' limited capacity to apply for ECF. The market is not providing for clients whose fundamental rights are at risk without access via ECF.

A **place-based drought** is one centred on a geographical area which has insufficient capacity to meet demand. If there is only one provider, or all local providers are in a similar position, this can happen across an entire area. Place-based droughts almost certainly affect all of the areas on the map with only one or two providers. They also affect some areas with multiple providers, particularly where some of the contracted providers are inactive, as in Mariam and Zainab's story.

The South West of England offers another example. Much of the region is desert and the entire region is a place-based drought. The county of Devon has a single provider, in Plymouth, consisting of a single caseworker in a single-roomed office. Like the East of England, Devon has suffered a persistent shortage of advice. In 2010, Devon Law Centre had to close when it lost its housing law contract, since immigration work alone could not sustain it (demonstrating the interdependence of different categories of law). The last private provider withdrew from legal aid in the same year. There were periods when there was no advice, interspersed with temporary interim provision from a London firm, until the current not-for-profit organisation opened in Plymouth. As Figure 3.1 shows, there are no providers in the surrounding counties, as far up as Bristol. The sole provider in Swindon, Wiltshire, has been unable to do any immigration legal aid work since obtaining its contract because it cannot recruit an immigration solicitor. Both Plymouth and Swindon are dispersal areas for asylum seekers, meaning there is constant high demand.

Towards the upper end of the South West region, Bristol has, on paper, nine providers. With dispersal numbers similar to Plymouth, it is clearly much better supplied than the rest of the South West. Of those nine, however, one did no legal aid immigration work in the contract year from September 2018 to August 2019 (nor in the following year); the remaining eight reported 505 matter starts between them (491 in the following year). They are mainly small organisations. Bristol Law Centre, with one full- and two part-time workers, is among the largest teams. Four of the organisations have a single office and four are multi-office providers, but two of the latter have only a part-time presence in Bristol, with staff shared with other offices and office space shared with other organisations. That means even in Bristol it can be hard to find a provider, despite supply appearing to increase in September 2018, from seven providers sharing 502 matter starts to nine providers sharing 1,650 matter starts. Despite seeming well supplied, Bristol is an advice drought within a desert. This reflects the position Mariam and her daughter faced in the East of England: the firm representing her consisted of a single self-supervising solicitor, and the appearance of plentiful provision in areas neighbouring the advice desert was illusory.

Even in the North West, where there appears to be a particularly robust provider base, a barrister described how lack of capacity had "brought the North West to a virtual standstill", such that "the tribunal even had to adjourn a lot of appeals because no one could take them on". The barrister noted that there were also numerous adjournments because of a shortage of judges, which made the picture more confusing. Greater Manchester had 14 providers at the time, whereas Merseyside had another four. Some of the legal aid providers in that region confirmed (in private email communications) that they had had matter starts remaining, but no capacity to open new cases.

This illustrates the irrelevance of matter starts as an indication of supply in both the pre- and post-September 2018 market. The combined matter start allocation for London's providers was 30,735 in September 2018, but barely over one third of these (10,412) translated into actual cases in the first year. North East Wales' sole provider was given an increase from 21 (plus the automatic 50 per cent uplift) to 300 matter starts, but only actually reported 30 in the first year and 14 in the second. The same pattern occurs across most (though not all) access points. Matter start allocations do nothing apart from create a false impression of capacity.

Place-based drought regions experience sharp fluctuations of supply, whereby changes to one individual practitioner's work patterns has an impact on the whole region. As a solicitor in the South West put it: "Any movement in one bit of the region causes problems for the rest." An NGO worker in Bristol described the effect when the Plymouth provider lost its supervising caseworker:

> 'A couple of things happened at once: MLP [the Plymouth provider] shrinking and a knock-on effect of cases from Plymouth coming up to Bristol, then someone going on maternity leave from [a small firm] in Bristol. MLP in Cardiff and Bristol having absorbed cases from Plymouth meant they were less able to take on new cases.'

The solicitor approaching maternity leave had to run down her caseload and refuse new cases, until eventually the firm was able to recruit a replacement as a permanent post. That meant they were able briefly to take on new cases, including from Plymouth, until the new practitioner reached capacity. Shortly afterwards, a large multi-office firm closed its Cardiff office. Although it appears to have distributed its open cases to its other offices, the closure reduced the regional capacity for new cases. In Bristol, an NGO took on a triaging role, finding representatives with capacity for unaccompanied children. That succeeded in placing children with lawyers and saving social workers trawling through lists of providers, but inevitably displaced adult cases as a consequence. Where providers are already struggling to remain in the market, seemingly small changes (like the resignation or maternity leave of one staff member) can become tipping points which make the organisation or office unsustainable, with effects throughout the supply side of the entire regional market.

Why has supply not increased to meet demand? Most of the private immigration firms in Devon had previously done legal aid work (before 2010), and said they withdrew because of the overwhelming stress of the auditing regime or the frequent clawbacks of money, in the context of low rates of pay which did not mitigate these. As of December 2019, none was willing to consider going back into legal aid work. This comment, from a self-employed private immigration solicitor, was typical:

> 'I had 500 files for people with immigration and asylum problems, but only one client – the LSC. Would I go back

to having one client? I have about 20 clients and they pay their bills and those who don't, I send to a debt collector. You can't do that with the Legal Aid Agency. There's no way I could go back to it commercially. My money was all in work-in-progress and I was up against the buffers on my overdraft. I ran up accountancy bills trying to restructure. In the end I had to put my firm into liquidation. It was technically profitable but it had a cash-flow crisis. I've never had a problem since I left legal aid.'

The legal aid providers for other categories of law in Devon felt that, despite the demand for immigration work, they were already struggling financially and could not afford the investment to expand into another unprofitable category.

'We do housing because we've done it a long time, but we can just about break even. We're now a housing team of three, and that's up from one and that cost a lot, and we need to make that back. If we were to start a fresh area – that could be mental health – we would have to invest a lot in the training, and the bureaucracy of getting a contract is also extensive. They *say* they want more people to do legal aid.'

The migrant support organisations in the county which undertook lower-level casework similarly said they could not afford to take on the liabilities of obtaining a legal aid contract. One said they had already run out of funding for their drop-in and were keeping it running on reserves. Another pointed out that trying to take on a legal aid contract would displace vital work they were already doing:

'We're doing level-one general casework. We deal with biometric residence permits, chasing the Home Office, extending NASS asylum support, dealing with social services, people who are disabled, and it takes up time. It would be wrong to close our doors and do something else instead. Our caseworkers are stretched to the limit, with clients with mental health difficulties attempting suicide in front of them. I've sectioned about ten people in here. A woman had a miscarriage right here. So we can't mess about trying to do something else.'

The two most feasible ways of increasing capacity appeared to be expansion of the sole existing provider or attracting a multi-office provider from outside the access point to open an office in Devon. For the existing provider, there were two main obstacles to expansion: it could not recruit new workers, and it needed more space. Its premises consisted of a single room, meaning that when there were two workers, they had to take turns working from home so the other could see clients in the office. When the supervising caseworker left, attempts to recruit a replacement failed and the remaining worker had to be supervised from the organisation's other offices. The salary which the organisation could afford did not reflect the demands of a role as supervising caseworker, almost certainly requiring relocation, let alone having to subsidise the operation by working half the time from home. The higher office costs of renting more space were also unaffordable, meaning that realistically, the existing provider could only expand if grant-funding was available to cover larger premises and a higher salary for a supervisor. In other words, demand could only be met through charity.

None of the multi-office providers from Bristol or South Wales was in a position to set up an office in Devon: again, some were already operating part-time offices and another was closing its Cardiff office. Joint working between support organisations and an outreach provider appeared to offer some respite, with a caseworker travelling to Devon to offer face-to-face advice instead of doing so remotely. But it proved difficult in practice to arrange suitable borrowed premises with appropriate reception or waiting facilities when all organisations were struggling financially, and when the outreach provider was already near full capacity. The long lead-in time for a new office or organisation to break even with immigration legal aid work creates an insurmountable obstacle, in this regional context, for a new provider to enter the market. It was expected to take at least two years to start breaking even and no organisation, private or not-for-profit, had the funds to sustain an office for that long.

Devon's geographical isolation, combined with the lack of other providers, means any organisation or individual taking up work there would face professional isolation as well. A solicitor who had previously worked in Plymouth explained:

> 'Psychologically it's hard being that isolated. It's far from everywhere and there are barriers in terms of getting what you need to run asylum cases – there are no interpreters, no experts, no psychologists. There is one good psychologist

now in Plymouth, but it was incredibly difficult. You can't even go for a coffee with [another practitioner] from down the road. And anyone starting a satellite office would be starting from scratch and who wants to do that in this climate? Someone in Bristol started as private for a while and then got a legal aid contract, but it's hard to get that in Plymouth.'

Without wanting to labour the drought metaphor, it becomes difficult to replenish the legal aid sector once the 'ecosystem' is lost. In regions where there are few providers, there is little movement between organisations, little opportunity to enter as a caseworker and work towards a professional qualification or a supervisor role. In Devon, in Wales, in the East of England, law graduates from good universities move away because there are no local training contracts (for solicitors) or pupillages (for barristers). One non-legal aid advice organisation in Plymouth was exploring the possibility of taking on a trainee solicitor on a Justice First Fellowship, which pays the trainee's salary costs, partnering with legal aid providers who could provide supervision in different categories of law. The difficulty for immigration was that there were no potential supervisors for 120 miles. Loss of experienced lawyers to mentor newcomers has previously been identified as a threat to quality (Byrom, 2013, 2017), but here also appears as a serious threat to supply. Geographical remoteness may limit more experienced practitioners' willingness to move, especially for stressful work on low pay, with professional isolation thrown into the mix. Since the closure of RMJ and IAS, there are no large-scale training programmes and no central support for training. It becomes difficult to either recruit or 'grow your own'.

The lack of supply in geographical areas where demand exists is a market failure. The market-based system is failing to ensure supply (let alone high-quality supply) in areas where it is needed, either because the marginal returns of provision are not sufficient to cover the marginal costs of doing it, or because some other factor, such as the audit regime, is causing providers to leave the market – or both. The system of dispersing asylum seekers is incompatible with this geographical pattern of legal aid availability: as we saw in Mariam's case, it leaves people isolated from desperately needed advice, with obstacles to travel and sometimes serious mental health consequences to the isolation.

An unsympathetic reader might argue that, since people had already reached the UK to seek asylum, they should be able to travel 100 or so miles for legal advice. This ignores the fact that most subsist on asylum support, or receive only food and board and no cash, meaning they cannot pay for travel. That means the costs of travel often falls on the support organisations or the advice providers. At an initial accommodation centre in Yorkshire, support organisations described people having to choose between legal advice and eating, because food was only available at certain hours and no cash was given to residents, so if they travelled to get legal advice they would have to miss meals. For children, too, the distance is problematic. One solicitor describes:

> '... an argument over whether a young person can go by bus from Plymouth to Bristol for an appointment. He would be waiting around for hours in Bristol for an appointment, plus hours on the bus. His social worker is not available to accompany him because it's too long out of the day, and his foster carers refuse to drive that distance, so I have to travel to him. And the LAA won't pay for my travel for a visit to him because they say it's reasonable for him to come to me!'

It is of course theoretically possible to ignore the boundaries of geography by using remote means of communication. This raises particular difficulties in the context of asylum cases, however. Practically, it demands a private room with good internet and a suitable device, either in the client's accommodation or provided by a support organisation. This alone may be insurmountable. An interpreter who meets the LAA criteria needs to be either physically present with the lawyer or join the call remotely. Beyond that, it is an obstacle to building the good rapport and trust which are crucial to enabling people to give an account of what has happened to them. As a solicitor put it:

> 'It's not fair on anyone and it affects the way we work. We try to avoid Skype because it's not conducive. We try to be person-centred and trauma-informed, but we're having to consider it because we're spending so much time trying to organise appointments.'

The use of remote access causes problems of its own, especially when distress and technical problems combine to cause frustration for the client, perhaps intensifying mental health difficulties. One support organisation worker described having had to ban a client from their premises for safeguarding reasons after a remote appointment with his lawyer from one of their rooms, but then continuing to try to facilitate his access from elsewhere. In any event, given a capacity shortage throughout England and Wales, the best that could be achieved through remote advice is to reduce the relevance of geography; it does nothing to actually increase supply.

Quantifying demand, on the other hand, is a matter of informed guesswork. The LAA receives information about supply, in the form of matter starts opened and costs per case, but there is no count of people turned away, no measure of people not applying for asylum, not appealing a refusal, or instructing private representatives because they cannot find legal aid representatives – all of which are reported by practitioners and support organisations who try to refer cases. It is impossible without data of this sort to quantify the effect of either the geographical gaps in supply or the discrepancy between matter-start availability and actual capacity (though any such data collection should not involve another unpaid reporting demand on providers).

Whether as a matter of policy or not, the LAA appears to devolve responsibility for providing information about system capacity onto a disparate provider base, which has neither the remit nor resources to collect that information. Practitioners and support organisations argue that there is an undersupply so that providers turn clients away and support organisations struggle to refer clients to providers with capacity. The ILPA representative said:

'The LAA has said before, when we've raised this issue about people finding it difficult to find lawyers, "Well we never have any evidence of this. You show us." And I think that's not a helpful response because it's not recognising that we aren't the state here and we can't take on that huge coordinated research task on top of providing the service.'

An LAA official explained that quarterly capacity reviews ask: "By category, have we lost providers? How many providers are running out of matter starts? How many haven't opened any matter starts?" This does not reveal how much functional capacity is available in the system, nor the extent of unmet demand. LAA officials do receive predictions from the Home Office about how many cases they expect and to where they intend to disperse people. But as LAA interviewees point out, this is often too late for them to begin any meaningful procurement, even if procurement under current conditions was capable of producing a sustainable increase in supply.

The contract-management system might be expected to feed information in both directions, but information flow and use appeared erratic. There is no systematic process for feeding providers' concerns about the contract back to policy makers. Representatives of various parts of the LAA and a number of practitioners' representative groups meet bimonthly at meetings of the Civil Contracts Consultative Group, where information can be shared in both directions. However, an ILPA representative explained that the main issues are ones which the LAA considers simply outside its remit, like rates of pay and the fixed fee, which providers are told to "take up with the Ministry of Justice". An LAA official believed there had been less "clamour" recently about issues like the quality of detention advice or the adequacy of the fixed fee, which may be an example of power being exercised through 'non-decision-making' by deflecting challenges or complaints (Bachrach & Baratz, 1962).

Advice deserts exist in other categories of law in England and Wales. The Law Society (2020) reported that 78 per cent of local authority areas had no community care legal aid providers, and 37 per cent of the population lived in local authority areas with no housing legal aid provision. Although provision is planned by procurement areas, not by local authority, the 2018 contract round left 39 procurement areas with insufficient bids for housing and debt work. The not-for-profit sector, which has always been central to social welfare legal aid provision, experienced 'a double whammy of LASPO and local authority cuts' (Robins, 2019), leaving Wales with no law centres at all doing legal aid work.

The issue of dormant contracts also arises in other categories of law.[3] In some, this is because there is a mandatory telephone gateway before clients can access face-to-face advice, meaning there is very little work available for providers. However, it also occurs in housing law, where 57 of the 130 procurement areas have at least one provider that reported no matter starts in the first year of the contract. In fourteen procurement areas, more than half of providers were inactive. Similarly in family law, 96 out of 108 procurement areas had providers who reported no matter starts in the first year of the contract. In East London, exactly half of the 136 providers reported no matter starts, although just over half of the 35 providers in Bridgend, Cardiff and the Vale were in that position. This illusory supply may mean there is simply not enough demand, or not enough *eligible* demand because of the extreme narrowing of scope, or may mean providers are unable to offer services for other reasons (recruitment, supervision, capacity).

---

[3] Ministry of Justice, FOI response 191197918 to author, dated 5 December 2019.

Any of those explanations means that wasted transaction costs are being incurred in tendering, awarding and managing contracts which are unused, as well as raising doubts over clients' ability to access advice and representation.

The evidence suggests that the LAA has the wrong, or ineffective, feedback loops in place. Advice droughts go unidentified because it has no formal feedback loops for unmet demand. It fails to collect critical information about system capacity or the actual functioning of the contract or the market. It has no explicit duty and no specific resources to research demand. It receives constant feedback about what does get done, for whom, by whom, but effectively none about what does not get done, for whom and why. Although the LAA has duties to consult with the profession, and does so through the Civil Contracts Consultative Group and other meetings, Smith and Cape (2017) point out that it rarely carries out research and knows little about how policy affects access and provision. Consequently, the LAA's annual report is criticised as 'very narrowly focused on corporate concerns' and 'about administrative and operational concerns, rather than giving a view of how citizens are (or are not) being assisted by legal aid' (Partington, 2015: unpaginated).

This lack of detailed understanding of whether and how people are being assisted by legal aid is a critical point. It is why stories like Mariam's need to be heard. The interplay of functional capacity, financial viability and client access has been underexplored, let alone the relationship between these and quality, which is the focus of Chapter 7.

7

No Choice, no Voice, no Exit

To what extent is the market, in its current form, capable of ensuring that the quality of work done on legal aid is adequate? It has been argued throughout the book that the funding regime creates an explicit conflict between financial rationality and quality in the sense of 'doing all the work the case needs' and responsiveness to in-case demand. The peer-review criteria used by the LAA's independent peer review panel have been validated in other research and are applied by both practitioners and funders for substantive quality assessments, so are treated here as a reasonable framework for discussing quality (see Appendix). The market-based system of procurement introduced following the Carter review (2006) was intended to maintain quality through market mechanisms and that system of peer review.

The fundamental idea behind public-choice markets is that users have a choice of providers, who therefore have to compete for custom. They may compete for clients directly, or they may compete for a contract to provide a service to everyone who qualifies for it. In either case, the competition (hypothetically) means that providers have to offer a good quality of service (whatever 'quality' means to the choosers) at a reasonable cost (whatever that means to the payer).

Choice, **Voice** and **Exit** are the main strategies supposedly available to members of the public to maintain quality in public services (Hirschman 1970). They make a Choice of provider when they enter the market, based on reputation and whatever other factors are important to the user. If the service is not good enough, they exercise Voice, in the form of formal or informal complaints to the provider, community action, through elected representatives or via the media. If the service fails to improve, they Exit to another provider. A provider which is inadequate should lose more users, attract fewer new users, and be dogged by complaints until it is forced out of the market.

More recently, Le Grand (2007) incorporated these into his four overlapping models for achieving good public services:

1. **Trust**, where professionals are facilitated to deliver the service with minimal state or other interference;

2. **Command and Control**, where targets and performance-management requirements are imposed through a hierarchical structure which controls service delivery;
3. **Voice**; and
4. **Choice**, which includes **Exit**.

Rather than two separate models, this chapter treats Command and Control and Trust as the opposite ends of a spectrum. All systems of administration and regulation will appear somewhere along that spectrum. As explored in Chapter 2, legal aid services have moved from close to the Trust pole to very near the Command and Control pole. Le Grand advocates choice-based competition as the most effective model, but acknowledges that, in reality, all public services incorporate some combination of these models so that – as with the 'market or state' debate – it is really a question of where the balance should lie, rather than which model to adopt to the exclusion of the others. Inevitably, users vary in their ability to exercise these strategies, and Exit may have financial and non-financial costs.

These analyses are certainly not the final word on what works in public services, but they are helpful for structuring the discussion of how market forces influence quality in asylum and immigration legal aid services. The current market structure in immigration legal aid is contradictory. It relies on Choice, Voice, and Command and Control to maintain quality, as follows:

• Choice of providers by the Legal Aid Agency, and Choice between providers by clients.
• Voice, including the complaints systems of providers, professional regulators, and the Legal Ombudsman, as well as wider voice through the media and elected representatives.
• Command and Control, manifested through the legal aid contract, auditing, performance targets and also professional entry controls and regulation, on both organisations and individual practitioners.

Command and Control in legal aid largely misses the issue of substantive quality. At the same time, the costs of Command and Control, combined with low fees and high financial risk, have driven providers out of the market, thus reducing Choice. Since the Exit strategy is effectively barred by the rules of the legal aid contract, this protects the market position of poor-quality providers. In doing so, it creates a false reassurance that fees are adequate and the market is working, in turn accelerating the loss of good-quality providers. The overall effect is that bad quality drives out good, at the same time reducing Choice, which in turn lowers the effectiveness of Voice, in a downward spiral.

Before examining these models and strategies in turn it is important to note that, within managerialism and marketisation of public services, the 'real client' is constructed not as the end user or recipient of the service but rather as the 'taxpaying citizen' (Sommerlad, 2004:p358). It is the taxpayer to whom the service must account for value for money, while the user is at best a 'flawed consumer' (Bauman, 1997:p14; Crouch, 2004; Sommerlad, 2004); yet the migrant or asylum-seeking service user is even more flawed, as a non-citizen and perhaps a non-taxpayer. Even on this basis, though, it is argued in the following sections that Choice, Voice, Exit, and Command and Control are ineffective mechanisms for the taxpayer to ensure quality or value.

Choice

First, there is often literally no choice of provider within a geographical area. Figure 3.1 shows that large areas of the country have no providers or only one provider. Even where there are multiple providers, the capacity and prioritisation issues discussed in Chapter 6 mean that there may be only one provider who can take on new clients. In practice, this often means clients go to the largest provider in the area, or one which maximises potential-client capacity by minimising the amount of work it does on each case. For people in immigration detention, there is usually no choice of provider at all and they have to take whichever provider is on the rota, unless they have time to wait for a preferred provider.

There is also reduced scope for choosing between *types* of provider, because the unified contract since 2007 has forced not-for-profits to behave more like private firms (see Chapter 4). Yet the market-based reforms expressly called for a variety of types of provision. The regulation of non-lawyer advisers was part of an agenda of 'de-professionalisation' in the sense of opening up the market to non-lawyer providers. The policy justification for introducing non-lawyer agencies was, in part, that they would take a more holistic approach, therefore increasing client choice (Moorhead et al, 2003). Instead, many have been driven out of the market and others forced to abandon the features which made them distinctive.

Second, even where there is a real choice of providers, most clients have no meaningful information on which to base their choice. Newly arrived asylum seekers do not read *Chambers and Partners* or the *Legal 500* and, in any case, these say too little about social welfare law to be useful. Peer-review scores are not published and, apart from peer review, there is no monitoring of substantive quality of work.

There is not much evidence about how asylum seekers do choose their lawyers. The 123 asylum-seeker interviews in the QALSS research suggested that few first-time asylum applicants felt they had *chosen* a lawyer. Some had gone down a list given to them at the accommodation centre and gone to the first provider which accepted them. Others had followed the recommendation of other residents at the initial accommodation centre, who were newly arrived themselves and had no real idea about the quality of the lawyer. Interpreters working at the initial accommodation centres sometimes touted for business on behalf of firms. A few had been referred by Refugee Action, Migrant Help, a trafficking support organisation or social services. The interviews indicate that many did not understand the basis on which they instructed a lawyer at all, saying that the Home Office, LSC or support organisation had "given" them the lawyer. In the main, the only interviewees who felt they had made a choice were those who were making fresh claims after some years in the country and taking a friend's recommendation.

The purchaser, the LAA, does not choose providers based on quality. That means that, even if we view the taxpayer as the real client, choice of provider is not an effective strategy within the current market structure. It is true that there are entry standards for the legal aid market, such as obtaining the SQM, supervision requirements in the contract, and demonstrating threshold competence on peer review roughly every three years (LAA, 2017). But there is no incentive in the contracting process, the fee regime or the auditing system to do better quality work. Of course, if peer-review scores were the basis for winning or losing a contract or preferential terms, there would need to be an appeals system whereby providers could challenge their scores, which would add to the cost and complexity of the system. At present this only exists for the lowest two peer-review levels. But it may be possible to develop preferential terms or earned autonomy, like less audit activity, for the providers which submit the most escape files for assessment, or receive the highest peer-review scores.

Third, the LAA explicitly rules out exit to another provider, except where a formal complaint has been made and upheld. The contract specifies that a new provider cannot take a case on legal aid where an existing provider has already granted it. Dissatisfaction with the existing provider's service is not sufficient reason to change provider (Ling & Pugh, 2017). Provider interviewees explained that they would rarely take over a case from another provider unless the client had been moved (by the accommodation provider) to a different geographical area, or (rarely) if the previous provider had failed them. That means choice is exercised only at the beginning of the process, when it is least likely to be effective.

With barristers, choice manifests differently. They are instructed by solicitors and caseworkers, who are repeat-buyers in the market, have access to information about the barrister's reputation and can switch to another barrister if they are unhappy with the first. Several barristers said that, "You get one chance" with a solicitor, and "if you don't do a good job, they don't instruct you again". The providers in the study explained that they tended to call on certain sets of barristers' chambers, unless there was a specific barrister they wanted, and trusted that "everyone there is good". In theory, the market for barristers should ensure quality.

But that system is also flawed for three reasons. First, the low level of pay on legal aid means that many more experienced barristers have reduced their own availability for this work because they make a loss on it. Many chambers only make their more junior barristers available for fixed-fee work (see Chapter 6). That limits the choice available to providers seeking barristers. Second, barristers who specialise in immigration and asylum work are concentrated in London and, to a lesser extent, Manchester and Birmingham. There are few barristers close to some of the other tribunal hearing centres and the LAA does not pay travel expenses for appeals advocacy, meaning few barristers can afford to travel far for a tribunal appeal hearing. This means providers with cases in more remote centres have a limited choice of barristers and may not have any access to specialists. Third, not all solicitors and caseworkers are adequately knowledgeable and skilful. This may mean they make an ill-informed decision about whether a barrister is doing a good job or not, just as the client does about the provider, so that there remains a market for barristers who are less competent – a point supported by practitioner interviewees who also sit as tribunal judges.

These are emphatically not arguments against choice in the legal aid market. There has been a great deal of debate about whether or not there should be user choice in other public services previously delivered directly by the State without user choice. This has never been the case with legal aid. In fact, the government decided, after the Carter Review in 2006, to remove users' choice of criminal lawyer. It proposed to award huge contracts based on Best-Value Tendering and to allocate clients to lawyers by rota, month of birth, initial or some other random method. Legal professionals fiercely advocated for choice, arguing that there would be no incentive for these firms to make an effort if they won contracts by promising to do the work cheaply and were allocated clients regardless of reputation. The government proposed to remove choice from legal aid users at the very time it was expanding user choice in other services on the basis that it was the only way to ensure quality. The argument here is that Choice is ineffective as a mechanism for producing quality in the current market system, because of the way it has been operationalised.

Voice

Asylum clients rarely make formal complaints about their lawyers. This was the main reason why the Legal Ombudsman co-commissioned the QALSS research in 2014, with the SRA. The Legal Services Board (LSB, 2012) had already noted that there were few complaints compared with other areas of law, which seemed inconsistent with other information about quality across the immigration legal services field. The Board was concerned that asylum seekers did not understand the different types of practitioner and regulator, or the redress available. It also questioned whether regulators were assessing quality adequately, or were instead relying on the LAA to deal with risks (at least in the publicly funded section of the market; LSB, 2012). But when clients do not understand their right to complain or have the time or necessary knowledge to complain, only the worst conduct will ever reach the attention of the regulators (Sommerlad & Sanderson, 2004; Gibbs & Hughes-Roberts, 2012). Regulation is more an element of Command and Control but is relevant to Voice because, unless proactive expert monitoring is implemented, only Voice activates regulation (see next section).

Yet there is no legal aid to help people to make complaints against their lawyers. For most asylum seekers, there is a language barrier. The process itself is intimidating, since it requires the person to complain first to the firm or organisation that represents them, then wait four weeks for a response before going to the regulator or ombudsman. This may be longer than the client has available before their hearing or removal from the UK. The complexity of immigration law means that support organisations are often unable to help with complaints against lawyers. It is also far from easy to understand which body a complaint should go to, since the ombudsman deals with issues around practitioners' work or services and the regulators deal with dishonesty or malpractice. Providers are required to send a client care letter including information about how to complain, but many of the QALSS interviewees said they did not know they had a right to complain, suggesting that they either did not understand or did not remember what was in the client care letter.

All of this, of course, assumes the client realises there is a problem. Without understanding the process, the law or what they are entitled to expect from a lawyer, they may not realise the quality is inadequate until potentially irreparable damage is done (Dingwall & Fenn, 1987; Hill & Varone, 2017). For example, one of the QALSS interviewees was happy with his solicitor because, every time his fresh claim was refused, the solicitor made another application for him, and had done so four times already. To the informed eye, it appears that the solicitor was submitting serial claims of inadequate quality, either failing the client (because he had a good fresh claim) or giving him false hope (because he did not).

Even if clients realise quality is poor, they may 'regard the problem as the lesser of two evils', the other being no representation at all (Hill & Varone, 2017:p299). Indeed, support workers interviewed in the QALSS research said they usually tried to work with a provider on a specific case rather than complain, because there was little chance of finding an alternative provider.

It is no exaggeration to say that Voice is wholly ineffective as a strategy for this client group. Indeed, as Crouch (2004) describes it, Voice is a mechanism of citizenship, exercised through voting and campaigning as much as through individual complaint mechanisms. So perhaps Voice was never intended to be available to the non-citizen who needs immigration and asylum advice. Even taxpayers, though, have Voice only in a very remote sense: their only information about the quality of services is mediated through, for example, the NAO or other reports on legal aid. Although barristers have Voice to complain about poor-quality solicitors and caseworkers, and vice versa, the regulators do not act on third-party complaints per se. Beyond that, it would be problematic to put the burden of dealing with poor quality onto already-pressured legal aid practitioners without legal aid (or similar) funding to support them doing so. Clients need expert third parties to assist with complaints, which realistically means legally aided lawyers, combined with an Exit route.

Command and Control versus Trust

At the beginning of legal aid, from 1949 to 1988, solicitors administered the fund themselves through the Law Society, using the Green Form scheme from 1973 to provide time-limited advice in any area of law, with minimal oversight (see Chapter 2). Lawyers were self-regulated until 2006–07. On Le Grand's classifications (2007), this was a system characterised primarily by Trust, with minimal Command and Control. As shown in Chapter 2, the role of Trust has much diminished since then and the system is based increasingly heavily on Command and Control, manifested through the monopsony market, the rules of the legal aid contract and the audit regime linked to it, plus independent regulation.

The auditing regime was described by case-study interviewees as "zero-tolerance" and "focused on clawing back money" (see Chapters 3 and 4). There are ten different types of audit for immigration and asylum practitioners, some of which happen automatically, while others are triggered by the provider doing higher-value or higher-level work, or by an issue arising on another audit.[1] The majority of audits, however, are carried out by non-lawyers who are neither required, nor able, to judge whether the advice given was legally correct. Rather, the focus is on whether the provider has the right evidence on file of the client's financial means, whether the correct outcome code was used, whether all of the right boxes were ticked. One of the case-study providers had been refused payment on a file, given a contract notice and been compelled to self-review other files before a follow-up audit, because, as the solicitor explained:

> 'One of the files didn't have "nil" written in the partner-assessment section. There was no partner but the legal aid form had not been filled in correctly because they hadn't put "nil, nil, nil, nil, nil" down one side. And so that file was non-compliant. ... We'd have been told off for that in the past but ... we would've got paid for the work because it was clear that we'd done it and that we had evidence of income on file. They are *very* particular.'

These audit issues described by interviewees are not unique to legal aid: there is a vast amount of academic literature on the distorting effect of audits which focus on procedural or peripheral matters and ignore substantive quality (Bevan & Hood, 2006; Hood, 2006; Shore, 2008 for example). It is easy to see why the providers in the BAJ study "tightened up" their procedures, by either employing a practice manager or diverting a relatively senior practitioner into managing these issues, because they could not afford to be penalised. Immigration

---

[1] Legal Aid Agency: https://www.gov.uk/guidance/legal-aid-agency-audits.

providers in Plymouth said they withdrew from legal aid not because of the low fees, but because of the risks of financial clawbacks. Yet those who ticked all the boxes but failed to obtain crucial evidence for the client, gave incorrect advice, or used an interpreter who spoke the wrong dialect could pass an audit without difficulty.

The only monitoring of substantive quality is through peer review, which is relatively expensive and little used. Peer reviews rate providers from level one, the highest, down to five (see Appendix for criteria). The Carter Review advocated a minimum peer-review level of two. Instead, level three – threshold competence – was adopted as sufficient. A level four review triggers a follow-up review in six months; a second level four or a level five review means loss of the contract. As set out in the *Independent Peer-Review Process* guidance (LAA, 2017:paragraphs 2.26–2.30), indicators of level two (Competence Plus) performance include: 'Clients are advised correctly and in full'; 'Issues are progressed comprehensively, appropriately and efficiently'; 'Advice and work is tailored to the individual client's circumstances'; and, perhaps most importantly, 'The provider adds value to cases and takes a proactive approach'.

Providers can pass a peer review at level three when, 'There is adequate but limited communication with the client', and 'The advice and work is adequate, although it may not always be extensive and may not deal with other linked issues other than the presenting issue'. There is no need, at this level, for the provider to add value, nor to tailor the work to the client's circumstances. Clients need not even be advised 'correctly and in full'. In other words, mere processing is sufficient.

This concept of 'processing' is important, because it describes a level of work that is sufficient to pass a peer review and maintain a contract, but without necessarily adding value to the case, beyond acting as a conduit between applicant and Home Office. The fee is the same, whether providers operate this processing model or carry out meticulous expert work. Clearly, there are disincentives to quality in the contractual relationship with the LAA, but not all providers respond to them in the same way.

It would be difficult to incentivise quality through a fee regime per se. BAJ interviewees in solicitors' firms, not-for-profits and barristers' chambers argued that quality came through the ethos and commitment of an organisation, whether private or not-for-profit. It was built through supervision and training, careful recruitment of staff who shared that commitment, as well as a culture of sharing knowledge and experience and of being allowed to learn from mistakes. It was maintained through a determined effort to cross-subsidise legal aid work so that it could be done to a high standard.

In other words, the drivers of quality could not be instilled through a Command and Control system. Of course, they could not be instilled by Trust alone either, but the contradiction is that those providers which most deserved to be trusted (based on the quality of their work) were subject to even more Command and Control, because of the assessment of escape fee and Upper Tribunal files, than those who merely processed clients. It may be impossible to use contract rules to incentivise quality, but a problem arises when systems are designed primarily to guard against deliberate misconduct, rather than facilitate the work.

Compared with solicitors and caseworkers, Trust plays a greater role for barristers doing legal aid work. They are instructed by contracted providers and have no direct contractual relationship with the LAA. The control responsibility is delegated to the instructing solicitor or caseworker. All barristers pay for a practising certificate and professional indemnity insurance, but those doing legal aid work face no more regulatory activity or expense than those only doing private work. Research on the effectiveness of representation concluded that barristers (and other specialist advocates) did provide effective representation at tribunals, contributing to the quality and accuracy of decisions by addressing the tribunal on relevant law and clarifying relevant issues (Genn & Genn, 1989). Direct observation and peer review, however, have proved impractical as a means of researching quality in barristers' work (Sherr & Paterson, 2008), perhaps explaining why there is little academic literature on quality in the work of barristers in civil cases.

What is the role of regulation in balancing Trust with Command and Control? Regulation is multi-layered (see Chapter 2): every practitioner is regulated individually by the Solicitors Regulation Authority, Bar Standards Board, Chartered Institute of Legal Executives, or the Office of the Immigration Services Commissioner. The first three are regulated by the Legal Services Board, which is advised by the Legal Services Consumer Panel, with the Legal Ombudsman service sitting alongside these to deal with complaints from the public about legal services. Providers doing immigration legal aid work (though not private work) also need to go through the Law Society's accreditation scheme.

Each layer of regulation and accreditation has financial and resource costs, nearly all falling on practitioners and their organisations. As the Bar Standards Board (BSB, 2016) identified, there is a risk that any new regulatory barriers would further reduce supply. Either regulation needs to take account of the price paid for the work (but this implies that costs would be cut by downgrading quality standards) or the price paid needs to take into account the costs of whatever regulation is needed to maintain quality. The Legal Services Board (LSB, 2012) and others were also concerned that asylum seekers in particular did not understand this complex, overlapping regulatory system, the different types of practitioner and regulator, or the redress available to them (Migration Work et al, 2016). In other words, despite the expense of regulation, it is of doubtful effectiveness.

The correct weighting between Trust and Command and Control will always be a matter of judgement, but evidence and cost should certainly be taken into account. Otherwise the high cost of Command and Control, relative to the price paid for the provision of services, forces high-quality providers to leave the market, reducing Choice and, in turn, the effectiveness of Voice (see next section).

Poor quality in the market

There are consequences, at market level, to the conflict between quality and financial viability. As we have seen, the failure of the 'swings and roundabouts' principle (see Chapter 4) means that providers who "do the work the case needs" lose money on every legal aid case they do, and have to rely on subsidy from private clients, grant-funding or higher-paid work (including winning costs in higher court cases), if available to them. As a result, some have left the market, either suddenly as a result of a cash-flow crisis or in a more controlled way. Others have restricted their legal aid market share by capping their total capacity, to limit their legal aid losses to the amount they can raise in subsidy, and by limiting the kind of case they will take on to avoid making losses. In other words, they reduce their responsiveness to potential-client demand in order to maintain responsiveness to in-case demand.

Although the BAJ research focused on high-quality providers, many of the interviewees were able to reflect on quality in other organisations, which helps to build an understanding of how quality differs across the market. Some of the evidence of poor-quality work has appeared throughout this book. In particular, there is fairly robust evidence to suggest that the fixed fee acts as an attractor point or a cap, beyond which some providers do not go, regardless of in-case demand: the practitioners who were told during job interviews that the firm did not work beyond the fixed fee; "escapees" from firms which produced poor-quality work; barristers' accounts of the work of some firms which instruct them; and the comment of the MoJ official in the QALSS research that "most cases" cost about the level of the fixed fee.

It is, of course, difficult to criticise any business for not doing substantial amounts of unpaid work or handing out free goods and services. That is also a reason why regulators have limited scope to increase quality, since they cannot reasonably order private businesses or charities to undertake unpaid overtime. Control of prices by a government department means quality is, "inherently prescribed by the economic parameters of the service" (Sherr et al, 1994:p141), unless providers strategically evade that prescription. All of the BAJ interviewees believed that the low fees were therefore a real disincentive to do good work on files and felt obstructed by the LAA, but some were also concerned that other firms used low fees as an "excuse" for doing the "bare minimum" of work.

One of these interviewees, a solicitor with 23 years' experience, had resigned from her most recent job in a large legal aid firm outside London because of its tolerance, and even encouragement, of poor-quality work. This included neglecting basic steps like taking detailed instructions from clients or allowing interpreters to read back the asylum interview without a legal caseworker present. In one case, her colleague failed to request an interpreter in the correct language for the Home Office interview, despite that language being spoken exclusively by one Darfuri tribe in Sudan, whose members almost automatically qualify for asylum:

> 'I sat next to a guy who had a client who spoke Fur, and he'd got the Home Office interview record back. … He was doing a whole list of corrections and he gave this to me and it was like, "No, it wasn't a playground, it was a field". I said surely the big point here is he's a Fur speaker, not an Arabic speaker. Did you tell the Home Office he wanted a Fur interpreter? And he said, "Well, they should have found that out themselves at the screening interview". Well, maybe they should've done, but you're his representative. … And if they can't find a Fur interpreter, you compromise and say, okay, he'll do his interview in Arabic, but Fur is his first language. You've kind of got your claim in the bag at that point. And this had totally passed him by and constantly people [in that firm] would say, "Well, the Home Office should've done that". And in that case, what's the point of them?'

Yet this firm had unlimited demand because it was one of a few suppliers in a dispersal area where large numbers of new clients arrived daily. It had a highly critical peer review, but did not fall below the threshold for contract sanctions. The solicitor expressed concern to managers but said: "The response to it was always, this is the business model, and we can't afford to do it any other way. [And] there was a massive push against instructing counsel because it was cheaper to do it in-house, or the firm kept the fee."

The use of the lowest (level one) accredited workers to do the application stage meant it was often a "non-stage". These inexperienced staff did the bare minimum of work and billed the fixed fee, leaving any substantive work to the level two caseworker at appeal stage. As a result of this, the solicitor explained:

> 'There was a lot of discontentment among the level two people because they felt they had to do a lot of extra work [at appeal stage] to make up for the fact that nothing had been done on Legal Help. So you could bring in far more fees by being a level one than a level two. You could turn over lots of Legal Help and do 15 minutes on each one with no external scrutiny, whereas you couldn't get away with that at the appeal stage. So I think it led to two things: to a lot of [clients being dropped at appeal stage] because level two people looked at something and thought I can't turn this around in the time I've got available; but it also led to level two people having to spend a lot more time than they should have, so that meant that actually the more senior, committed people were bringing in far less money, not just because they were going over the fixed fee, but because they were having to compensate for everything that hadn't been done on the Legal Help.'

Another firm had taken decisive action in respect of those (committed) staff bringing in less money, as one of its former caseworkers described:

> 'They sent round an email, like every other day, and it had a league table of everybody's hours for the week or something, and then that was circulated to everybody with everybody's name on it! And the idea was it would motivate the people at the bottom – they don't want to be at the bottom so they're going to do more hours so they try and get higher – which is just like extra stress, like internal shaming or something.'

At this micro-level, one begins to see how the individual pressures to meet billing targets manifest as a pressure on even the most committed workers within an incentive-responsive business model. It is perhaps the inevitable consequence of the situation observed by Sommerlad whereby, with team-billing targets leading to individual billing targets, 'each worker is becoming her own cost centre' (2001:p351). This then leads to the refusal to continue representing clients at appeal stage, not because the client genuinely has less than a 50 per cent chance of succeeding before an immigration judge, but because too little work has been done on their case so far. This sheds light on the representation in Mariam's case (see Chapter 6), where it was clear how cheap, low-value work at application stages not only causes distress and anxiety for asylum applicants, but also drives failure demand for work at appeal stage, by lawyers, Home Office and Tribunal, and potentially for work on a fresh asylum claim or emergency work to prevent removal.

Poor quality is not always linked to case-by-case financial incentives, but can nevertheless be defined as incentive-responsive provision. The solicitor quoted previously mentioned another firm, also outside London, which also had a poor reputation, whose files she had regularly taken over at appeal stage. This firm also had limited local competition and effectively unlimited demand, particularly from unaccompanied children, whose cases are exempt from the fixed-fee scheme:

> 'I think they really didn't know what they were doing. They had some people with really good intentions but ... they were just processing. It was almost as if they didn't know they were supposed to be adding value. And it was interesting because that was all hourly rates work, so I don't think it's necessarily more profitable [to do it badly].'

At organisational level, this can only occur because work which is too complex is delegated to a worker not competent to do it, or the training or supervision within the organisation are inadequate. Although these firms did not necessarily profit from doing the work badly, the entire business model results from an incentive-responsive choice to employ cheap, inexperienced staff and failing to invest in the training and supervision needed to ensure its workers respond appropriately to the in-case demand. There is a more general incentive to save on costs because of fixed fees, and no market incentive to improve quality.

A junior solicitor contrasted the position on supervision at the large firm where he began his career, where "to a large extent you were just left to your own devices and you very much learnt by making mistakes and finding out the hard way". At this previous firm he "didn't know any better" than to work in the way he saw around him, where he noted that "the emphasis and the work culture is very different" and the lawyers who were "passionate about it" were in the minority. The physical environment reflected and influenced that work culture, with open-plan offices and limited client-meeting space, which made it more difficult to spend time with clients taking detailed statements. His current firm, by contrast, had a weekly meeting which functioned as regular support and peer-checking for all workers, from junior to senior. The supervision structure was laid out in the staff handbook and supplemented by a culture of sharing information and informal passing of knowledge and materials between staff. These findings echo other researchers' conclusions about recruitment, training, commitment to clients and social aims, and environment (McConville et al, 1994; Sommerlad, 2001).

There is some conflict between supervision as a driver of quality and financial viability. The LAA contract sets out minimum requirements for supervision which, both in this research and in the QALSS interviews, were widely seen as a positive thing.[2] But supervision is not chargeable on legal aid files (unless the supervision also amounts to casework *and* the case escapes the fixed fee). Although supervision is not necessarily required on every individual file (depending on the experience of the caseworker), nevertheless there is a discrepancy between the level of supervision the LAA requires and the amount it is willing to pay for. For firms with private income as well as legal aid, the cost is absorbed, in effect, by private clients paying towards legal aid supervision. For the not-for-profits in the study, however, it was an additional cost which had to be raised from another source. Organisations did not identify supervision specifically as problematic, since it contributes to quality, but rather the overall volume of unpaid tasks required, which create a real difficulty in covering the costs.

Two main reasons for poor work emerge from these accounts: first, a business model which minimises the work done or the costs of that work, in order to make a profit on the fixed fee; and second, an apparent failure to understand how to do casework well (despite the accreditation requirements). Many of these firms were said to have

---

[2] One full-time-equivalent supervisor to a maximum of four full-time-equivalent caseworkers; supervisor to conduct file reviews and record the outcomes of these; the number of file reviews must reflect the skills, knowledge and experience of the caseworker, but a minimum of one face-to-face supervision session per month.

"some good people", but those few could not "turn around" a whole firm unless they were at partner level. Those "good people" outside London were further disadvantaged by being at a distance from the core professional network with its training and support.

Development of a 'lemon market'

George Akerlof's 'lemon market' metaphor (1970) helps to explain what is happening. Akerlof drew on the used-car market to show how, when quality is not readily inspectable by a purchaser or the purchaser cannot determine the quality, purchasers will only be willing to pay the value of an average item. This means those who have a poor-quality car – 'a lemon' – have an incentive to sell, because they will receive the average price, which is more than their car is worth. Those who have a high-quality car – 'a peach' – have an incentive to withdraw it from the market, since the average price is below its value. Over time this leads to the withdrawal of high-quality cars and the prevalence of poor-quality cars in the market: that is, a lowering of overall quality. Potentially, it drives a reduction in the price a buyer is willing to pay for the average car left in that market. As Akerlof put it, 'Both the supply of used cars and also the average quality will depend upon the price' (1970:p490).

Asylum legal services are obviously very different from used cars, but this metaphor helps to make sense of the market. The fixed fee represents the notional average cost of a case. The purchaser (the LAA) does not distinguish between suppliers on the basis of quality, beyond imposing certain minimum standards. The service user (the client) is usually unable to distinguish between suppliers on the basis of quality at the time they make their 'purchase' or choice, and usually has no option to choose a better service at a higher price. Auditors who are unable to distinguish between high- and low-quality providers treat all providers as average, implementing a level of monitoring which is disproportionate in resource terms to the risk posed by the high-quality providers, but fails to identify the defects in the poor-quality services. Where the costs of this monitoring are passed on to the provider, it exacerbates the financial pressures on those who are already reliant on cross-subsidy.

Providers then face a choice of whether to:

1. trade services in the market which are worth more than the price they will receive and make a loss;

2. trade services in the market which are worth no more than the price available; or
3. stop trading in that market.

RMJ was forced to stop trading in the legal aid market. The other BAJ providers, except Firm Z, took Option 1: trading services at a loss but capping those losses at the amount they could raise in subsidy. Some took a partial version of Option 3: stopping trading certain services in the legal aid market, taking only work that would be paid for at hourly rates, enabling them to do fewer cases but do them well. All of these strategies involve a reduction in market share.

Providers who are willing to take Option 2 and deliver a service by capping their work at the level paid for, which breaks even despite the fixed fee, are incentivised to enter the market or to maintain or increase their market share. They incur no contract sanctions for the paucity of their work. In many areas there is more demand than supply, from clients who are unaware of the quality of their work and are unable to move to another provider if they realise that the service is poor. If fewer high-quality services (or matter starts) are put into the market, while the same or a higher number of poor-quality ones are performed, overall quality in the market goes down.

Of course, numerical data do not exist to prove or disprove that average quality is declining, nor that high-quality providers have left the market in greater numbers than poor-quality ones. Peer review is conducted on a small sample each year, and that sample is a mix of random selection and providers about whom concerns have been expressed, so the peer-review statistics are not representative of the whole field. Since sampling is not the same each year, and since peer review rests on subjective judgements against the criteria, it cannot be compared accurately across time either.

Nevertheless it is worth looking at the peer-review data given to the Civil Contracts Consultative Group for 2017–18.[3] In immigration, 15.15 per cent of providers reviewed (5 out of 33) received the top rating (Excellence). This was more than in any other area of law (7.5 per cent, 5.4 per cent and 0 per cent for family, mental health and housing, respectively). The same proportion received the second level (Competence Plus). No providers received the bottom rating, level

---

[3] Legal Aid Agency: Audit report attached to minutes of Civil Contracts Consultative Group meeting, 24 January 2018. All minutes available at: https://www.gov.uk/government/publications/contracts-consultative-groups.

five (Failure in Performance), but 36 per cent (12 out of 33) received level four (Below Competence). Again, this was much higher than in any other area of law (2.5 per cent, 8.1 per cent and 15.16 per cent, respectively). This represented just over 5 per cent of the 234 providers which held immigration contracts in August 2017 (a year before the 2018 contracts were awarded). The figures suggest that, in immigration law, the LAA has contracted with too many providers who are not competent, raising the inference that either quality barriers to enter the market are too low, or the contract terms cause quality to drop to an unacceptable level.

But even without numerical data, it is self-evident that those who do the least work per case, or use the cheapest staff, make the most profit from fixed-fee cases. The LAA, being unable to discern substantive quality, does not know whether it is paying for real excellence, mere processing that adds no value or even harms the case, or anything in between. Since providers are guaranteed a contract if they meet a minimal quality standard, and are therefore guaranteed clients in a market where demand exceeds supply, and since clients are denied a viable exit route from poor-quality providers, the organisations which mediate demand primarily with a view to maximising profit have the best chance of survival. High-quality providers become the outliers, hence some in the BAJ research had been asked to explain why they were 'expensive' compared with the average.

Akerlof's lemon market has occasionally been applied to public-service provision before (Jackson & Price, 1994) but, when compared with private goods and services markets, a key difference exacerbates the lemon market effect in legal aid (and perhaps other services), namely the LAA's position as a monopsonist. It uses this power to force down prices, impose performance targets and enforce various ways of working, but does not use it to distinguish on grounds of quality, either in terms of access to the market (awarding contracts) or preferential contract terms. In effect, through the use of its monopsony power, it has unintentionally protected the market position of poor-quality providers so that bad quality drives out good.

Conclusion

It is important to acknowledge that there were concerns about quality in legal services, including publicly funded services, long before contracting and fixed fees existed. As far back as 1975, Bridges et al discussed the 'fruit machine' providers where quality was a gamble, as well as the 'sausage machines' which provided routinely poor services.

There is no past golden age when services were uniformly excellent, to which we could all return with a sigh of relief. But several decades of reforms – including independent regulation, an accreditation system, contracts and auditing – at great public and private expense, ought to have produced a clear improvement in quality, unless they were entirely the wrong reforms or something else (like price or market conditions) was confounding those positive changes.

Even if one accepts the characterisation of taxpayers as the client of publicly funded services, the strategies of Choice, Voice and Exit are ineffective for them too in the current market structure. If taxpayers are to pay for work that is of value, rather than mere processing or worse, then the purchaser has to take action to ensure that it only buys work which is of value. Legal aid (across categories) has moved from a model dominated by Choice and Trust, via some attempts to increase Voice, to a scenario dominated by Command and Control, in which Choice has been displaced by scarcity, and Trust has been largely ousted in favour of risk. Yet Command and Control is expensive, with little evidence that it is effective in ensuring quality.

This discussion highlights one of the 'wicked problems' of marketised professional services for vulnerable people: regulation is already enormously expensive and paid for by levies on professionals. Yet it can only really take aim at the 'dreadful', rather than the merely inadequate. More regulation, to get at the inadequate, means more expense for professionals (unless the cost is shifted back to government), yet legal aid professionals are already only marginally profitable, or subsidising legal aid work from other sources. The Bar Standards Board concluded that any additional restrictions on barristers' ability to practise in that field would create a serious threat to the already precarious supply (BSB, 2016), and the SRA's reports and responses similarly identified little more which could be done by way of regulation within the existing system to protect asylum and immigration clients, without further reducing supply (Migration Work et al, 2016; SRA, 2016).

As a result, neither regulation (except in extreme cases) nor the market are effective mechanisms for ensuring quality in legal aid services. The purchaser, the LAA, operates as a de facto regulator since it has monopsony power to determine the economic incentives, the performance targets, the audit issues, the entry and exit standards for providers, and the mechanisms for clients to exercise the Choice and Exit strategies. As operated currently, this prevents market forces from operating positively on quality, but also overwhelms any practical effectiveness of regulatory powers in the specific arena of publicly funded asylum legal services.

The answer, at its broadest, is to increase Choice, strengthen Voice, allow Exit, and rebalance the system among Trust, Command and Control, and Risk. Exit could be enabled by changing a clause in the legal aid contract, but making it into a viable option demands shoring up Choice, by rebuilding the provider base with a fee regime and auditing system that supports good-quality providers. Choice can only exist, and control for quality, where there is a robust supplier base with the ability for the most popular providers to expand to meet demand. This means facilitating, rather than blocking, the best-quality practitioners and organisations and developing a more proportionate auditing system with a focus on substantive quality – and improving or removing the lemons.

8

Why we need to think about systems

In 2019, the Tribunal and Home Office began piloting a new system for appeals, aiming to promote early review of the evidence and withdrawal of poor-quality decisions, or those where the new evidence and legal arguments suggested the appeal should succeed. In the new model, the Home Office should upload all of its paperwork to a shared platform. The appellant's representatives should respond with all the evidence that they wish to rely on and an Advance Skeleton Argument (ASA). The Home Office should review all of this before the hearing and, if appropriate, withdraw the refusal decision and grant asylum.

This would have been an entirely positive development, except that legal aid payments were not aligned with the in-case demands of the pilot scheme. The barrister had to review all of the papers, then write and submit a skeleton argument as if attending court. If the Home Office decided to grant asylum, the barrister would not get paid because the hearing would not go ahead. The problem was brought to the attention of the LAA, the Home Office and the Tribunal. Barristers from some of the main immigration teams said they would not participate until legal aid funding was amended to fit the new demands. Consultation, through the Civil Contracts Consultative Group, was ongoing and the Group was assured in the March 2020 meeting that: 'The policy team were keen to take on board the rep bodies' views and so would consult with them *before* implementing the changes' [emphasis added] (CCCG, 2020).

The procedure was suddenly made compulsory in May 2020, apparently in response to the COVID-19 pandemic and the need to deal with more cases remotely. The new scheme did not in itself mean that cases *would* be heard remotely, but might mean that some would be conceded by the Home Office without a hearing. The pilot data, though not fully evaluated, indicated the Home Office was accepting around 19 per cent of appeals on review. At this stage, however, no amendments had been made to the funding scheme. The President of the Immigration and Asylum Chamber of the Tribunal acknowledged in letters to ILPA that the new procedure created unpaid demands, but that, 'I hope you will understand that that is not an issue with which the Tribunal can or should be directly concerned'.[1] It is of course not within the Tribunal's gift to change legal aid fees, but it does have the power to decide whether and when its procedures – and in-case demands – will be changed. In other words, the President of the Tribunal was comfortable with making significant amendments to appeal procedures, placing significant extra in-case demand on practitioners, without any provision for them to be paid for any of their work at all.

A new fixed fee was then implemented as from the beginning of June 2020[2] with very limited consultation with practitioners and in the face of opposition from ILPA. There were now three possible fees for the appeal stage of a case:

- The **Stage 2A fee** of £227 for a case under the old procedure which did *not* end in a full hearing.
- The **Stage 2B fee** of £567 plus the £302 advocacy bolt-on for a case under the old procedure which *did* end in a full hearing.
- The new **Stage 2C fee** of £627 for all cases under the new procedure.

On the face of it, the new Stage 2C fee looked like an increase in remuneration. In reality, because the £60 increase failed to offset the loss of the £302 advocacy bolt-on, it placed even greater financial risk on practitioners and failed to reflect the real in-case demand.

The in-case demand on the provider, up to the point where the evidence and Advance Skeleton Argument (ASA) are submitted, is for all of the same work they would do under the old procedure. The in-case demand after the Home Office review, if the case is to be heard in court, is for additional preparation work updating the evidence if necessary, liaising with the client and instructing the same barrister, if available, and a new one if not. The in-case demand on the barrister, up to the Home Office review, is to do all of the preparation as if for the hearing, including reading all of the papers, liaising with the provider over evidence, and drafting a detailed skeleton argument to comply with the practice direction relating to the new procedure.

If the Home Office accepted the appeal at the review stage, there were three possibilities:

---

[1] Letters dated 1 April 2020 and 17 April 2020.

[2] In the Civil Legal Aid (Remuneration) (Amendment) (Coronavirus) Regulations 2020.

- The barrister went unpaid altogether.
- The barrister received the extra £60 in the Stage 2C fee.
- The provider and the barrister negotiated splitting the Stage 2C fee in some other way.

A fee of £60 was clearly inadequate for the work required of the barrister. Assuming they pay the typical management fee of around 20 per cent into chambers, the remaining gross fee is £48. Barristers interviewed in the BAJ study, which is the only evidence currently available on the matter, said that four hours' preparation would be the minimum, but six to ten hours would be more common. Six hours' work for £48 would be £8 per hour, compared with a National Minimum Wage (at the time of writing, age 25+) of £8.72 per hour. It goes without saying that being unpaid altogether is also unacceptable.

The fee-splitting option is also problematic. Since the fixed fee scheme was introduced, the practice throughout the country has been that the stage 2B fee was for the solicitor/caseworker and the bolt-on hearing fee was for the barrister. There has never been a further process of fee-splitting or negotiation over who gets what. Following the practice direction and procedure rules to meet the new requirements, both parties will do at least the same amount of work to prepare the case as under the old procedure. Although the advocacy, travel and waiting are avoided, the barrister still undertakes all of the preparation work that they would do for a hearing, for the purpose of drafting the ASA. As detailed in Chapter 4, demand-responsive providers already lose money on each of these cases. Under the new procedure and fee, they would lose more when the case was decided without a hearing. Negotiations over sharing out the losses would take up extra time and resources (that is, they would amount to a new transaction cost) and risk undermining professional relationships. It would also put pressure on chambers to offer out junior counsel at cut rates, potentially amounting to less than minimum wage, and on providers to accept more junior counsel because they cannot afford the cost of experience.

Even when the hearing does go ahead, the new procedure means some preparation will have to be duplicated. Whoever prepares the skeleton argument has to read all the paperwork: statements, interview transcript, refusal letter, country background evidence, any other medical or expert evidence, and so on. It will then be at least several weeks, and often months, before the hearing in that case, so that person would need to prepare again before presenting the case. In some cases, updated evidence will be needed to reflect a change in circumstances, or to confirm that circumstances like an appellant's mental health have not changed. That means, even where a case goes to a full hearing, the fixed fee was unlikely to cover the total work now required. What was more, under the new fixed fee, there was no provision for separate payments if one barrister drafted the ASA and another ended up presenting the case at Tribunal. Yet there was no provision either for ensuring that hearings are listed on a date when the barrister who drafted the ASA is available.

Another point of concern was the effect of the Stage 2C fee on the 'risk zone' between the fixed fee and the escape threshold. Although the percentage risk stayed the same, with up to 199 per cent of the work at risk, the absolute sums at risk became larger with the stage 2C fee. For example, on the old fee regime, the risk zone in an asylum case which did proceed to a Tribunal hearing was £1,134, this being the gap between £567 (the old fixed fee) and £1,701 (triple that fixed fee). Under the new fee regime, the risk zone was between the new fixed fee of £627 and £1,881 (that is, a gap of £1,254). Providers now stood to lose up to an additional £120 per case, more than a 10 per cent increase on the sum at risk.

For cases which do not proceed to a substantive hearing, the increase in the risk zone was over 176 per cent. Under the old fee regime, the risk zone was between £227 and £681 (that is, £454 at risk). A provider who has done most of the work to get a case ready for hearing would be quite likely to cross the escape threshold and receive hourly rates. The new risk zone, however, was between £627 and £1,881. A provider now stood to lose up to £1,254 per case in this category, which should be more common under the new procedure. Those organisations which cross-subsidise legal aid work would have to further limit the number of fixed-fee cases they take on. That was likely to mean demand-responsive providers undertaking even fewer fixed-fee cases, because they cannot afford to do them, leaving more adult first-time asylum applicants unrepresented or poorly represented.

The new Stage 2C fee was largely based on guesswork, partly informed by tentative estimates provided by representative bodies, added onto the guesswork which determined the original fixed fee. Guesswork is a bizarre way of setting prices, at least when actual cost data could reasonably be obtained by paying hourly rates for a trial period or to certain trusted providers. As discussed in Chapter 4, basic economic understandings tell us that there is a high risk of market failure when prices are imposed which do not match the cost of providing a service.

The new fixed fee was to be reviewed after one year, in June 2021, and the MoJ intended to gather views and data about the adequacy of the new fee over the course of that year. This book has set out evidence that some providers (those referred to as incentive-responsive) deliberately work within the fixed fee, or cap their work at the level of the fixed fee. This meant that the fixed fee would have determined the amount of time that (at least some of) those providers would spend on the case. The new fixed fee would become a new attractor point around which the data would cluster. The LAA and MoJ would receive an artificially high amount of data on cost *confirming* that the new procedure took almost precisely the time covered by the new fee. The time reported would look remarkably consistent across providers and across cases, except from a small number of demand-responsive firms and not-for-profits, who were likely to further reduce the number of fixed fee cases they take on, to minimise their exposure to risk. As a result, there would never be accurate data on how long it took or how much it cost to meet the in-case demand for the work under the new procedure. Worse, one year of the new fee was likely to leave some demand-responsive providers unable to survive financially, exacerbating the lemon market effect discussed in Chapter 7.

Most of the larger teams of immigration specialist barristers published a joint statement stating that they would not take on cases which were subject to the new procedure, 'other than in exceptional circumstances' (ILPA, 2020). As several barristers pointed out, the better the quality of their work, the more persuasive their written argument, the less chance they had of being paid for it.

There followed a series of conflicting directions from Tribunal hearing centres. The pilot directions, undated but drafted for the start of the pilot scheme in January 2019 (and now removed from the website), set out points with which an ASA 'must comply'. In particular, it must 'engage expressly with the decision under challenge' (as opposed to being generic), and must be cross-referenced to documents in the bundles. It 'must' contain a summary of the facts the appellant relies on, a schedule of issues in numbered points, and submissions. In these submissions, 'it is imperative that the ASA engages expressly with each of the grounds upon which the appellant's application was refused' [paragraph 1.3.4]. Furthermore:

> In an appeal against the refusal of a protection claim, for example, the ASA must engage with questions of credibility, sufficiency of protection and internal relocation where such issues have been raised by the respondent. In an appeal against the refusal of a human rights claim, for example, the ASA should identify the articles of the [Human Rights Act]

relied upon, the manner in which any qualified articles are engaged and the reasons why any decision taken under the Immigration Rules is said to be wrong. [paragraph 1.3.5]

A sample skeleton argument was also made available: a six-page document comprising the required summary, schedule of issues and submissions for a fictional case. This fictional case included only two issues on which the Home Office disputed credibility, which barristers considered to be far fewer issues than they usually had to address. It was clear from the example and the pilot directions that the requirement was for a skeleton argument based on a thorough understanding of the appellant's case, including their witness statement, any other evidence (including expert and country background material), and the Home Office's reasons for refusal. It is difficult to read these directions as requiring anything other than the full skeleton argument that would be required for a hearing. The Presidential Practice Statement (No.2 of 2020),[3] which made the new procedure compulsory for all new appeals, outlined a similar requirement, saying that where an appellant is represented, the Tribunal:

> will accept as an Appeal Skeleton Argument ('ASA') a document that answers the following question: 'Why does the appellant say that the decision of the respondent is wrong?' In answering this question, the appellant should set out concisely the reasoning in the respondent's decision letter to which objection is taken. Anything that is relevant should be identified and the answer to the question should be given with sufficient particularity to enable the respondent to conduct an effective review of the decision under appeal.

Nevertheless, when barristers said that they would not do the work unless paid, various Tribunal hearing centres sent out communications suggesting barristers had misunderstood these detailed directions. A set of directions from Manchester, shared by the recipient barrister, and unpublished, stated that:

> There has been misunderstanding about what is meant by a skeleton argument and perhaps, with hindsight, the title

---

[3] https://www.judiciary.uk/publications/immigration-and-asylum-tribunal-chamber-presidential-practice-statement-note-covid-19-pandemic/

is unfortunate. It is not the skeleton argument, traditionally prepared by the advocate attending the hearing. Rather it should be a brief statement as to what is wrong with the decision …. A simple statement that the reasons given by the respondent are wrong and why and brief reference to the evidence will suffice. … Basically it should set out, by reference to the evidence, why the decision was wrong. [paragraph 9]

However, the same document states that, if the case does end in a hearing, 'The Tribunal … does not want any further skeleton argument'. On that basis, the appellant was not to have a skeleton argument prepared on their behalf at all. Directions from another hearing centre, London's Taylor House, did not even refer to an ASA, but required preparation of a 'case summary' with contents described in essentially identical terms to the ASA. London's Hatton Cross hearing centre, however, directed submission of:

A typed case-specific Appeal Skeleton Argument identifying the disputed issues specific to the Appellants' cases clearly saying why the Respondent's decision is wrong in each case and setting out the evidence that will be advanced in relation to each point. A generic skeleton argument will not help with managing the case.

These conflicting directions, and accusations of having misunderstood the Practice Statement, prompted one barrister to comment that: "It is correct it's misnamed as a skeleton; it's actually full written submissions. We did not misunderstand anything. It's disrespectful and borderline gaslighting to say that we did."

In addition to barristers' refusal to take on the work, and a Labour Party 'prayer' (a type of formal objection) against the new regulations in June 2020, two judicial review applications were lodged against the Lord Chancellor in late June and early July. On 4 August 2020, the Lord Chancellor conceded both applications, accepting that he had failed to carry out adequate consultation and satisfy his duty of enquiry. The new regulations were revoked and hourly rates payments were implemented by way of a temporary amendment to the legal aid contract, from which data was to be collected to inform the setting of a new fee. Even this, however, is not problem-free. Because barristers have to bill their Tribunal appeals work via their instructing solicitor, in hourly rates cases the solicitor has to monitor the costs throughout the case, and apply for an extension before exceeding the initial cost ceiling. In fixed fee cases, they do not. This is yet another transaction cost on providers; there is no reason barristers could not be permitted to bill for their Tribunal appeals work directly, as they do in Crown Court criminal cases and many other categories.

This story illustrates precisely why change needs to be planned systemically and why it does not work at present. The pilot scheme and the new procedure rightly attempt to divert demand out of the system, reducing in-case demand for appeal hearings without reducing access to justice. All of this derived from the recommendations of the JUSTICE Working Party on immigration appeals (JUSTICE, 2018). Reducing the need for appeals will reduce stress for applicants. It will reduce the demands on Tribunal and Home Office time and should enable quicker hearings of those appeals which do need to be in the Tribunal system. That should also save money for taxpayers.

Yet the savings cannot reasonably be at the sole personal expense of legal aid practitioners who are crucial to the functioning of the system. It would be considered unacceptable to save money on local government house-building budgets by requiring all plumbers to do their part of the work earlier and unpaid. It would be considered unacceptable to save on hospital budgets by not paying the doctor if the patient survived. The risks are placed on the wrong part of the system and create the wrong incentives.

The *Droughts and Deserts* report (Wilding, 2019) contained detailed recommendations, many of which could be implemented quickly to ease difficulties, such as changing the audit regime, reducing the escape threshold, and shifting some risk away from practitioners. These would help with short-term sustainability, but they are not the long-term solution.

Conclusion

The current market is dysfunctional. It does not work for practitioners. It does not, for the most part, work for clients. Often it does not work for the courts. It does not even work for the funders, the LAA and MoJ, who spend more public funds than necessary on dormant or unsustainable contracts, untargeted auditing and failure demand. This being the case, it cannot possibly work for the taxpayer.

As argued in the Introduction, instead of a coherent policy based on need, the legal aid scheme is littered with the debris of old policy directions and distorted by hostility. Fixed fees were, largely, part of an attempt to implement Best-Value Tendering (BVT), which would have led to a catastrophic acceleration towards a lemon market. They were also part of an attempt to tackle the largely illusory (at least in social welfare law) issue of supplier-induced demand. Matter starts were part of the old rationing system, which is no longer relevant. The unified contract, which put private and not-for-profit providers onto the same terms, was similarly part of the move towards BVT, though it confounded the earlier policy aim of having a range of types of provider in the market.

Similarly, the zero-tolerance auditing regime is left over from the NAO qualifying the LSC's accounts, but now tells the public nothing about access to justice or the impact of public funding. The lack of earned autonomy for providers may have made sense at the time of the Carter Review, when the LAA was expected to contract only with providers who reached levels one or two on peer review, and to trust them. It no longer makes sense. There are many more examples.

It is not possible simply to re-incentivise private providers back into the legal aid market, re-incentivise quality, continually retender for work in advice drought areas when the work is not financially viable, because history matters. It is no use tinkering at the edges, reforming legal aid as if it existed in a vacuum, because the system matters. The whole system needs rebuilding around a real and data-informed understanding of demand, supply, quality, financial viability for legal aid providers and access for clients, freed from the politics of blame against lawyers or clients, and infused with a humane and pragmatic approach.

Appendix: Independent peer-review criteria and guidance

This is a direct reproduction of the peer-review criteria published by the Legal Aid Agency, for use by members of the independent peer review panel. The parts relating solely to non-immigration categories of law have been left out. In the original, this forms an appendix to detailed guidance to reviewers.[1] The non-sequential numbering in this document refers to sections of that guidance. This section contains public sector information licensed under the Open Government Licence v3.0.[2]

Peer-review criteria – civil files

A. Communication with the Client:

  1. How well does the adviser appear to have understood the client's problem?

  2. How effective were the adviser's communication and client-handling skills?

  3. How effective were the adviser's fact- and information-gathering skills?

  4. How effectively was the client informed of:

    a) The merits (or not) of the claim? and

    b) All developments?

B. The Advice:

  1. How legally correct was the advice given?

  2. How appropriate was the advice to the client's instructions?

  3. How comprehensive was the advice? (For Family, see over.)

  4. Was the advice given in time/at the right time?

---

[1] Available at https://assets.publishing.service.gov.uk/government/uploads/system/uploads/attachment_data/file/620110/independent-peer-review-process-guidance.pdf

[2] https://www.nationalarchives.gov.uk/doc/open-government-licence/version/3/

C. The Work/Assistance:

1. If no other work was carried out, was this appropriate?
2. If any further fact-finding work was carried out:
   a) How appropriate? and
   b) How efficiently executed was the work?
3. If any other work was carried out:
   a) How appropriate was the work? and
   b) How efficiently executed was the work?
4. How effective in working towards what the client reasonably wanted/needed was any further work carried out?
5. If no disbursements were incurred was this appropriate?
6. How appropriate were any disbursements incurred?
7. Where this is necessary, did the adviser consider/advise on/act on an effective referral?
8. Throughout the file how effectively did the organisation use resources?
9. Did the adviser or their work in any way prejudice the client? If yes, provide details overleaf.

Immigration:

The following generic criteria should be amplified in immigration cases:

A3. Should include consideration of whether the adviser fully investigated the client's immigration history, status etc. In terms of section A generally, there should be evidence on file that the adviser has ascertained how the client and any dependants are being maintained and accommodated, and that the adviser has addressed, either by action or referral, any issues this raises.

Q1, 2 & 4. It would be appropriate for the adviser to take the necessary steps to obtain all relevant supporting documents. Use of the correct forms by the adviser is of critical importance, and the reviewer should be alert to Home Office return of incorrect forms.

C5. In considering disbursements, you should consider whether an interpreter was instructed, if required. If so, was the interpreter appropriate in all the circumstances (for example linguistic ability and independence)?

C7. 'Referral' includes referring the client to other helping organisations.

The criteria are marked either Yes/No or on a sliding scale of 1–5:
1 = Excellence; 2 = Competence Plus; 3 = Threshold Competence;
4 = Below Competence; 5 = Failure in Performance.

A. Communication with the Client:

1. Understanding the problem includes identifying the issues.
   The most effective way of assessing these issues from the file is to
   look for:

   1. A clear note of all interviews, either in original form or as part
      of the letters sent to the client confirming the instructions.
   2. A clear record of all advice given, either on attendance notes or
      as part of the letters sent to the client confirming instructions,
      or on a statement or in supporting documents.

If it is noted on the file that the client has any particular communication
problems (for example with language or literacy), it is appropriate to
consider whether the chosen methods of communication were suited
to the client.

Any statement taken from a client would need to show that the
adviser had a good grasp of the client's needs and problems, and that
the client had the opportunity to convey sufficient details, given the
particular circumstances of the client. A statement should be checked
with the client and an interpreter if needed.

B. The Advice:

This section applies to the initial and subsequent advice, and should
include a clear explanation of the options open to the client, and what
immediate action needs to be taken, and by whom.

3. Comprehensiveness – This should include: consideration of whether
   the adviser identified issues other than the immediate presenting
   problem, possibly necessitating separate advice or referral elsewhere
   (overlap with C8; consideration of whether the adviser used a
   holistic approach and (if different) whether the adviser considered
   all the client's problems, both legal and other, when formulating
   the advice.
4. Timing – This relates directly to the adviser's knowledge and
   understanding of procedure and its practical application.

C. The Work/Assistance:

2. Refers to fact-finding work that has been carried out since the first interview.

2 & 3. Efficiently – Inherent in the definition of efficiency is promptness.

4. Effective – For example communications should be accurate, comprehensible and clear. In some cases, where no amount of letter-writing etc. will overcome the other side's intransigence, the reviewer will need to consider whether the adviser adopted tactics that would be effective to achieve what the client reasonably wanted/needed.

8. In considering this question, the reviewer should look at the chances of success of the case, and whether the case was a reasonable use of public funds, taking into account the importance of the issue to the client.

Overall mark – This is the mark the reviewer allocates to the case as a whole, having already assessed the file against the review criteria, but is not necessarily an arithmetical averaging of the other marks.

References

Abel, R.L. 1986. The decline of professionalism? *Modern Law Review*, 49(1), 1–41.

Abel, R.L. 2003. *English Lawyers between Market and State: The Politics of Professionalism*. Oxford University Press.

Akerlof, G.A. 1970. The market for 'lemons': Quality uncertainty and the market mechanism. *Quarterly Journal of Economics*, 84(3), 488–500.

Alcock, P. & Scott, D. 2007. Voluntary and community sector welfare. In: Powell, M. (ed) *Understanding the Mixed Economy of Welfare*. Policy Press. pp 83–105.

Anderson, B.L. 2015. *Us and Them?: The Dangerous Politics of Immigration Control*. Oxford University Press.

Asylum Aid. 2010. *Annual Report*. [No longer publicly available].

Bach Commission. 2017. *The Right to Justice*. Fabian Society.

Bachrach, P. & Baratz, M.S. 1962. Two faces of power. *American Political Science Review*, 56(4), 947–52.

Baksi, C. 2013. Tooks Chambers to resurrect as low-cost Mansfield Chambers. *Law Society Gazette*. 23 September 2013. Available at: https://www.lawgazette.co.uk/practice/tooks-chambers-to-resurrect-as-low-cost-mansfield-chambers/5037829.article [Accessed 24 May 2020].

Bauder, H. 2014. Domicile citizenship, human mobility and territoriality. *Progress in Human Geography*, 38(1), 91–106.

Bauman, Z. 1997. *Postmodernity and its Discontents*. Polity Press.

Bennett, H. 2017. Re-examining British welfare-to-work contracting using a transaction cost perspective. *Journal of Social Policy*, 46(1), 129–48.

Bevan, G. 1996. Has there been supplier-induced demand for legal aid? *Civil Justice Quarterly*, 15(April), 98–114.

Bevan, G. & Hood, C. 2006. What's measured is what matters: Targets and gaming in the English public health care system. *Public Administration*, 84(3), 517–38.

Bevan, G. & Fasolo, B. 2013. *Models of Governance of Public Services: Empirical and Behavioural Analysis of 'Econs' and 'Humans'*. Cambridge University Press.

Bevan, G., Holland, T. & Partington, M. 1994. *Organising Cost-effective Access to Justice*. Social Market Foundation.

BID (Bail for Immigration Detainees). 2019. *Position Paper: Spring 2019 Legal Advice Survey, May 2019*.

Boon, A. 2014. *The Ethics and Conduct of Lawyers in England and Wales.* 3rd edition. Hart.

Boulton, J.G., Allen, P.M. & Bowman, C. 2015. *Embracing Complexity: Strategic Perspectives for an Age of Turbulence.* Oxford University Press.

Bowcott, O. 2019. Homelessness lawyers complain of legal aid culture of refusal. *The Guardian.* 26 June 2019. Available at: https://www.theguardian.com/law/2019/jun/26/homelessness-lawyers-complain-of-legal-aid-culture-of-refusal [Accessed 24 May 2020].

Bowles, R.A. & Perry, A. 2009. *International Comparison of Publicly Funded Legal Services and Justice Systems.* Ministry of Justice.

Bozeman, B. 2002. Public-value failure: When efficient markets may not do. *Public Administration Review*, 62(2), 145–61.

Bozeman, B. & Johnson, J. 2015. The political economy of public values: A case for the public sphere and progressive opportunity. *The American Review of Public Administration*, 45(1), 61–85.

Bridges, L., Sufrin, B. & Whetton, J. 1975. *Legal Services in Birmingham.* University of Birmingham.

Bridges, L., Meszaros, G. & Sunkin, M. 2000. Regulating the judicial review case load. *Public Law*, (4), 651–70.

Brooke, H. 2017. *The History of Legal Aid 1945–2010.* Bach Commission on Access to Justice. Appendix 6. Available at: https://fabians.org.uk/publication/the-right-to-justice/ [Accessed 1 October 2020].

BSB (Bar Standards Board). 2016. *Immigration Thematic Review Report.* Available at: https://www.barstandardsboard.org.uk/resources/resource-library/immigration-thematic-review-report-may-2016-pdf.html [Accessed 1 October 2020].

Burnham, J. & Horton, S. 2012. *Public Management in the United Kingdom: A New Introduction.* Palgrave Macmillan.

Burton, M. 2013. *The Politics of Public Sector Reform: From Thatcher to the Coalition.* Palgrave Macmillan.

Byrom, N. 2013. *The State of the Sector: The Impact of Cuts to Civil Legal Aid on Practitioners and their Clients.* Centre for Human Rights in Practice, University of Warwick.

Byrom, N. 2017. Cuts to civil legal aid and the identity crisis in lawyering: Lessons from the experience of England and Wales. In: Flynn, A. & Hodgson, J. (eds) *Access to Justice and Legal Aid Comparative Perspectives on Unmet Legal Need.* Hart. pp 231–8.

Cape, E. & Moorhead, R.L. 2005. *Demand Induced Supply? Identifying Cost Drivers in Criminal Defence Work.* Lord Chancellor's Department.

Care, G. 2016. *Migrants and the Courts: A Century of Trial and Error?* Routledge.

Carr, A. 1999. Fat cats, thin kittens: A portrait of life at the junior Bar. *Medicine, Science and the Law*, 39(1), 2–4.

Carter of Coles, Lord. 2006. *Legal Aid: A Market-based Approach to Reform.* Department for Constitutional Affairs.

Caulkin, S. 2016. Everything you know about management is wrong. In: Pell, C., Wilson, R. & Lowe, T. (eds) *Kittens are Evil: Little Heresies in Public Policy*. Triarchy Press. pp 29–36.

CCCG (Civil Contracts Consultative Group). 2020. Meeting minutes, March 2020. Available at: https://www.gov.uk/government/publications/contracts-consultative-groups [Accessed 15 April 2021].

Cilliers, P. 2000. What can we learn from a theory of complexity? *Emergence*, 2(1), 23–33.

Citizens Advice Bureau. 2004. *Geography of Advice: An Overview of the Challenges Facing the Community Legal Service* (Evidence report).

Civil Exchange. 2016. *Independence in Question: The Voluntary Sector in 2016.* Civil Exchange.

Clarke, J. & Newman, J. 1997. *The Managerial State: Power, Politics and Ideology in the Remaking of Social Welfare*. Sage.

Clarke, J. & Newman, J. 2012. The alchemy of austerity. *Critical Social Policy*, 32(3), 299.

Clayton, G. 2016. *Textbook on Immigration and Asylum Law.* Oxford University Press.

Clementi, D. 2004. *Report of the Review of the Regulatory Framework for Legal Services in England and Wales*. Department for Constitutional Affairs.

Cornford, T. 2016. The meaning of Access to Justice. In: Palmer, E., Cornford, T., Marique, Y. & Guinchard, A. (eds) *Access to Justice: Beyond the Policies and Politics of Austerity*. Bloomsbury. pp 27–40.

Crouch, C. 2004. *Post-Democracy.* Polity Press.

De Grauwe, P. 2017. *The Limits of the Market: The Pendulum Between Government and Market.* Oxford University Press.

Dingwall, R. 2010. The inevitability of professions? In: Currie, G., Ford, J., Harding, N. & Learmonth, M. (eds). *Making Public Services Management Critical*. Routledge. pp 71–85.

Dingwall, R. & Fenn, P. 1987. A respectable profession? Sociological and economic perspectives on the regulation of professional services. *International Review of Law and Economics,* 7(1), 51–64.

Drakeford, M. 2007. Private welfare. In: Powell, M. (ed) *Understanding the Mixed Economy of Welfare*. Policy Press. pp 61–78.

Economist. 2015. Turned away. 10 December 2015. Available at: https://www.economist.com/news/britain/21679843-thin-evidence-britain-declares-its-biggest-source-refugees-safe-after-all-turned-away [Accessed 1 May 2018].

Evans, K. 2016. Public service markets aren't working for the public good ... or as markets. In: Pell, C., Wilson, R. & Lowe, T. (eds) *Kittens are Evil: Little Heresies in Public Policy.* Triarchy Press. pp 19–28.

Evans, S. 2017. A reflection on Case Study One: The barriers to accessing advice. In: Kirwan, S. (ed) *Advising in Austerity: Reflections on Challenging Times for Advice Agencies.* Policy Press. pp 23–7.

Fenn, P., Gray, A. & Rickman, N. 2007. Standard fees for legal aid: An empirical analysis of incentives and contracts. *Oxford Economic Papers,* 59(4), 662–81.

Flood, J. 2007. 'He's fucking marvellous!' The fall and rise of barristers' clerks. *Counsel Magazine.* Available at: https://www.researchgate.net/publication/228135504_'He's_Fucking_Marvellous'_The_Fall_and_Rise_of_Barristers'_Clerks [Accessed 1 October 2020].

Flood, J. & Whyte, A. 2009. Straight there, no detours: Direct access to barristers. *International Journal of the Legal Profession,* 16(2–3), 131–52.

Flood, J. & Hviid, M. 2013. *The Cab Rank Rule: Its Meaning and Purpose in the New Legal Services Market.* Available at: SSRN 2205124.

Flood, J.A. 1983. *Barristers' Clerks: The Law's Middlemen.* Manchester University Press.

Fouzder, M. 2019. Legal aid practitioners test replacement billing system. *Law Society Gazette.* 6 December 2019. Available at: https://www.lawgazette.co.uk/practice/legal-aid-practitioners-test-replacement-billing-system/5102422.article [Accessed 24 May 2020].

Free Movement blog. 2020. Pioneering immigration judge Hugo Storey retires. 2 October 2020. Available at: https://www.freemovement.org.uk/pioneering-immigration-judge-hugo-storey-retires [Accessed 8 October 2020].

Garden Court Chambers. 2019. Ian MacDonald QC: Obituary. 15 November 2019. Available at: https://www.gardencourtchambers.co.uk/news/ian-macdonald-qc-1939-2019 [Accessed 24 May 2020].

Genn, H. 1993. Tribunals and informal justice. *The Modern Law Review,* 56(3), 393–411.

Genn, H. & Genn, Y. 1989. *The Effectiveness of Representation at Tribunals: Report to the Lord Chancellor.* Lord Chancellor's Department.

Gibbs, J. & Hughes-Roberts, D. 2012. *Justice at Risk: Quality and Value for Money in Asylum Legal Aid.* Runnymede Trust.

Gibney, M.J. 2004. *The Ethics and Politics of Asylum: Liberal Democracy and the Response to Refugees.* Cambridge University Press.

Gill, N., Rotter, R., Burridge, A., Griffiths, M. & Allsopp, J. 2015. Inconsistency in asylum appeal adjudication. *Forced Migration Review*, 50, 52–4.

Goriely, T. 1998. Revisiting the debate over criminal legal aid delivery models: Viewing international experience from a British perspective. *International Journal of the Legal Profession*, 5(1), 7–28.

Goriely, T. 2002. *The English Approach to Access to Justice.* Paper presented to a World Bank Workshop, Washington, 11 December 2002.

Goulandris, A. 2020. *The Enterprising Barrister: Organisation, Culture and Changing Professionalism.* Bloomsbury.

Gray, A., Rickman, N. & Fenn, P. 1999. Professional autonomy and the cost of legal aid. *Oxford Economic Papers*, 51(3), 545–58.

Gray, A.M. 1994. The reform of legal aid. *Oxford Review of Economic Policy*, 10(1), 51–67.

Griffiths, D., Sigona, N. & Zetter, R. 2005. *Refugee Community Organisations and Dispersal: Networks, Resources and Social Capital.* Policy Press.

Guardian, 2010. Collapsed charity 'Unable to manage its affairs'. *The Guardian.* 17 June 2010. Available at: https://www.theguardian.com/law/2010/jun/17/rmj-kenneth-clarke.

Hansen, O. 1992. A future for legal aid. *Journal of Law and Society*, 19(1), 85.

Harris, L.C. & Piercy, N.F. 1998. Barriers to marketing development in the barristers' profession. *Service Industries Journal*, 18(4), 19–37.

Harvey, A. 2010. Closure of Refugee and Migrant Justice and the legal aid tenders. *Journal of Immigration Asylum and Nationality Law*, 24(3), 230–2.

Harvey, A. 2013. Legal aid: Welcome to Laa Laa Land. *Journal of Immigration, Asylum and Nationality Law*, 27(2), 102–5.

Haynes, P. 2012. *Public Policy beyond the Financial Crisis: An International Comparative Study.* Routledge.

Hill, M. & Varone, F. 2017. *The Public Policy Process.* 7th edition. Taylor & Francis.

Hirschman, A.O. 1970. *Exit, Voice, and Loyalty: Responses to Decline in Firms, Organizations, and States* (vol 25). Harvard University Press.

Hood, C. 1991. A public management for all seasons? *Public Administration*, 69(1), 3–19.

Hood, C. 2006. Gaming in targetworld: The targets approach to managing British public services. *Public Administration Review*, 66(4), 515–21.

Hood, C., James, O., Jones, G., Scott, C. & Travers, T. 1998. Regulation inside government: Where new public management meets the audit explosion. *Public Money and Management*, 18(2), 61–8.

House of Commons Constitutional Affairs Select Committee. 2004. *Civil Legal Aid: Adequacy of Provision. Fourth Report of Session 2003–04* (HC391-I).

House of Commons Constitutional Affairs Select Committee. 2007. *Implementation of the Carter Review of Legal Aid. Third Report of Session 2006–07* (HC223-II).

House of Commons Public Accounts Committee. 2015. *Implementing Reforms to Civil Legal Aid. Thirty-sixth Report of Session 2014–15* (HC784).

House of Commons Public Accounts Committee. 2020. *Immigration Enforcement. Seventeenth Report of Session 2019–21* (HC407).

Hubeau, B. & Terlouw, A. (eds) 2014. *Legal Aid in the Low Countries*. Intersentia.

Hughes-Roberts, D. 2013. *Rethinking Asylum Legal Representation: Promoting Quality and Innovation at a Time of Austerity*. Asylum Aid.

Hunter, R. & McKelvie, H. 1999. Gender and legal practice: The relevance of gender to practice as a barrister. *Alternative Law Journal*, 24(1), 57–61.

Hyde, J. 2018a. London firm shut down over dishonesty suspicions. *Law Society Gazette*. 19 April 2018. Available at: https://www.lawgazette.co.uk/practice/london-firm-shut-down-over-dishonesty-suspicions/5065717.article [Accessed 4 October 2018].

Hyde, J. 2018b. Ban upheld for immigration solicitor who brought useless claims. *Law Society Gazette*. 26 April 2018. Available at: https://www.lawgazette.co.uk/news/ban-upheld-for-immigration-lawyer-who-brought-useless-claims/5065861.article [Accessed 4 October 2018].

Hyde, J. 2018c. Judge slams 'game-playing' immigration lawyers and refers three firms to SRA. *Law Society Gazette*. 27 April 2018. Available at: https://www.lawgazette.co.uk/law/judge-slams-game-playing-immigration-lawyers-and-refers-three-firms-to-sra/5065881.article [Accessed 4 October 2018].

Hynes, S. 2012. *Austerity Justice*. Legal Action Group.

Hynes, S. & Robins, J. 2009. *The Justice Gap: Whatever Happened to Legal Aid?* Legal Action Group.

IARLJ (International Association of Refugee Law Judges), European Chapter. 2016. *An Introduction to the Common European Asylum System for Courts and Tribunals: A Judicial Analysis*. European Asylum Support Office.

ICIBI (Independent Chief Inspector of Borders and Immigration). 2017. *Inspection Report on Asylum Intake and Casework.* ICIBI.

Jackson, P. & Price, C. 1994. *Privatisation and Regulation: A Review of the Issues.* Addison-Wesley Longman.

James, D. & Killick, E. 2010. Ethical dilemmas? UK immigration, Legal Aid funding reform and caseworkers. *Anthropology Today,* 26(1), 13–15.

James, D. & Killick, E. 2012. Empathy and expertise: Case workers and immigration/asylum applicants in London. *Law & Social Inquiry,* 37(2), 430–55.

JCWI (Joint Council for Welfare of Immigrants). 2017. *Annual Report.* Available at: https://www.jcwi.org.uk/annual-reviews-and-audited-accounts [Accessed 1 October 2020].

John, G. 2019. A walk down a long road with Ian Macdonald QC: Tribute letter. 19 November 2019. *Garden Court North Chambers.* Available at: https://gcnchambers.co.uk/walk-down-long-road/ [Accessed 9 July 2020].

JUSTICE. 2018. Immigration and asylum appeals: A fresh look. 2 July 2018. Available at: https://justice.org.uk/new-justice-working-party-report-on-immigration-and-asylum-appeals/ [Accessed 1 October 2020].

Kirkup, J. & Winnett, R. 2012. Theresa May interview: 'We're going to give illegal migrants a really hostile reception.' *The Telegraph.* 25 May 2012. Available at: http://www.telegraph.co.uk/news/uknews/immigration/9291483/Theresa-May-interview-Were-going-to-give-illegal-migrants-a-really-hostile-reception.html [Accessed 20 August 2020].

Kritzer, H.M. 1999. The professions are dead, long live the professions: Legal practice in a post-professional world. *Law & Society Review,* 33(3), 713–59.

Kritzer, H.M. 2002. Lawyer fees and lawyer behavior in litigation: What does the empirical literature really say. *Texas Law Review,* 80(7), 1943.

Kritzer, H.M. 2009. Fee regimes and the cost of civil justice. *Civil Justice Quarterly,* 28(3), 344–66.

LAA (Legal Aid Agency). 2017. *Independent Peer Review Process, June 2017.* Legal Aid Agency.

LAG (Legal Action Group). 2018a. Advice deserts set to grow as LAA tenders fail to attract bids. April 2018. Available at: https://www.lag.org.uk/article/204777/advice-deserts-set-to-grow-as-laa-tenders-fail-to-attract-bids [Accessed 22 July 2020].

LAG (Legal Action Group). 2018b. Civil legal advice education and discrimination tenders abandoned. February 2018. Available at: https://www.lag.org.uk/article/204486/civil-legal-advice-education-and-discrimination-tenders-abandoned [Accessed 22 July 2020].

Lane, M., Murray, D., Lakshman, R., Devine, C. & Zurawan, A. 2013. *Evaluation of the Early Legal Advice Project: Final Report.* Home Office.

Langdon-Down, G. 2006. Knockout punch? *Law Society Gazette.* 3 November 2006. Available at: https://www.lawgazette.co.uk/analysis/knockout-punch/2910.article [Accessed 20 August 2020].

Law Society. 2020. Legal aid deserts. April 2020. Available at: https://www.lawsociety.org.uk/campaigns/legal-aid-deserts [Accessed 1 October 2020].

LCD (Lord Chancellor's Department). 2003. *Public Consultation on Proposed Changes to Publicly Funded Immigration and Asylum Work*, CP 07/03. LCD.

Le Grand, J. 2007. *The Other Invisible Hand: Delivering Public Services through Choice and Competition.* Princeton University Press.

Le Grand, J. & Bartlett, W. (eds) 1993. *Quasi-markets and Social Policy.* Macmillan.

Ling, V. & Pugh, S. 2017. *Legal Aid Handbook 2017/18.* Legal Action Group.

Lipsky, M. 1980. *Street Level Bureaucracy: Dilemmas of the Individual in Public Services.* Russell Sage Foundation.

Lowe, T. 2016. Outcomes-based performance management makes things worse. In: Pell, C., Wilson, R. & Lowe, T. *Kittens are Evil: Little Heresies in Public Policy.* Triarchy Press. pp 37–52.

LSB (Legal Services Board). 2012. *Regulation of immigration advice and services: Summary of responses to consultation and LSB response.* Available at: https://www.legalservicesboard.org.uk/our-work/consultations/closed-consultations [Accessed 1 October 2020].

Lyons, K. 2016. UK 'using misleading information' to return Eritrean asylum seekers. *The Guardian.* 22 January 2016. Available at: https://www.theguardian.com/uk-news/2016/jan/22/uk-using-misleading-information-return-eritrean-asylum-seekers-home-office-guidance [Accessed 1 May 2018].

Maclean, M. & Eekelaar, J. 2009. *Family Law Advocacy: How Barristers help the Victims of Family Failure.* Bloomsbury.

Mayo, M. 2013. Providing access to justice in disadvantaged communities: Commitments to welfare revisited in neo-liberal times. *Critical Social Policy*, 33(4), 679–99.

Mayo, M., Koessl, G., Scott, M. & Slater, I. 2015. *Access to Justice for Disadvantaged Communities*. Policy Press.

Mayson, S. 2007. *Legal Services Reforms and Litigation*. College of Law Legal Services Policy Institute.

McConville, M., Hodgson, J., Bridges, L. & Pavlovic, A. 1994. *Standing Accused: The Organisation and Practices of Criminal Defence Lawyers in Britain*. Oxford University Press.

Meadows, D.H. & Wright, D. 2008. *Thinking in Systems: A Primer*. Chelsea Green.

Migration Work, Refugee Action & Asylum Research Consultancy. 2016. *Quality of Legal Services for Asylum Seekers*. Solicitors Regulation Authority.

Ministry of Justice. 2019. *Post-Implementation Review of Part 1 of LASPO*. Available at: https://www.gov.uk/government/publications/post-implementation-review-of-part-1-of-laspo [Accessed 15 April 2021].

Moorhead, R. 1998. Legal aid in the eye of a storm: Rationing, contracting, and a new institutionalism. *Journal of Law and Society*, 25(3), 365–87.

Moorhead, R. 2001. Third way regulation? Community legal service partnerships. *Modern Law Review*, 64(4), 543–62.

Moorhead, R. 2004. Legal aid and the decline of private practice: Blue murder or toxic job? *International Journal of the Legal Profession*, 11(3), 159–90.

Moorhead, R., Sherr, A. & Paterson, A. 2003. Contesting professionalism: Legal aid and non-lawyers in England and Wales. *Law & Society Review*, 37(4), 765–808.

Morison, J. & Leith, P. 1992. *The Barrister's World and the Nature of Law*. Open University Press.

Mullen, T. 2016. Access to justice in administrative law and administrative justice. In: Palmer, E., Cornford, T., Marique, Y. & Guinchard, A. *Access to Justice: Beyond the Policies and Politics of Austerity*. Bloomsbury. pp 69–103.

Mullings, S. 2020. Legal aid deserts and a culture of refusal. *The Justice Gap*. 2 March 2020. Available at: https://www.thejusticegap.com/legal-aid-deserts-and-a-culture-of-refusal/ [Accessed 20 August 2020].

NAO (National Audit Office). 2004. *Improving the Speed and Quality of Asylum Decisions* (Session 2003–04).

NAO (National Audit Office). 2009. *Management of Asylum Applications by the UK Border Agency* (HC 124 Session 2008–09).

OECD/Open Society Foundations. 2019. *Legal Needs Surveys and Access to Justice*. OECD. Available at: https://doi.org/10.1787/g2g9a36c-en [Accessed 26 July 2020].

Partington, M. 2015. Who is doing legal aid? The statistical evidence. *Martin Partington: Spotlight on the Justice System*. 4 August 2015. Available at: https://martinpartington.com/2015/08/04/who-is-doing-legal-aid-the-statistical-evidence/ [Accessed 26 July 2020].

Paterson, A. 2011. *Lawyers and the Public Good: Democracy in Action?* Cambridge University Press.

Pleasence, P., Balmer, N.J., Buck, A., O'Grady, A. & Genn, H. 2004. Multiple justiciable problems: Common clusters and their social and demographic indicators. *Journal of Empirical Legal Studies*, 1(2), 301–29.

Rees, J., Miller, R. & Buckingham, H. 2017. Commission incomplete: Exploring the new model for purchasing public services from the third sector. *Journal of Social Policy*, 46(1), 175–94.

Refugee Action. 2018. Tipping the scales. Access to justice in the asylum system. Available at https://www.refugee-action.org.uk/resource/tipping-scales-access-justice-asylum-system/ [Accessed 2 October 2020].

Rickman, N., Fenn, P. & Gray, A. 1999. The reform of legal aid in England and Wales. *Fiscal Studies*, 20(3), 261–86.

Robertson, G. 2019. Ian Macdonald: Obituary. *The Guardian*. 26 November 2019. Available at: https://www.theguardian.com/law/2019/nov/26/ian-macdonald-obituary [Accessed 20 August 2020].

Robins, J. 2019. Justice gap: The towns where there's no access to free legal advice. *The Guardian*. 27 March 2019. Available at: https://www.theguardian.com/society/2019/mar/27/justice-gap-towns-no-access-to-legal-aid-wales-england [Accessed 20 August 2020].

Robinson, J. 1933. *The Economics of Imperfect Competition*. Macmillan.

Robinson, V., Andersson, R. & Musterd, S. 2003. *Spreading the 'Burden'? A Review of Policies to Disperse Asylum Seekers and Refugees*. Policy Press.

Rogers, J. 2010. Shadowing the bar: Studying an English professional elite. *Historical Reflections/Réflexions Historiques*, 36(3), 39–57.

Rogers, J. 2012. Representing the Bar: How the barristers' profession sells itself to prospective members. *Legal Studies*, 32(2), 202–25.

Rose, N. 2017. Langdon sounds warning over 'shrinking' junior bar. *Legal Futures*. 6 November 2017. Available at: https://www.legalfutures.co.uk/latest-news/langdon-sounds-warning-bell-shrinking-junior-bar [Accessed 4 October 2018].

Sandel, M.J. 2012. *What Money Can't Buy: The Moral Limits of Markets*. Macmillan.

Seddon, J. 2003. *Freedom from Command and Control*. Vanguard Press.

Seddon, J. 2008. *Systems Thinking in the Public Sector*. Triarchy Press.

Seelhoff, A. 2018. Immigration JRs: Paramount duty is to the court. *Law Society Gazette*. 1 May 2018. Available at: https://www.lawgazette.co.uk/commentary-and-opinion/immigration-jrs-paramount-duty-is-to-the-court/5065917.article [Accessed 4 October 2018].

Self, P. 1993. *Government by the Market? The Politics of Public Choice*. Macmillan.

Sherr, A. & Paterson, A. 2008. Professional competence peer review and quality assurance in England and Wales and in Scotland. *Alberta Law Review,* 45(5), 151–68.

Sherr, A., Moorhead, R. & Paterson, A. 1994. Assessing the quality of legal work: Measuring process. *International Journal of the Legal Profession*, 1(2), 135–58.

Shore, C. 2008. Audit culture and illiberal governance: Universities and the politics of accountability. *Anthropological Theory,* 8(3), 278–98.

Singh, A. & Webber, F. 2010. Excluding migrants from justice: The legal aid cuts. *IRR Briefing paper*, 7.

Slocock, C. 2010. *History of Closure of RMJ*. Unpublished, not publicly available.

Smith, C. 2015. Mansfield team moves chambers. *Law Society Gazette*. 9 November 2015. Available at: https://www.lawgazette.co.uk/practice/mansfield-team-moves-chambers/5052068.article [Accessed 28 July 2020].

Smith, T. & Cape, E. 2017. The rise and decline of criminal legal aid in England and Wales. In: Flynn, A. & Hodgson, J. (eds) *Access to Justice and Legal Aid: Comparative Perspectives on unmet Legal Need*. Bloomsbury. pp 63–86.

Sommerlad, H. 2001. 'I've lost the plot': An everyday story of legal aid lawyers. *Journal of Law and Society*, 28(3), 335–60.

Sommerlad, H. 2004. Some reflections on the relationship between citizenship, access to justice, and the reform of legal aid. *Journal of Law and Society*, 31(3), 345–68.

Sommerlad, H. 2008. Reflections on the reconfiguration of access to justice. *International Journal of the Legal Profession*, 15(3), 179–93.

Sommerlad, H. 2016. The new 'professionalism' in England and Wales. In: Headworth, S. (ed) *Diversity in Practice: Race, Gender, and Class in Legal and Professional Careers*. Cambridge University Press. pp 226–60.

Sommerlad, H. & Sanderson, P. 2004. *Cultures of Professional Knowledge and Competence: Issues in the Training and Regulation of Legal Advice Providers in the UK*. Unpublished. Available at: http://eprints.hud.ac.uk/id/eprint/5569/ [Accessed 2 October 2020].

Sommerlad, H. & Sanderson, P. 2009. *Training and Regulating those Providing Publicly Funded Legal Advice Services: A Case Study of Civil Provision*. Ministry of Justice.

Sommerlad, H. & Sanderson, P. 2013. Social justice on the margins: The future of the not for profit sector as providers of legal advice in England and Wales. *Journal of Social Welfare and Family Law*, 35(3), 305–27.

Spencer, M. 2002. Public subsidies without strings: Labour and the lawyers at the birth of legal aid. *International Journal of the Legal Profession*, 9(3), 251–81.

Spencer, S. 2011. *The Migration Debate*. Policy Press.

SRA (Solicitors Regulation Authority). 2016. Asylum report: The quality of legal service provided to asylum seekers. Available at https://www.sra.org.uk/sra/how-we-work/reports/asylum-report/ [Accessed 2 October 2020].

Stephen, F.H., Fazio, G. & Tata, C. 2008. Incentives, criminal defence lawyers and plea bargaining. *International Review of Law and Economics*, 28(3), 212–19.

Sterett, S. 1990. Keeping the law up to date: The idiom of legalism and the reform of administrative law in England and Wales. *Law & Social Inquiry*, 15(4), 731–64.

Sterett, S. 1998. Caring about individual cases: Immigration lawyering in Britain. In: Sarat, A. & Scheingold, S.A. *Cause Lawyering: Political Commitments and Professional Responsibilities*. Stanford University Press. p 293–316.

Stewart, J. 2007. The mixed economy of welfare in historical context. In: Powell, M. (ed) *Understanding the Mixed Economy of Welfare*. Policy Press. pp 23–40.

Sturge, G. 2020. Asylum statistics. *House of Commons Library Briefing SN01403*. 17 March 2020. Available at: https://commonslibrary.parliament.uk/research-briefings/sn01403/ [Accessed 2 October 2020].

Sunkin, M., Bridges, L. & Meszaros, G. 1993. *Judicial Review in Perspective: An Investigation of Trends in the Use and Operation of the Judicial Review Procedure in England and Wales*. Public Law Project.

Tata, C. 2007. In the interests of clients or commerce? Legal aid, supply, demand, and 'ethical indeterminacy' in criminal defence work. *Journal of Law and Society*, 34(4), 489–519.

Tata, C. & Stephen, F. 2006. 'Swings and roundabouts': Do changes to the structure of legal aid remuneration make a real difference to criminal case management and case outcomes? *Criminal Law Review*, 2006 (August), 722–41.

Taylor, D. 2016. Gap-year students deciding asylum claims. *The Guardian*. 28 February 2016. Available at: https://www.theguardian.com/uk-news/2016/feb/27/gap-year-students-deciding-asylum-claims [Accessed 4 October 2018].

Thaler, R.H. 2015. *Misbehaving: The Making of Behavioral Economics*. WW Norton.

Thaler, R.H. & Sunstein, C.R. 2008. *Nudge: Improving Decisions about Health, Wealth, and Happiness*. Penguin.

Thomas, R. 2005. Evaluating tribunal adjudication: Administrative justice and asylum appeals. *Legal Studies*, 25(3), 462–98.

Thomas, R. 2006. Assessing the credibility of asylum claims: EU and UK approaches examined. *European Journal of Migration and Law*, 8(1), 79–96.

Thomas, R. 2011. *Administrative Justice and Asylum Appeals: A Study of Tribunal Adjudication*. Bloomsbury.

Thomas, R. 2015a. Administrative justice, better decisions, and organisational learning. *Public Law*, 1, 111–31.

Thomas, R. 2015b. Mapping immigration judicial review litigation: An empirical legal analysis. *Public Law*, 4, 652–78.

Thomas, R. 2016. Immigration and access to justice: A critical analysis of recent restrictions. In: Palmer, E., Cornford, T., Marique, Y. & Guinchard, A. (eds) *Access to Justice: Beyond the Policies and Politics of Austerity*. Bloomsbury. pp 105–34.

Trude, A. 2009. *Cost of Quality Legal Advice: Literature Review*. Information Centre about Asylum and Refugees.

Trude, A. & Gibbs, J. 2010. *Review of Quality Issues in Legal Advice: Measuring and Costing Quality in Asylum Work*. Information Centre about Asylum and Refugees.

Wall, D.S. 1996. Legal aid, social policy, and the architecture of criminal justice: The supplier-induced inflation thesis and legal aid policy. *Journal of Law and Society*, 23(4), 549–69.

Walsh, P.W. 2019. Migration to the UK: Asylum and resettled refugees. *Migration Observatory*. Available at: https://migrationobservatory.ox.ac.uk/resources/briefings/migration-to-the-uk-asylum/ [Accessed 20 August 2019].

Webber, F. 2012. *Borderline Justice: The Fight for Refugee and Migrant Rights*. Pluto Press.

Welch, M. & Schuster, L. 2005. Detention of asylum seekers in the US, UK, France, Germany, and Italy: A critical view of the globalizing culture of control. *Criminal Justice*, 5(4), 331–55.

Wilding, J. 2017. Unaccompanied children seeking asylum in the UK: From centres of concentration to a better holding environment. *International Journal of Refugee Law*, 29(2), 270–91.

Wilding, J. 2019. *Droughts and Deserts: A Report on the Immigration Legal Aid Market*. Available at: https://www.researchgate.net/publication/333718995_Droughts_and_Deserts_A_report_on_the_immigration_legal_aid_market [Accessed 2 October 2020].

Williams, G. 2011. Don't go that way. *Charity Finance*. July 2011. Not publicly available.

Williamson, O.E. 1975. *Markets and Hierarchies*. Macmillan.

Williamson, O.E. 2000. The new institutional economics: Taking stock, looking ahead. *Journal of Economic Literature*, 38(3), 595–613.

Whitfield, D. 2007. Marketisation of legal aid. *Legal Action*, 2007(March), 6–8.

Yeo, C. 2020. *Welcome to Britain. Fixing Our Broken Immigration System*. Biteback Publishing.

Zander, M. 1978. *Legal Services for the Community*. Temple Smith.

Zander, M. 2000. *The State of Justice: The Hamlyn Lectures*. Sweet & Maxwell.

Index

References to figures appear in *italic* type;
those in **bold** type refer to tables.